DICTIONARY

OF

AMERICAN PHILOSOPHY

DICTIONARY
OF
AMERICAN PHILOSOPHY

by

ST. ELMO NAUMAN, Jr.

Philosophical Library
New York

To

CONNIE & APRIL

The best two daughters

PREFACE

AMERICAN PHILOSOPHERS: American philosophers are
defined as those thinkers who are significant for the progress of human thought, whether native-born Americans,
as in the case of Jonathan Edwards and Ralph Waldo Emerson, or long-term residents, such as Albert Einstein and
Rudolph Carnap. To be included in this study it is not necessary for a man to be a systematic thinker. It is enough to
be significant. Thus several of those considered were literary or political figures, such as William Penn, Benjamin
Franklin, Ethan Allen, Walt Whitman, and others. They
all were, however, original and influential for a given line
of thought.

Philosophy may be defined either as the analysis of concepts or the construction of speculative systems. If the
former were to be emphasized, to the exclusion of the latter,
we would include only the mathematical logicians, seman-
ticists, and linguistic analysts: Tarski, Quine, Chomsky, and
the others. If the latter, speculative philosophy, were to
be emphasized, we would include Royce, Tillich, Lonergan, and the rest. In practice, however, both methods owe
a great deal to each other. There is no such thing as an
uncritical system, nor is there an unsystematic criticism.
Both methods imply each other. Seldom is a system so
carelessly conceived that its major concepts are nameless.
Seldom is analysis conducted with the narrow single-mind-
edness characteristic of the medieval angel-mongers. A
true system wants clarity and true analysis wants breadth.

Therefore, we have combined both lists for our purposes,
believing that both are characteristic of American philosophy. For that matter, if we are to offend, we shall offend
both sides equally.

One further comment needs to be made. We decided, despite all the inherent pitfalls, to include eminent living philosophers as well. It seems to be a shame that one need die first, before becoming notable. Our only regret was the lack of information available in some cases. Therefore, the length of the article does not necessarily indicate relative importance.

DICTIONARY

OF

AMERICAN PHILOSOPHY

I

CHRONOLOGY OF AMERICAN PHILOSOPHERS

This chronological listing is presented as a useful tool to orient the reader in the sequence necessary for the full comprehension of the development of American thought. The names listed in capitals signify major thinkers.

1576-1663	William Ames
1644-1718	William Penn
1656-1743	James Blair
1662-1717	William Brattle
1688-1776	Cadwallader Colden
1696-1771	Samuel Johnson
1703-1758	JONATHAN EDWARDS
1703-1767	Thomas Clap
1706-1790	BENJAMIN FRANKLIN
1720-1766	Jonathan Mayhew
1720-1772	John Woolman
1723-1794	John Witherspoon
1733-1804	Joseph Priestly
1734-1775	William Small
1735-1826	John Adams
1737-1809	THOMAS PAINE
1738-1789	Ethan Allen
1743-1806	THOMAS JEFFERSON
1745-1813	Benjamin Rush
1750-1814	Samuel Stanhope Smith
1752-1817	Timothy Dwight
1758-1808	Fisher Ames
1759-1840	Thomas Cooper
1764-1806	Elihu Palmer

1766-1844	Levi Hedge
1777-1845	Frederick Beasley
1780-1842	William Ellery Channing
1785-1829	Joseph Buchanan
1794-1842	James Marsh
1796-1840	Karl T. C. Follen
1796-1865	Francis Wayland
1799-1888	Amos Bronson Alcott
1800-1872	Francis Lieber
1801-1888	Rowland Gibson Hazard
1802-1846	Thomas Roderick Dew
1802-1887	Mark Hopkins
1803-1882	RALPH WALDO EMERSON
1804-1882	William Barton Rogers
1806-1841	Frederick Augustus Rauch
1807-1873	Jean Louis Rodolphe Agassiz
1809-1865	Abraham Lincoln
1809-1877	Albert Taylor Bledsoe
1810-1860	Theodore Parker
1811-1882	Henry James the Elder
1811-1892	Noah Porter
1811-1894	James McCosh
1812-1883	Alexander Hamilton Stephens
1813-1887	Henry Ward Beecher
1817-1862	HENRY DAVID THOREAU
1819-1892	Walt Whitman
1823-1900	Johann Bernhard Stallo
1823-1901	Joseph LeConte
1828-1906	Henry Conrad Brokmeyer
1829-1900	Charles Carroll Everett
1830-1875	Chauncey Wright
1832-1918	Andrew Dickson White
1833-1885	Elisha Mulford
1833-1899	Robert Green Ingersoll
1834-1916	George Holmes Howison
1834-1826	Charles William Eliot
1835-1909	William Torrey Harris

1835-1910	Mark Twain
1836-1903	Francis Ellingwood Abbot
1839-1897	Henry George
1839-1914	CHARLES SANDERS PEIRCE
1840-1900	Thomas Davidson
1842-1901	John Fiske
1842-1910	WILLIAM JAMES
1842-1914	Ambrose Bierce
1847-1910	BORDEN PARKER BOWNE
1851-1933	Felix Adler
1852-1919	Paul Carus
1854-1926	Albion Woodbury Small
1855-1916	JOSIAH ROYCE
1856-1906	William Rainey Harper
1857-1929	Thorstein Veblen
1859-1952	JOHN DEWEY
1861-1924	James Edwin Creighton
1861-1947	ALFRED NORTH WHITEHEAD
1863-1916	Hugo Münsterberg
1863-1930	Mary Whiton Calkins
1863-1931	George Herbert Mead
1863-1952	GEORGE SANTAYANA
1867-1940	F. E. Woodbridge
1868-1936	Arthur K. Rogers
1869-1950	John Elof Boodin
1871-1938	William McDougall
1871-1960	Ralph Tyler Flewelling
1872-1944	Walter T. Marvin
1872-1970	BERTRAND RUSSELL
1873-1939	Edward G. Spaulding
1873-1946	Edwin B. Holt
1873-1962	Arthur O. Lovejoy
1873-1966	William Ernest Hocking
1873-1953	William Pepperell Montague
1875-1944	James Bissett Pratt
1876-1957	Ralph Barton Perry
1878-1933	Durant Drake

3

1878-1953	Walter B. Pitkin
1879-1955	ALBERT EINSTEIN
1880-1947	Morris R. Cohen
1880-	Roy Wood Sellars
1882-1961	Percy Williams Bridgman
1883-1931	Kahlil Gibran
1883-1964	Clarence Irving Lewis
1884-1953	Edgar Sheffield Brightman
1885-	Will Durant
1886-1965	PAUL TILLICH
1888-	Rosenstock-Huessy
1891-1970	RUDOLPH CARNAP
1892-1966	Brand Blanshard
1892-	Herbert W. Schneider
1895-	Susanne K. Langer
1897-	V. J. McGill
1899-	John Herman Randall, Jr.
1899-	HERBERT MARCUSE
1899-	Robert Maynard Hutchins
1901-	Marvin Farber
1901-	Paul Weiss
1901-	Ernest Nagel
1902-	Dagobert D. Runes
1902-	Mortimer J. Adler
1902-	Sidney Hook
1902-	Alfred Tarski
1902-	John D. Wild
1902-	Herbert Feigl
1902-	Corliss Lamont
1902-	ERIC HOFFER
1904-	Bernard Lonergan
1905-	Ayn Rand
1905-	Paul Kristeller
1905-	Carl Gustav Hempel
1906-	Nelson Goodman
1907-	Mircea Eliade
1907-	Gregory Vlastos

1908-	Willard Van Orman Quine
1908-	Maurice H. Mandelbaum
1908-	Charles Leslie Stevenson
1909-	Max Black
1911-	Norman Malcolm
1912-1971	Adrienne Koch
1913-	Lewis White Beck
1914-	Stuart Hampshire
1915-	Alan Wilson Watts
1916-	Roderick Milton Chisholm
1921-	Walter Kaufmann
1928-	Avram Noam Chomsky

II

THE TEN GREATEST AMERICAN PHILOSOPHERS

In the preceding chronology, at least nineteen names seemed to stand out as highly significant in American philosophy, and many more could be added. Of these, ten may be singled out by general consensus as the most outstanding representatives of American thought. Granting the essential subjectivity of any such process, we can say that without doubt these ten have had the greatest influence on the course of thought, both within this land and throughout the world. These are:

   (1) Jonathan Edwards
   (2) Ralph Waldo Emerson
   (3) Charles Sanders Peirce
   (4) William James
   (5) John Dewey
   (6) Alfred North Whitehead
   (7) George Santayana
   (8) Albert Einstein
   (9) Paul Tillich
 (10) Rudolph Carnap

Of these ten, five were born in the United States, and five were born abroad. Since the last five were from other lands, we might remark on the significant improvement which has been observed in America's place in the world marketplace of free and unobstructed thinking. Four of the ten, surprisingly enough, were not associated with colleges in any significant way: Edwards, Emerson, Peirce, and Einstein. Einstein did research rather than teaching, Peirce never could get a decent academic job, Emerson supported himself, and Edwards died almost as soon as he was connected with a college. There may be some sort of parable there, but we will leave it to someone else to discover.

AMERICAN PHILOSOPHY: A familiar quotation describes America's self-image as it was at one point in time:

> We are the Americans.
> We flatten mountains.
> We build bridges.
> We dam the rivers.
> We irrigate the fields.
> If there is an obstacle, we surmount it.
> If there is an objection, we override it.

This boundless optimism seems curiously out of style now, much as if it were the concluding remarks in the speech of the Last American talking to the final meeting of the sole surviving Kiwanis Club. We have lost our innocence. The American experiment appears to have passed its prime.

However, there are advantages in this condition. For now, for the first time, it is possible to state definitively the nature of American philosophy. We may make with confidence a generalization concerning its source and distinctive character.

American philosophy is the result of a continuous interaction between American and European lines of thought. It is an equation that includes itself as a variable. Within the general context of this interaction we can discern the continuous obsession with the practical that is the distinctive characteristic of all American thought. A theory must always have a "cash value" of some sort to satisfy the American mind. Let us examine these characterizations in more detail.

1

American philosophy is the result of a continuous interaction between American and European lines of thought. There were nine major stages in this process: (1) Puritan, (2) English, (3) Scottish, (4) French, (5) German, (6) Transcendental, (7) Pragmatic, (8) Scientific, and (9) Existential. Before we examine these mutual influences in more detail, let us make one important observation.

We have said that the interaction was with European lines of thought. That means that non-European systems were not considered significant except insofar as they had first become European (as in the case of Schopenhauer's admiration for Buddhism, for example). In this sense American philosophy remains as stubbornly colonial as in the days when the settlers owed formal allegiance to the Crown. The myriad ideas from Indian cultures, Navaho, Hopi, and the rest, have no part in American thinking. If they are studied at all, it is by the anthropologists. Similarly with the Chinese and Japanese immigrants who poured into the west. They could work on the railroads, or cook and do the laundry, but their civilizations were considered far inferior to European civilization. Thus Japanese is not taught in many high schools. German is. American philosophy steadfastly contemplates its European roots, until at last students begin looking longingly at the oriental mysteries. It has been a kind of Captain Kangaroo approach to world thought, piously provincial. This will change, but no one can say how soon. It is not the academicians, but authors such as Eliade and Watts who are thinking across cultural lines. We are too largely occupied with science to invest much time in the analysis of comparative mythology (as in the case of Schelling's later thought).

(1) The first school of thought that did influence American philosophy was Puritanism. The colonists looked back with deep and genuine affection to the glorious days of

the Puritan martyrs, who stood for conscience against the coercive might of the English state and church. They wrote for advice on practical matters to the Puritans living in Holland, and the Puritans in England felt bonds of spiritual kinship with those in the New World. Cambridge was their school, and Cambridge, Massachusetts, was the town where they founded their new school. Ames and Edwards represent this period best.

(2) The second main phase of American philosophy is the English. This is best exemplified by Samuel Johnson, who deserted the true faith, Puritanism, to return to the Church of England and spread the doctrines of Berkeley upon the land. Locke, both through his empiricism and his political thought, also was tremendously influential in America. Beasley held Locke's philosophy with a single-minded reverence usually reserved to religious fanatics.

(3) Scottish common-sense realism was the third stage of American thought. John Witherspoon and Samuel Stanhope Smith were among the first to advocate the virtues of this down-to-earth method of thinking, far superior in every way, they held, to the immaterialism of Berkeley. This mode of philosophizing gained a tenacious hold on the American consciousness, and enjoyed a long life, extending to the time of James McCosh of Princeton.

(4) French influences were predominant in the American Enlightenment, both avidly pursued (by Franklin, Jefferson, et al.) and roundly denounced as subversive and alien to clean wholesome thinking by others (such as Fisher "Squire" Ames).

(5) German philosophy came to this country largely due to the kind influence of the Prussian police, who so hounded and harrassed its own citizens that talented young men fled to America by the boatload. Karl Follen, Francis Lieber, Stallo, and Brokmeyer belong to this era, educat-

ing the American public in the pleasures of one German thinker after another.

(6) With Transcendentalism, American thought came into its own, and directly influenced European thought. When Emerson traveled to England, he found that he was already famous through his books, which was more than could be said in some parts of Illinois at the same time. Much later, and more unexpectedly, we find Heidegger quoting Emerson, in his famous statement, "the half-gods are gone, and the new gods have not yet arrived."

(7) Pragmatism, similarly, had a deep influence on European thought. William James was highly regarded, and was, at least in his upbringing, a kind of citizen of the world.

(8) By "scientific" influence, in this context, we mean to denote the influence both of Einstein on the one hand and the logical positivists on the other. When they came to America, they made significant and lasting contributions to American thought. The Vienna Circle, transplanted, became the Los Angeles Loop. Carnap and his contemporaries conducted their various programs of clarification and mathematization with vigor and enthusiasm. The state universities, before anyone else, caught the spirit of semantic clarification, and declared symbolic logic to be the new first principle of philosophic inquiry.

(9) At about the same time, Existentialism reached these shores. If logical analysis came with the intelligent and sophisticated men driven from the continent by political disasters, Existentialism came because of the war that followed. The ideal of progress was gone, and the new mood of pessimism and despair found its mirror in the translations by David Swenson and Walter Lowrie of the melancholy Dane, Kierkegaard.

Currently, of course, there is no school as such dominating

11

American philosophy. As each of the systems and methods has been examined, each has been found wanting to one degree or another, this one needing more precision, that one needing more breadth. It may be said, without too much fear of exageration, that we are on the threshold of some new and significant philosophical insight. Langer, Kaufmann, Chomsky — so many of the new thinkers seem on the verge of some important new discovery. But let us leave the future to its own devices and examine next the character of American thought up to now.

2

American philosophy has been continually obsessed with the practical. Jonathan Edwards and the other New England divines were intensely interested in how to make theology practical. He chose the subject of the freedom of the will for his major work. The will was a distinctively practical concern, both for religious leaders attempting to convince their parishoners to stop stealing watermelons and also for the members of the community who were responding to a revival with more fervor than within living memory, the "Great Awakening."

A more sceptical group of men, the leaders of the American Revolution, were not so much concerned with theology, and how to make that practical, as they were with society. They proposed to make a more perfect society. Franklin, Paine, Adams, and Jefferson, to name only a few, investigated the very practical problem of the distribution of political power. Society would become responsive to their desires or they would make another society.

The Transcendentalists, in their turn, concentrated on the practical art of sound living, viewing philosophic doctrines as a great help and solace in life.

Pragmatism, of course, is named after the practical. One of the most theoretical departments of philosophy, epistemology, was entered by these practical men and declared captive to the idea that the truth of the matter lies in its practical application. If it works, it's true. They almost applied for a patent on their philosophy.

The last phase we shall note in the development of American philosophy is the effort by logical analysts to clarify science by sharpening the tool, mathematical logic, which can best define its operations. This is an intensely practical pursuit, whether performed with or without an anesthetic.

America has never, at any stage in her development, considered philosophy a mere game to be indulged in by men of leisure. Philosophy, like life, has been a practical affair. It is engaged in for important stakes, issuing in concrete results, in science, politics, and education.

A

ADLER, MORTIMER J. (1902-   ): I have seen students at the University of Chicago, famous across the country for their lack of interest in religion, pack a lecture hall to hear Mortimer J. Adler lecture on God. Speaking with a trace of scholasticism, he nevertheless had a breadth of mind which communicated the ability to perform conceptual analysis with an existential enthusiasm unique in its time.

Born in New York, Adler graduated from Columbia (Ph. D. 1928) and taught there until 1929. He then taught philosophy of law at the University of Chicago from 1930 to 1952, and has been director of the Institute for Philosophical Research since that time. He has written over fourteen books, including *Dialectic* (1927), *The Idea of Freedom* (1958), *The Revolution in Education* (1958), and *The Conditions of Philosophy: Its Checkered Past, Its Present Disorder, and Its Future Promise* (1965).

•   •   •

AGASSIZ, JEAN LOUIS RODOLPHE (1807-1873): "Harvard is a respectable high school," Agassiz said, referring to the required courses in classics, "where they teach the dregs of education." He strongly advocated the empirical teaching of natural history as the best possible preparation for any sort of mental work. Agassiz's biology classes became crowded with eager students, which aroused the intense jealousy of his colleagues, who complained that the college was becoming "lopsided."

The science taught in the lower schools at the time consisted of periods of "fourteen weeks", routinely memorizing one subject after another. This practice was vigorously opposed by Agassiz. The key to good education, he said, lay in doing advanced and original work.

Besides helping to spark Harvard College into becoming a great University, Agassiz provided his version of ideal education on an island in Buzzard's Bay which had been given him by an admirer. On this endowed paradise, Agassiz conducted his summer school of science (1873) for teachers, students, and naturalists, fifty select participants.

His philosophical position was idealistic (which led him to oppose Darwinian evolutionary theory):

> I feel more vexed at impropriety in a scientific laboratory than in a church. The study of Nature is intercourse with the Highest Mind. You should never trifle with Nature. At her lowest her works are the works of the highest powers, the highest something in the universe, in whatever way we look at it.... This is the charm of study from Nature herself; she brings us back to absolute truth whenever we wander.

A naturalized citizen of the United States by the beginning of the Civil War, Agassiz was born in French Switzerland on May 28, 1807. His mother was a Mayor, Rose Mayor, the daughter of a country doctor. His father was the last of a line of Protestant clergymen.

A great naturalist, Agassiz became famous for his studies of fossil fish, and the fishes of Brazil. He formulated the controversial theory of the "Ice Age." However, the outcome of fourteen brilliant years at Neuchâtel had been financial disaster. In 1845 the expenses of the lithographic establishment (which printed the beautiful illustrations for his studies) outran its income, and it was closed. Dinkel and Vogt (his two associates) left and even his wife went back home. Agassiz departed for America to start again. His wife never joined him, dying in 1848, the year of the European revolutions. Tuberculosis claimed her life. In due time his three children did join him at Cambridge.

A great lecturer, Agassiz had contagious enthusiasm and warmth. Someone remarked: "One has less need of an overcoat in passing Agassiz's house than by any other in Cambridge."

Scientific investigation, according to Agassiz, was not the study of plants and animals as such, but rather glimpses into the divine plans of which their structures are the expression.

Agassiz's philosophical influence extended to Joseph Le Conte (*q.v.*), one of his pupils who in turn was the teacher of Josiah Royce in California. William James (*q.v.*) was another celebrated student influenced by Agassiz.

•   •   •

ALCOTT, AMOS BRONSON (1799-1888): Carlyle (1842) wrote of:

> The good Alcott; with his long, lean face and figure, with his gray worn temples and mild, radiant eyes; all bent on saving the world by a return to acorns and the golden age; he comes before one like a venerable Don Quixote, whom nobody can laugh at without loving.

Alcott was one of the New England Transcendentalists, friend of Emerson and Thoreau, founder of the Concord Summer School of Philosophy, and of several other schools which passed into oblivion. Overshadowed (justly) by his associates, Alcott nevertheless presents a significant view of nineteenth-century American thought.

Born in Connecticut on the 29th of November, he had only the most meager education, consisting of a few months here and there and culminating in a mere desire (which was never realized) to go to Yale. At nineteen he went to Virginia hoping to find a schoolteaching post. Instead he found a peddling position. For four and a half years he traveled over Virginia and North Carolina, gaining courtly manners from the one and Quaker sympathies from the other, and not much money from either. He retained all these qualities steadfastly. In 1823 he read Penn (*q.v.*) and returned to New England with higer things in mind than peddling.

For the next ten years he taught school in Bristol, Wolcott, and Cheshire, Connecticut; in Boston, and in Germantown, Pennsylvania (1831-33). His daughter Louisa May was born at this time, the most successful of all his many enterprises.

He reformed education by introducing such novelties as organized play, gymnastics, the honor system, children's libraries, less corporal punishment. He believed schoolrooms could be attractive and instruction ought to be designed to make learning a pleasant experience in itself. Naturally enough, these changes convinced people that Alcott was unfit to teach.

His school in Boston failed because of his inclusion of sex education, and, even worse, the admission of a black girl. The Alcott family moved to Concord (1840), where he farmed rather half-heartedly.

In 1844 (Lousia May was 11) they established the utopian community of Fruitlands, thirty miles south of Boston, in the township of Harvard (no connection with the University). Louisa May Alcott's *Transcendental Wild Oats* describes it well. Starting with eleven people, the Utopia lasted only six months. Crops were planted late and carelessly and at harvest time the men all had more important things to do, such as attending a reform meeting. Mrs. Alcott and the girls were left to harvest what they could before a storm hit. By January they were out of food.

Back in Concord (and other places), Alcott again tried his hand at education and lecturing. They were gradually losing their war on poverty. Is was not until 1868, with the success of Louisa May's third book, *Little Women*, that the family became financially independent.

Alcott's philosophy of transcendental idealism was almost

Neo-Platonic, teaching that the world is the visionary creation of the fallen soul of man, which was in turn a distant emanation from the deity. He firmly believed in the pre-existence of the soul.

Spirit was imprisoned in matter. It could only be freed by intuitive self-knowledge and complete devotion to spiritual inspirations. Life was to be lived in a kind of quiet ecstasy.

Eighteen-seventy-nine saw the establishment of the Concord Summer School of Philosophy and Literature (which functioned until 1888). Those who came included William James, Noah Porter, W. T. Harris, James McCosh, Emerson, and others. Attendance ranged as high as 3000.

In 1882, while writing two sonnets on Immortality, Alcott suffered a stroke from which he never recovered. He died March 4, 1888.

●   ●   ●

AMES, FISHER (1758-1808): Born in Dedham, died in Dedham, Ames looked upon the outside world with suspicion and dislike. A Massachusetts malcontent, "Squire" Ames was sent to Congress, which he regarded as the instrument to save the country from the dangers of democracy. He wrote:

> The most ferocious of animals when his passions are roused to fury and uncontrolled, is man; and of all governments, the worst is that which never fails to excite, but was never found to restrain those passions, that is, democracy. It is an illuminated hell.

A brilliant student, he entered Harvard at twelve and graduated with the class of 1774. He considered living at home better than going to war (except for a short tour of duty with the militia) and used his time to advantage by learning law. He practiced law, which he disliked, and was later elected to serve the people, whom he also disliked. His political thought was expressed in these terms:

We cannot live without society. . . . The liberty of one depends not so much on the removal of all restrain from him, as on the due restraint upon the liberty of others. Without such restraint, there can be no liberty.

A rising young Federalist, his ideal of government was the Roman Republic, in a form, ironically enough, that had never actually existed. An aristocracy of talent and virtue, he believed, must govern. Wanting Congress to be intimately connected with the executive (with the department heads as a recognized ministry of the executive), his hopes were dashed in 1795 when a ways and means committee was created. Ames predicted that:

> our government will be, in fact, a mere democracy, which has never been tolerable, nor long tolerated.

When Madison, reacting with indignation to the Anglo-American incidents of 1793-4, proposed the declaration of a commercial war, Ames spoke against the plan, saying it would be foolish to try to "quarrel ourselves into their good will:"

> I hope we shall show, by our vote, that we deem it better policy to feed nations than to starve them, and that we shall never be so unwise as to put our good customers into a situation to be forced to make every exertion to do without us.

His reward for this speech, besides having a definite impact upon the issue at hand, was to be burned in effigy in Charleston, South Carolina, together with Benedict Arnold and the Devil.

Ames was opposed to Jefferson and other Southern Radicals. Jefferson, for his part, considered Ames one of the "paper men" in Congress. Ames strongly supported the Sedition Act. He considered Gallomania poisonous in its influence upon American politics. Thus the same French influence which had led to the American enlightenment, to men like Franklin and Jefferson, Ames considered a menace to be opposed by every means:

> The Federalists must entrench themselves in the State governments, and endeavor to make State justice and State power a shelter of the wise, and good, and rich, from the wild destroying rage of the Southern Jacobins.

This, then, was the thought of Fisher Ames. Elected president of Harvard, he declined on the ground of his advancing age (47). He coveted government by the "wise and good and opulent," saying:

> It is the almost universal mistake of our countrymen, that democracy would be mild and safe in America.

It was surely one of the ironies of history that he died, in 1808, on the fourth of July.

• • •

AMES, WILLIAM (1576-1633): Though William Ames never reached America (he died *en route*), he was one of the formative influences on early New England thought.

Dr. Matthew Nethen writes in his preface to the 1658 edition of Ames' collected works:

> (to the studious reader): William Ames, dear reader, was a great man, a great theologian, as we shall show! I will certainly not say too much if I call him the light to theologians, the show-piece of professors, the immovable pillar of truth and piety, the enemy of falsehood and impiety, the unrelenting hammer against Papists and Pelagians and Remonstrants, the fearless advocate and protector of the cause of God, the invincible soldier of Christ, the most remarkable hero and prince in the camp of God. He made Papists, Remonstrants, and Church Officials quake with terror along with all their swarms of apologists. He was a

21

star of good omen to the Belgian [Dutch] Church in the season when it was subjected to the grave dangers of Arminianism during its wild fluctuations. And as this involved even danger to the Republic, he was the singular ornament of our age. This most excellent theologian was given to us by England, the fertile mother and nurse of so many other exceptional theologians.

I. Life

Ames was born in 1576 at Ipswich, in Suffolk, England. His father was a prosperous merchant notorious for his radical Puritan sympathies. His parents died young, and he was raised by an uncle, Robert Snelling of Oxford.

He attended Christ College at Cambridge *(Cantabrigia).* In later years, Bertrand Russell would attend and teach at Cambridge. For the moment, the school's reputation was a hotbed of Puritanism. Both the Crown and the Church were having difficulty controlling such an independent university.

"The Great Perkins" taught there, deeply influencing Ames. In 1607 he received his A.B. degree. According to Nethen:

> Because of his outstanding progress in the studies, (he) was elected one of the Teaching Fellows *(socii conregentes)* of the College. He would have been elected successor to the Master in the event of his death, if he would only conform to the Heirarchy. However, to defeat the Puritan party, they plotted that a certain person named [Valentine] Cary, an unworthy fellow as compared with Ames, be thrust in. (Cary) was later made a bishop.
>
> Ames loved the simplicity of the Apostles and Christians and was an enemy of idle and pompous ceremony, and refused to wear a surplice at the services which were conducted on holy days. This new

John Dewey

Jonathan Edwards
(Painting by Joseph Badger, Yale University Gallery)

Master set in motion a serious controversy against him on this account, threatening to expel him from the College, if he did not conform in these matters. These threats did not succeed in changing him. He was strong and constant in good. Furthermore, because Ames was in good standing among the students, he did not dare expel him from the College as threatened. Therefore he altered his tactics to smooth sailing so that [Ames] would leave voluntarily. Which happened.

Now that [Ames] was ripe in mental power, knowledge, and exercise of the mind for public office in school or church, his non-conformity — that is, his cultivation of primitive and Apostolic simplicity in public worship — stood against him. He could not secure a place worthy of his virtue in his native land. Meanwhile, he spoke at public meetings in Cambridge and elsewhere, according to the custom of the Fellows. One occasion was at a brilliant and distinguished occasion called the feast of St. Thomas' Day, shortly before Christmas. He spoke with great acclaim before the whole assembled University. He shrewdly pointed out with cutting but wholesome censure the frivolous dicing and paganism of the students as they celebrated (debacchantium) at the College for twelve whole days.

He had to answer for this before the Senate of the University. He defended his cause well, an acute and wise man.

Because of his sound doctrine, upright life, and outstanding gifts in preaching the word of God powerfully to his hearers and applying it to their consciences, he won the admiration of bishops and the Hierarchy. More than once it was said among them: How great a man could Ames be if he were a son of the church!

He was called by the people of Colchester to be the "lecturer" of the city. But the Bishop of London, whose diocese included that city, blocked the appointment.

Since Ames had already resigned his teaching post at this time, he was in a difficult position, which rapidly became dangerous. He was soon hunted by the authorities.

Before the end of the year 1610, he had to flee the country, following the path of many before him, to Holland.

For a while, he supported himself as chaplain to the British community at The Hague. He entered the theological disputes on the continent.

He stood for the cause of God in our time, against the enemies of divine grace and friends of the free will of man. In that struggle, Ames effectively made known his hand to all who wavered. Those first meetings were almost fights with the rash and proud Nicolas Grevinchovy at Rotterdam.

Ames married the daughter of Dr. Burgess, spiritual advisor to Horatio Veere, Commanding General of the English garrison in that country. Soon afterward she died, childless.

Political pressures from England in 1618 forced his dismissal from even this modest post. Many whom he thought friends were really spying on him for the Crown.

He pamphleteered against the so-called "Remonstrants," a rational group arguing for free will against the Calvinistic doctrine of predestination.

On the 23rd of July, 1619, as the Synod of Holland gathered at Leiden, Ames was recommended for the post of professor of ethics. Another candidate, Tisius, was also proposed. The trustees ("their Lordships") were consulted. They decided to consult the Prince, who consulted the English government. They said Ames was a dangerous fugitive, a subversive Puritan, who should not be employed. Although the church preferred Ames, political resistance decided the case.

One trustee, sympathetic to Ames, employed him to tutor his son.

One of the teachers, Festus Homius, then arranged to

have Ames succeed him in a position technically outside the university, therefore not subject to political veto. In this capacity, Ames gave courses for young men, and wrote his influential book, the *Medulla (The Marrow of Theology)*.

When an opening developed in Friesland, at the University of Franeker, Ames was officially employed, although matters were in such doubt that he was not allowed to enter the classroom.

In 1622, at last, he gave his inaugural address, entitled, "Urim and Thummim," arguing for curriculum reform by adding the Old and New Testaments to the course of study, and by requiring knowledge of Greek and Hebrew.

In characteristically moralistic fashion, he decried the low state of student morals. The school motto, he said, should be changed from "Christo et Ecclesia" (For Christ and Church) to "Baccho et Buchacibus" (For Wine and Drunkenness).

Ames strongly disapproved of Machovius, one of his colleagues who liked to drink. The students on one occasion got him so dead drunk that when it was time for class, the students, saying that they were taking him back to the university, instead took him down a country road and dumped him. Ames, like all Puritans, insisted upon the ethical expression of religious belief.

During this time, he wrote a text-book on the subject of logic, *The Demonstration of True Logic*, which will be reviewed below.

He also indulged in the great outdoor sport of Protestants, writing against Rome. The official Roman Catholic pamphleteer was Belarminus. Ames' book was *Belarminus ennervatus (Belarminus dissected)*.

So far as major works are concerned, following the *Marrow*, Ames' second great work was *On the Conscience*. This book went through a dozen editions, and was found in the libraries of most educated men in colonial America.

While at this rural university, Ames married an Englishwoman, who strongly felt the isolation, and said so from time to time.

Ames had remained in close contact with the settlers in New England. Governor Winthrop and others asked his advice on matters of importance. In December of 1630 Ames wrote that it was his intention to leave the following summer for New England.

Meanwhile, in Rotterdam, Ames met Hugh Peters, a popular preacher who had returned from New to Old England to become one of Cromwell's right-hand men. At the time Peters was starting a school in Rotterdam, and he urged Ames to stay for a while and teach there. In October of 1632 the city government approved, and Ames agreed to teach temporarily, on his way to America.

In October of 1633, the River Maas flooded. Water poured into the house. Ames waded through the cold water. The shock produced a cold with high fever. His health was not good, and within a few days, he died, in the arms of his friend, Hugh Peters. The travel plans to the New World were never used.

His wife followed through with those plans, bringing many of Dr. Ames' books to America, one of the most valuable libraries available at that time.

At the time of Ames' death the little Spinoza boy, in Amsterdam, was nearly a year old.

II. Thought

Let us look at Ames' work with logic. The *Demonstratio logicae verae (Demonstration of True Logic)*, (1646) bears close similarities to the system of Peter Ramus (1515-1572), the popular alternative to traditional logic at the time. Since he was martyred during the St. Bartholomew's Day massacre in Paris, Ramus' works recommended themselves to the Puritan tutors at Cambridge and Oxford. Like the Bertrand Russell fans in later years, those who read Ramist logic believed they had found the alternative to Aristotelian logic.

In Ames' view:

1. Dialectic, otherwise called logic, is the art of treating of things well; that is, to discern well the reasons of things and to relate them to each other.

2. The reasons of things are thought of either simply and separately or in relation to each other... Therefore dialectic is divided into two parts: *finding* and *judging*.

3. *Finding* is... the part by which simple reasons are traced out.

73. The simple reasons when found must be related usefully to each other. This *relating* therefore is the second part of logic.

74. The *relating* of found reasons is for the purpose either of having made from them a judgment which grows naturally from the relation like a flower or of retaining them in memory; for the three tasks of reasoning are to find, to judge, and to hold in memory — served by the three inner senses: imagination, the cognitive faculty, and the sensory memory. Therefore the second part of logic is best divided into *judgment* and *method*.

129. When the purpose of treating of things is not simply to teach but to delight, move, beguile, then a *crypsis* (or concealment of this method) must be resorted to through transposing, exaggerating, emphasizing things according to the thought of the teacher, and prudently accommodating them to the wit of the hearers.

By treating logic in this way we take into account every form of reasoning that has to do in any way with any being. First come the simple elements of reason and then the relating of them to each other. Those simple elements are either in the fact and fabric of the thing or outside of it. We must indeed first know the fact of the thing before we can accept or use testimony concerning it.

The simple facts of things are either primary or secondary, the latter deriving from the former. We first see these facts as they are in themselves before comparing them with others; in themselves we first see what they are before we see what they are not; and in seeing what they are, we look both to their essence and existence and to their adjuncts, complements, and accessories. When we have thus seen what constitutes the thing, we mark that it is not another thing: it differs from all others, from some to a slighter, from others to a greater, degree — and not only from all other things but also from nothing, or the negation of itself.

After considering in this way what the thing is and what it is not, we compare it with others either in rank or nature and find it equal or unequal, similar or dissimilar. When, that is, we have examined the matters which are primary to the fact of the thing, we turn to consider the secondary matters which derive from them. We look at the thing as classified under some essential or complementary truth, at the relation of its class to other things, and at that which it has in common with many things, noting how it is an effect of many causes or a cause of many effects, or an adjunct to many subjects or finally a subject to many adjuncts. In this consideration we see that the thing is a whole and that it consists of members, which are the marks or contacts of its causes. We see it as a species of a certain genus, and that causes of the species correspond to the causes of the members of the whole, except that they are in a different mode.

Finally, after we have given the thing both primary and secondary contemplation, and by examining it inside and outside, up and down and sideways, have even as it were penetrated into and entered its very nature, we determine what it is and by giving it a definition set the ends of its essence; and these we designate either properly, that is, by precise definition of form and matter, or as it were in outline, suggesting their extent by description. After all these things have been looked into, one may safely give or accept testimony concerning the nature of the thing.

After these simple elements of reason have been found, we relate them fittingly to each other according to the nature of reason, and this either (and primarily) for purposes of judgment or (secondarily) for the uses of memory. To form a judgment truths are related as they appear in their own light, and in the thing so seen a "sentence" (or decision) immediately comes into being. The truths will be either connected or disconnected: this will be determined by either a simple or a composite process. If the thing is in doubt, then for light and conviction help is sought from some third truth, which is related to the others either singly, as in a simple syllogism, so that the light may shine on them one by one, or in connection with each other, as in a composite syllogism. After the things are so thought through, an accurate judgment can be given, as upon something clearly seen.

Method is a second arrangement, made for purposes of memory, in which truths, including established principles and judged either by themselves or in the light of other truths, are put in the order which is natural to them.

Now that we see the virtues of logic, let us sedulously study to keep the eye of our reason directed by this its proper rule. Let us exercise that reason in order to be able to see distinctly all that is in anything, judge it accurately, and hold it permanently in memory.

Ames charts his logical scheme in an illuminating manner. "In logic," he declares, "we consider what reason or understanding may be had in any way in respect of any being whatsoever."

To be specific, "There are understandings of being which (either) *discover the reality* of it, (or) *make a judgment* concerning it."

In the first case, we can discover the reality of a matter either *in the make-up* of the being or outside the make-up of the being, after the contemplation of everything else in the nature of the thing is completed, which is a direct understanding of the thing.

In the second case, we make a judgment concerning it by applying the understandings of things whose reality we have discovered to their fitting and natural uses, either in a primary or a secondary way.

If the judgment is made in a primary way, about matters that are and are seen to be, such judgments are concerning things which are either clear or obscure. If clear, they are obvious in themselves and in their own light, in which case the judgment (sentence) is made concerning them without further thought, and is called an IDIOM *(idioma)*.

If obscure and doubtful, the mind in this case gives more thought to them by means of some third direct understanding, which being applied, Judgment is made of them as of the obvious, and is called the SYLLOGISM *(syllogismus)*.

We will not explain all the kinds of understanding possible, in Ames' view. However, it may be instructive to list them, in ascending order, from the lowest to the highest:

(1) Instruction *(methodus)*
(2) Syllogism *(syllogismus)*
(3) Idiom *(idioma)*
(4) Evidence *(testimonium)*
(5) Definition *(definitio)*
   (a) Imperfect
   (b) Perfect
(6) Distribution *(distributio)*
   (a) of the genus into species *(genus in species)*
   (b) of the whole into parts *(totius in partes)*
(7) Denomination *(notatio)*
(8) Conjugates *(conjugata)*
(9) Dissimilars *(dissimilia)*
(10) Similars *(similia)*
(11) Unequals *(imparia)*
(12) Equals *(paria)*

(13) Negation *(negatio)*
(14) Opposites *(opposita)*
(15) Varieties *(diversa)*
(16) Adjunct *(adjunctum)*
(17) Subject *(subjectum)*
(18) Result *(causatum)*
(19) Cause *(causa)*

Following Ames' logic, a second topic of interest is certain aspects of his philosophy of religion. His academic aim, as he says in *An Exhortation to the Students of Theology* (1623), is:

(to) call theology away from questions and controversies, obscure, confused, and not very essential, and introduce it to life and practice so that students would begin to think seriously of conscience and its concerns.

According to Ames, it is less important to live happily, *eudamonein*, than it is to live well, *euzoein*. He is unwilling to combine Aristotle with religious teaching, as did St. Thomas Aquinas. Ames rejects Aristotle at this point.
"The end of doctrine," Ames says, quoting Peter Ramus with approval, "is not the teaching of the things which are subject to it, but their use and exercise."
Thus the ethical result of metaphysical doctrines was most important for Ames. Ethics was the logical conclusion and the necessary result of his religious inquiry:

50. Vertue (sic) is an habit whereby the will is inclined to doe well.
The cardinal virtues are Justice, Prudence, Fortitude, and Temperance. Justice is the inclination to do rightly, giving every man his own. Prudence means thinking to find out what is right, and "to direct aright all the meanes of it." Fortitude refers to a firm persistence in doing rightly, overcoming difficulties and impediments of any sort. Temperance means the restraining of whatever desires of men divert them from doing good.

31

Ames' influence lasted through several generations in the New World, first as text books for generations of students, then as source books for serious scholars. Most libraries of cultured and well-educated men of New England included his books among their contents.

ART (John Dewey):

1. Works of art are the only media of complete and unhindered communication between man and man that can occur in the world full of gulfs and walls that limit community of experience.—*Art as Experience*.

2. Because objects of art are expressive, they are a language. Rather they are many languages. For each art has its own medium and that medium is especially fitted for one kind of communication. Each medium says something that cannot be uttered as well and as completely in any other tongue.—*Ibid*.

3. The arts which today have most vitality for the average person are things he does not take to be arts: for instance, the movie, jazzed music, the comic strip, and, too frequently, newspaper accounts of love-nests, murders, and exploits of bandits. For, when what he knows as art is relegated to the museum and gallery, the unconquerable impulse towards experiences enjoyable in themselves finds such outlet as the daily environment provides. Many a person who protests against the museum conception of art, still shares the fallacy from which the conception springs. For the popular notion comes from a separation of art from the objects and scenes of ordinary experience that many theorists and critics pride themselves upon holding and even elaborating.—*Ibid*.

4. There must be historic reasons for the rise of the compartmental conception of fine art. Our present museums and galleries to which works of fine art are removed and stored illustrate some of the causes that have operated

to segregate art instead of finding it an attendant of temple, forum, and other forms of associated life. An instructive history of modern art could be written in terms of the formation of the distintively modern institutions of museum and exhibition gallery. I may point to a few outstanding facts. Most European museums are, among other things, memorials of the rise of nationalism and imperialism. Every capital must have its own museum of painting, sculpture, etc., devoted in part to exhibiting the greatness of its artistic past, and in other part, to exhibiting the loot gathered by its monarchs in conquest of other nations; for instance, the accumulations of the spoils of Napoleon that are in the Louvre. They testify to the connection between the modern segregation of art and nationalism and militarism.—*Art as Experience.*

5. A work of art no matter how old and classic is actually, not just potentially, a work of art only when it lives in some individualized experience. As a piece of parchment, of marble, of canvas, it remains self-identical throughout the ages. But as a work of art, it is recreated every time it is esthetically experienced.—*Ibid.*

6. There is a conflict artists themselves undergo that is instructive as to the nature of imaginative experience. . . It concerns the opposition between inner and outer vision. There is a stage in which the inner vision seems much richer and finer than any outer manifestation. It has a vast, an enticing aura of implications that are lacking in the object of external vision. It seems to grasp much more than the latter conveys. Then there comes a reaction; the matter of the inner vision seems wraith-like compared with the solidity and energy of the presented scene. The object is felt to say something succinctly and forcibly that the inner vision reports vaguely, in diffuse feeling rather than organically. The artist is driven to submit himself in humility to the discipline of the objective vision. But the inner vision is not cast out. It remains as the organ

by which outer vision is controlled, and it takes on structure as the latter is absorbed within it. The interaction of the two modes of vision is imagination; as imagination takes form the work of art is born.—*Ibid.*

7. We lay hold of the full import of a work of art only as we go through in our own vital processes the processes the artist went through in producing the work. It is the critic's privilege to share in the promotion of this active process.—*Art as Experience.*

B

BEASLEY, FREDERICK (1777-1845): A fearless defender of Locke's philosophy, Frederick Beasley wrote that it "never has been and never can be overthrown." With a kind of devotion usually reserved for the Bible, Beasley opposed the "detestable sophistries" of Berkeley and Hume. In fact it has been said that Beasley's contemplation of these two sophists caused him such pain that his own possession of the absolute truth (Locke) brought him little inner peace.

Beasley believed that the philosophies of Berkeley and Hume had caused Locke to be blamed for smuggling a kind of hidden skepticism within his own system of empiricism. If this opinion persisted, a political reaction could conceivably result. The dogmatism of continental thinkers could become a prop for monarchy. Worse, the beauties of common-sense empiricism would fall into disuse. Science would suffer. Errors in epistemology would grow. A new kind of scholasticism might return. The situation was critical.

Born near Edenton, North Carolina, educated at the College of New Jersey (Princeton), he studied under Samuel Stanhope Smith (q.v.). In 1813, Beasley became Provost of the University of Pennsylvania, occupying the chair of moral philosophy.

Proud of his conservatism in both thought and dress, he continued to powder his hair long after the custom had passed.

He rejected Scottish common-sense realism, as we have noted, in favor of the system of Locke. His most noted work was: *A Search of Truth in the Science of the Human Mind* (1822).

• • •

BECK, LEWIS WHITE (1913-   ): A noted contemporary American philosopher, Lewis White Beck is an expert on Kant, having written *Commentary on Kant's Critique of Practical Reason* (1960) and *Studies in the Philosophy of Kant* (1965), among other works. Born in Griffin, Georgia, Beck was educated at Emory, Duke (Ph.D. 1937), and Berlin (1937-38). He has taught at Emory, the University of Delaware, Lehigh, and the University of Rochester (from 1949). Another of his works is *Philosophic Inquiry* (1952).

• • •

BEECHER, HENRY WARD (1813-1887): The most influential preacher in all American history, Henry Ward Beecher's contribution to philosophical thought, such as it was, can be found not in the *Seven Lectures to Young Men* (1844) with its warnings against "the strange woman," but in *Evolution and Religion* (1885).

This marked the appropriation of evolutionary concepts for religious purposes. Forgotten were Spencer and Darwin, as the theologians expounded a Christian version of moral evolution.

BEHAVIORISM: A frame of reference in psychology (founded by J. B. Watson) which lays stress upon observations of overt behavior, derives the method of introspection, rules out consciousness, and emphasizes the theory of a machine-like quality in animal and human activity. — Harriman, *Dictionary of Psychology*.
Behaviorists completely reject consciousness and introspection as unsuitable to scientific treatment, regard psychology as the study of behavior by objective methods

exclusively. Watson treats psychological events — i.e., behavior — as reducible to the action of stimulus-response
mechanisms variously combined and conditioned. The
role of conditioning (learning) is emphasized, that of
heredity minimized. Instincts are denied. Many variants
of behaviorism have arisen, among them E. C. Tolman's
purposive Behaviorism which studies behavior not as a
composition of minute or 'molecular' stimulus-response
mechanisms, but as 'molar' wholes or behavior acts from
which immanent determinants such as purposes and
cognitions are inferred, not introspectively observed. —
Vergilius Ferm, *An Encyclopedia of Religion.*

BEING: The major topic of metaphysics (the other being
the world-view, or *Weltanschauung*), being is treated by
American philosophers in accordance with their school of
persuasion, idealistic, realistic, naturalistic, or analytic.

1. Jonathan Edwards' thought on the subject of Being
began quite early in his writing:

That there should absolutely be nothing at all is
utterly impossible, the mind can never let it stretch
its conceptions ever so much bring it self to conceive
of a state of perfect nothing, it puts the mind into mere
convulsion and confusion to endeavor to think of
such a state, and it contradicts the very nature of
the soul to think that it should be, and it is the greatest
contradiction and the aggregate of all contradictions
to say that there should not be. . . . A state of absolute
nothing is a state of absolute contradiction. . . . A state
of nothing is a state wherein every proposition in
Euclid is not true, nor any of those self-evident maxims
by which they are demonstrated and all other eternal
truths are neither true nor false. — *Of Being* (1720), in
Faust & Johnson, *Jonathan Edwards,* 18-20.

Being is also discussed under the topic of "the nature
of things" in his discourse on *Justification by Faith Alone:*

"The wisdom of God in his constitutions doubtless appears much in the fitness and beauty of them, so that those things are established to be done that are fit to be done, and those things are connected in his constitution that are agreeable one to another."

The discerning reader will understand that Edwards' answer to the question Socrates posed in the *Euthryphro* is that the gods do what is pious rather than the pious being what the gods choose to do.

2. Emerson:

The philosophy of six thousand years has not searched the chambers and magazines of the soul. In its experiments there has always remained, in the last analysis, a residuum it could not resolve. Man is a stream whose source is hidden. Our being is descending into us from we know not whence. The most exact calculator has no prescience that somewhat incalculable may not balk the very next moment. I am constrained every moment to acknowledge a higher origin for events than the will I call mine.

As with events, so is it with thoughts. When I watch that flowing river, which, out of regions I see not, pours for a season its streams into me, I see that I am a pensioner; not a cause, but a surprised spectator of this ethereal water; that I desire and look up, and put myself in the attitude of reception, but from some alien energy the visions come.

The Supreme Critic on the errors of past and the present, and the only prophet of that which must be, is that great nature in which we rest, as the earth lies in the soft arms of the atmosphere; that Unity, that Oversoul, within which every man's particular being is contained and made one with all other; that common heart, of which all sincere conversation is the worship, to which all right action is submission; that overpowering

reality which confutes our tricks and talents, and constrains every one to pass for what he is, and to speak from his character, and not from his tongue, and which evermore tends to pass our thought and hand, and become wisdom, and virtue, and power, and beauty. We live in succession, in division, in parts, in particles. Meantime within man is the soul of the whole; the wise silence; the universal beauty, to which every part and particle is equally related; the eternal ONE. And this deep power in which we exist, and whose beatitude is all accessible to us, is not only self-sufficing and perfect in every hour, but the act of seeing and the thing seen, the seer and the spectacle, the subject and the object, are one. We see the world piece by piece, as the sun, the moon, the animal, the tree; but the whole, of which these are the shining parts, is the soul. Only by the vision of that Wisdom can the horoscope of the ages be read, and by falling back on our better thoughts, by yielding to the spirit of prophecy which is innate in every man, we can know what it saith. Every man's words, who speaks from that life, must sound vain to those who do not dwell in the same thought on their own part. I dare not speak for it. My words do not carry its august sense; they fall short and cold. Only itself can inspire whom it will, and behold! their speech shall be lyrical, and sweet, and universal as the rising of the wind. Yet I desire, even by profane words, if I may not use sacred, to indicate the heaven of this deity, and to report what hints I have collected of the transcendent simplicity and energy of the Highest Law.
— "The Oversoul," *Essays*.

•   •   •

BIERCE, AMBROSE (1842-1914): Born in a log cabin, Ambrose Gwinnett Bierce did *not* become President of the United States. The son of Marcus Aurelius Bierce, a farmer at Horse Cave Creek, Ohio, he received no general education beyond his father's small library. He joined the Army (9th Indiana Infantry) at the outbreak of the Civil War. Severely wounded, he later went West to San Francisco with his brother and turned to journalism. He celebrated his success by getting married and having fun. He married Mary Day on Christmas Day, 1871, and for the next four years was on the staff of *Fun.*

He published *The Fiend's Delight, Nuggets and Dust Panned Out in California,* and *Cobwebs from an Empty Skull.* "Bitter Bierce," as he was called, then landed a job on the *Wasp* and continued to publish: *Tales of Soldiers and Civilians* (1891) and *Can Such Things Be?* (1893), the latter being weird stories of the supernatural.

His finest work was *The Devil's Dictionary* (1906, first published as *The Cynic's Word Book*). With an utter lack of reverence, he attacked pretension wherever he found it:

Faith, *n.*   Belief without evidence in what is told by one who speaks without knowledge, of things without parallel.

Life, *n.*   A spiritual pickle preserving the body from decay. We live in daily apprehension of its loss; yet when lost it is not missed.

Love, *n.*   A temporary insanity curable by marriage or by removal of the patient from the influences under which he incurred the disorder.

Funeral, *n.*   A pageant whereby we attest our respect for the dead by enriching the undertaker.

Grave, *n.*   A place in which the dead are laid to await the coming of the medical student.

Happiness, *n.*   An agreeable sensation arising from contemplating the misery of another.

At the age of seventy, Bierce said to some friends,

"Please forgive me for not perishing where I am," and disappeared (in 1913) into warring Mexico. He wrote:

Goodbye. If you hear of my being stood up against a Mexican stone wall and shot to rags please know that I think it a pretty good way to depart this life. It beats old age, disease, or falling down the cellar stairs. To be a Gringo in Mexico — ah, that is euthanasia!

He was never heard from again.

•   •   •

BLACK, MAX (1909-   ): A noted authority on analytic philosophy, Max Black has written *Problems of Analysis* (1954), translated portions from Gottlob Frege, and produced *A Companion to Wittgenstein's Tractatus* (1964). Born in Baku, Russia, Black was educated at Cambridge, Göttingen, and London (Ph.D. 1939). He came to the United States in 1940, and has taught at the University of Illinois (1940-46) and Cornell (1946-   ). Other of his books include *Language and Philosophy* (1949), *The Nature of Mathematics* (1950), *Critical Thinking* (1952), and *The Labyrinth of Language* (1968).

Max Black represents the influence of the later Wittgenstein and British "ordinary language" philosophy on America. Language, he maintains, is not a sort of mirror to reality. Rather, we should seek to classify words and expressions by their uses and functions, not overlooking the flexible ambiguities that characterize ordinary language.

•   •   •

BLAIR, JAMES (1656-1743): The first president of the College of William and Mary in Virginia, Blair illustrates the essential poverty of depending upon the mother country as the source of all that is good. He squandered his own potential contributions to the field of thought by an excessive interest in the thought patterns of the Old World.

The founder and president of the second major college in the colonies (Harvard being the first), he served at his post for forty years. During that time he spent his attention on endless quarrels with three successive governors. He appealed to the Crown for their removal for one reason after another.

I. Life

Born and bred in Scotland, Blair attended Marischal College at Aberdeen, and received his M.A. from the University of Edinburgh. Ordained into the Episcopal church, he had some unspecified difficulties and left for England about the end of the reign of King Charles II.

Dr. Henry Compton, Bishop of London, sent him to Virginia in 1685.

Blair conceived the need for a college at the capitol, "Williamsburgh," to be "for Professors and Students in Academical Learning." The General Assembly in Virginia approved the idea and sent Blair in 1691 to solicit funds from interested parties in England, including, of course, Queen Mary and King William.

Blair was successful in raising money. The estate of the great English scientist Robert Boyle contributed to the endowment. So did three pirates, whose contribution was extorted by the Crown as the price of pardon.

Blair's appointment to the presidency of the college was for life. He was much more secure than the governor, and sent complaint after complaint to the Bishop of London, to the king, and to the queen.

For example, Blair charged that Governor Andros was no longer able to ride horseback because of old age and "a fall he had from his horse, which they say has burst him." He has neglected the militia and the rangers. Another civil disorder like Bacon's Rebellion might break out if such an old and ineffective man is kept in charge of the government. He doesn't consult his own council. He no longer has any influence with the Assembly, and therefore is no service to the King. He has diminished the King's revenue. He has so angered the Indians that one of the Chiefs went into the Governor's kitchen after an interview and cut his own throat with a case knife. He doesn't follow instructions. He is suspicious and jealous, producing factions in the colony. In sum, he hasn't done anything good either for the king or the people. — reference in Morton, *Colonial Virginia* (Chapel Hill: The University of North Carolina Press, 1960), 354.

Andros, for his part, said that he had done all he could for both the College and the Church, but that he could never seem to please Mr. Blair.

Next, Blair helped get Colonel Nicholson appointed Governor (1698), then promptly quarreled with him.

In 1702, the students at the college wanted an early Christmas vacation. They locked the president out. He begged them in vain to open up. They refused. He then ordered two of his servants to break down the door. At this, students began firing with guns (loaded only with powder).

Blair stormed into the governor's office and angrily accused him of furnishing the boys with weapons for the purpose of assassinating the president.

Blair went to England to lobby for the governor's recall. At this, six ministers wrote to the Bishop of London, complaining: "Shall a Scotch Commissary have the making and unmaking of our governours? He was not (say they) pleased with the last, nor is with this, and will be as little with the next."

Nott was appointed Governor in 1705, but died the following year. Hunter, appointed to succeed him, was captured by pirates and taken to France. Blair did not quarrel with either of these two.

Besides, in 1705 the college burned. The large library of Mungo Ingles, among other things, was destroyed. Blair's efforts were diverted toward repairing this considerable damage.

However, as soon as Governor Spotswood arrived on the scene in 1710, Blair began his customary agitation once again. A specifically religious dispute arose, the question of who had the right to appoint clergymen to the parish, the governor (as the king's representative) or the commissary (as the bishop's representative). The matter was never resolved, and at Colonel Spotswood's removal in 1722 was still boiling.

The next governor was Major Drysdale. He deliberately followed the policy of not antagonizing Blair. Gooch, who followed, outlived Blair. Following this, Blair exerted relatively little influence on political life.

II. Thought

Blair was strongly anti-deist, when the gentle freethinking of such men as Franklin or Jefferson was in the process of developing. Blair condemned Sir John Randolph, one of the outstanding leaders of colonial Virginia, as being "no friend of religion" because of his tolerant rationalism: "Very wild, dissenting, and scarce Christian opinions," in Blair's view.

Blair also opposed the early age of reason, that part with which he was acquainted. Further, he opposed the pragmatic approach which could be faintly traced in the first stages of American thought.

He opposed absolutism in politics (his sermons on the accession of a new monarch have not survived) because he disliked its practice by the colonial governors. Perhaps it would be more precise to say that he opposed aristocracy in politics although he sanctioned it in religion. He was in favor of a sort of theocratic commonwealth, based on religious principles. He wanted as much as any medieval pope to control the political branch of government.

In his books, *Our Saviour's Divine Sermon on the Mount*

Contained in the Vth, VIth, and VIIth Chapters of St. Matthew's Gospel Explained And the Practice of it Recommended in divers Sermons and Discourses, first printed in 1722 and revised in 1732, can be found his ethical views and a sort of epistemology:

> We should aim at as high Degrees of moral Virtue as in this imperfect State we are capable of. — vol. I, p. 449.
> We are not to understand, that in this corrupt and depraved State, we are able of ourselves to yield any tolerable Obedience to the Laws of the Gospel; it is only by the Grace of God we are enabled to yield Obedience. — vol. IV, p. 306.
> When the inward Light of the Mind and Conscience is darkened, this occasions a vast Number of other Errors and Follies in the Life and Conversation. — vol. III, p. 290.
> All Vice vitiates the Faculty of the Understanding, that it sees things through a false Glass, and in a wrong Light; as a Man that has the Jaundice sees not Things in their true Colours, but as they are tinctured with that yellowish Disease which is in himself; so the vitious Man infuses a strong Tincture of his own Conceits into all Truth, that he cannot see Things in their native Beauty. — vol. II, 292.

The best source of information on Blair is the new biography on him: Park Rouse, *James Blair of Virginia* (Chapel Hill: The University of North Carolina Press, 1971).

•   •   •

BLANSHARD, BRAND (1892-1966): A classical rationalist, Brand Blanshard was born in Fredericksburg, Ohio, and educated at the University of Michigan (B.A. 1914 — the land grant colleges had really come into their own),

Columbia (M.A. 1914 – he was one of John Dewey's students), Oxford, and Harvard (Ph.D. 1921). He taught at Michigan, Swarthmore, and Columbia, writing, in the process, *The Nature of Thought* (1939). He restated idealism counter to the criticisms of realism, pragmatism, and behaviorism, maintaining that there are elements of judgment and thought, even at the level of perception.

In 1945 he went to Yale to teach. He has also written *Philosophy in American Education* (1945), *On Philosophical Style* (1954), *The Impasse in Ethics and a Way Out* (1955), *Reason and Goodness* (1961), and *Reason and Analysis* (1962).

Blanshard attempted to refute emotive and subjective ethical and political theories. Moral judgments, he held, express knowledge. Influenced, no doubt, by Dewey, his ethical theory has its naturalistic aspect. Ethics is related to human nature.

Against Hume, Blanshard maintained that there are necessary connections, causes, in the world, among them are logical and mathematical laws, connections between properties and attributes, and necessary connections in ethics and value.

• • •

BLEDSOE, ALBERT TAYLOR (1809-1877): Advocate of lost causes, as reactionary as Fisher Ames *(q.v.)*, Albert Taylor Bledsoe was assistant secretary of war for the Confederacy and afterwards editor of the *Southern Review*. He attacked Jefferson who, being dead at the time, never replied.

"The inalienable rights are neither life nor liberty," wrote Bledsoe, "but conscience, truth, honor may not be touched by man." All that equality can mean is that all men in civil society are equally subject to the general good.

Democracy, he maintained, is an impossible form of government which enthrones the tyranny of the mob.

Democracy is not the last hope of the world, but instead the last madness of a self-idolizing nation.

Bledsoe seems to have been everywhere: in West Point as a fellow student with Robert E. Lee and Jefferson Davis, in Springfield, Illinois, practicing law in the same courts with Abraham Lincoln and Stephen Douglas, Indian fighter in the West, professor of mathematics at the University of Mississippi and the University of Virginia, and minister to London.

According to Bledsoe, the Civil War was a struggle between moral principle and brute force. Principle meant that slavery was a moral right sanctioned by the Bible.

Bledsoe wrote an *Examination of President Edwards' "Inquiry into the Freedom of the Will"* (1845), *A Theodicy: or Vindication of the Divine Glory* (1853), *Essay on Liberty and Slavery* (1856), and *Is Davis a Traitor?, or Was Secession a Constitutional Right Previous to the War of 1861?* (1866).

In *The Philosophy of Mathematics* (1866) he adopts Berkeley's criticism of the calculus as concerned with the "ghosts of departed quantities," "somethings somewhere between something and nothing."

To avoid supposing that a variable will reach or coincide with its limit, Bledsoe argued that "if two variables always have the same ratio to each other, then, although they never reach their limits yet will these limits be in the same ratio." In stating the logic of motion, he may have influenced Peirce in the development of a logic of relations.

In *Theodicy* Bledsoe escapes the predestination of men by the bondage of God, declaring that God was under the necessity of creating the possibility of sin along with the possibility of holiness.

Freedom, he held, applied only to the will, not to the intellect or the appetite, both of which operate under the rigid order of absolute necessity. The will "is an *effort*, an *exertion*, an *act*, a *volition* of the mind."

With regard to education, Bledsoe opposed the uniformity and standardization of the infidel and utilitarian public school system, warned against teachers and books imported from abroad, and said that text-books could safely be written only by professors at the University of Virginia.

• • •

BOODIN, JOHN ELOF (1869-1950): Born in Sweden, educated at Minnesota, Brown, and Harvard, John Elof Boodin taught at the University of Kansas (1904-13) and Carleton College. He scorned "the philosophical disease, psychologitis," and wrote *Time and Reality* (1904), *Truth and Reality* (1911), *A Realistic Universe* (1916), *Creative Religion* (1922), *God and Creation* (1934), and *Religion of Tomorrow* (1943).

• • •

BOWNE, BORDEN PARKER (1847-1910): The founder of Personalism, which he had once called "transcendental empiricism," Borden Parker Bowne was the first of the triumvirate at Boston University: Bowne, Brightman, and Bertocci.

As the stronghold of Personalism since 1876, when Bowne was invited to head its department of philosophy (Personalism ended there in the mid-nineteen-sixties with the throrough-going modernization of the department), Boston University provides an interesting insight into the dialectical development of that philosophical position. Bowne was its chief expositor. When the criticism was pressed that personality cannot be the ultimate reality because of its destruction by natural evil and disaster, Bowne's successor, Edgar Sheffield Brightman *(q.v.)* devoted his attention to answering this objection. The answer was the doctrine of "surd evil" — a frank admission of the force of the problem — and the doctrine of the finite god. Personality is still ultimate, the argument held, as restated — as ultimate as

God, who, though limited by evil, is doing the best he can. As the new weaknesses of this formulation became apparent, the new standard-bearer, Peter A. Bertocci, shifted more and more into the frankly psychological studies, as if trying to create a new version of Fichtean idealism. The theoretical base was left unprotected in favor of the more practical and fruitful analysis of the human personality as such. The young man chosen as the successor began to analyze the nature of consciousness as such, but could not last in the new analytic department, and Personalism, institutionally, is dead, at its home.

Borden Parker Bowne was born in New Jersey and educated at the University of the City of New York, where he was valedictorian of the class of 1871. Two years later he went to Europe to study at Halle and Göttingen. There he learned the philosophy of Lotze (1817-1881), which became the basis for his thought.

Back in America, Bowne became assitant professor of modern languages at his alma mater. He was also religious editor of the New York *Independent*. He wrote a sharp criticism of Spencer, which undoubtedly helped him receive the invitation from Boston University.

He remained at Boston until he died.

His books include: *Metaphysics* (1882), *The Theory of Thought and Knowledge* (1897), and *Personalism* (1908).

Personalism is an attempt to defend the individual from the threats of naturalism and absolutism. It contends that the individual is the center of spiritual force, based ultimately upon the World Ground, God. The self, according to Bowne, must be our basic study, rather than categories of thought. Knowledge was not, as Spencer thought, the result of discrete sensations impressed upon the passive mind. If so, this would destroy the idea of the self as a substance of some sort, "the substantial self." Ultimate reality is personal, and the self is based on the world ground.

Not only is this scheme of thought susceptible of attack

by empiricists and naturalists, but it also makes theists uncomfortable, so much so that Bowne was tried for heresy by the Methodists of New York.

• • •

BRATTLE, WILLIAM (1662-1717): Connected with Harvard College, William Brattle's claim to fame as an early American philosopher rests entirely upon two events. The first is that he was born in Boston. The second is that he wrote a text-book.

Having been born in Boston, he naturally attended Harvard College, graduating when he was eighteen. Several years afterwards, he was employed as a tutor at the school for the ten years from 1686 to 1696. He was quite popular with the students, who nicknamed him, "The Father of the College," perhaps on the theory that he was on his last legs. He had reached the advanced age of 34. The nickname angered the president, who was an Increase Mather, and wanted *himself* to be Father of the College.

William Brattle received his taste of glory as acting president during the absence of Increase. His actions were quite liberal and easy-going. He was forced to pay the penalty for humanitarianism when President Mather returned, by resigning.

Brattle thereupon sank into oblivion, except for a little controversy-stirring in the Cambridge area. He was next heard from at the age of fifty-five when he died.

His book on the subject of logic was published posthumously; it was entitled: *Compendium Logicae Secundum Principia D. Renati Cartesii Plerumque Efformatum et Catechistice Propositum* (1734). Used as the logic text at Harvard for the next seventy-five years, it outlasted Increase.

Written on the principles of Descartes, the book was a notable improvement on the logic of Ramus which Ames used (*q.v.*). In the later editions, voluminous notes referring to Locke are added. Locke's essay on the Human Understanding was published in 1690. It is possible that it could have been available to Brattle in his pre-humous period.

The *Compendium Logicae* is only sixty octavo pages long, written in question-and-answer form. The Prolegomena defines the terms, explains the principles of the division of Logic, and gives the rules of certitude.

The main part is divided into four sections: (1) perception, (2) judgment, (3) reasoning, and (4) method.

Logic is defined as the art of thinking, the art of using reason in comparative cognition. The mind works through four operations: (1) apprehension, (2) judgment, (3) reasoning, and (4) construction *(compositio)*. The use of Logic is like medicine to the body, it helps free the mind from the defects of ignorance, forgetfulness, doubt, error, confusion, obscurity, and the like.

The rules of certainty are: (1) that nothing is to be admitted as true if it includes anything doubtful; (2) do not trust the senses too much; (3) what we perceive we perceive by the mind alone; (4) that is true that we know clearly and distinctly. The model of clear and distinct ideas is directly from Descartes.

(1) Perception. In this section Brattle discusses modes of perception, objects of perception, primary and secondary, and relations. The typical scholastic discussion of substance, affection and the various relations of perceptions is included.

(2) Judgment. Brattle considers here the various kinds of propositions.

(3) Reasoning. The kinds of argumentation, concluding with the syllogism, are presented in this part.

(4) Method is considered briefly.
Brattle's work was similar to the *Port Royal Logic*.
This is why he is here and what he did.

• • •

BRIDGMAN, PERCY WILLIAMS (1882-1961): Nobel Prize-winning physicist, Percy Williams Bridgman turned his talents to philosophical questions as well, authoring *The Logic of Modern Physics* (1927), *The Intelligent Individual and Society,* and *The Way Things Are* (1959). Born in Cambridge, Massachusetts, he attended Harvard and taught there. Drawing heavily upon Einstein's concepts, or his own view of them, Bridgman works out his epistemological operationalism. Concepts, to be meaningful, must be accounted for in terms of operations. Otherwise, concepts — or questions — are meaningless.

• • •

BRIGHTMAN, EDGAR SHEFFIELD (1884-1953): The second figure in Personalism at Boston University, Edgar Sheffield Brightman was the successor to Bowne, who died in 1910. Born at Holbrook, Massachusetts, Brightman studied at Brown and Boston University (S.T.B. 1910, Ph.D. 1912). He was a fellow at Berlin and Marburg. For four years he taught at two Wesleyans, Nebraska and Connecticut, and at Boston University from 1919. He married a German girl who died three years later. In 1918 he married a Connecticut girl.

He wrote some twelve books, including *Religious Values and Recent Philosophy* (1925), *The Problem of God* (1930), *The Finding of God* (1931), *Personality and Religion* (1934), *A Philosophy of Religion* (1940), and *The Spiritual Life* (1942).

An exceptionally clear writer, Brightman's philosophical task was to save Personalism from the problem of evil. He did so by conceding the force of the problem, and giving up the concept of an omnipotent God. By this means he thought to secure the theistic base of his philosophical position.

The problem of evil threatened the Personalistic assumption of the value of the individual spirit. The Personalist platform declared that "person is... dominant in power." Personal power is severely limited when shaking in an earthquake or being buried in an avalanche. If the individual person is the center of value and power for the universe, why is the universe so willing to destroy individual persons in natural disasters?

Brightman admitted the problem, rather than accept a pantheistic view that evil is somehow an illusion. He called such evil "surd" evil, meaning catastrophes such as floods, tidal waves, earthquakes, hurricanes, tornados, and volcanos. These cannot be blamed on human sins.

Therefore, he was driven to limit the power of God. He argued for a finite God, doing the best He can, but limited by "The Given." By so limiting God, Brightman reasoned, you could at least salvage God's goodness. Thus God becomes the architect of the universe rather than its creator. As he shapes the given and fashions it into the good, it resists. That resistance is the cause of evil.

Brightman appealed to Plato for confirmation of his theory, choosing the doctrine of the demiurge, the "divine craftsman" from the *Timaeus*.

•   •   •

BROKMEYER, HENRY CONRAD (1828-1906): In 1858 the most learned scholar in America on Plato and Aristotle, Goethe and Hegel, was employed at the Bridge, Beach & Company Stove Foundry, molding iron pots. Henry Conrad Brokmeyer, the founder of the "St. Louis Movement" in American philosophy, was born in Prussia on the 12th of August, 1828. When he was sixteen he fled his homeland to escape Prussian militarism. Stallo *(q.v.)* had done the same thing at the same time. Arriving in New York with twenty-five cents in his pocket, knowing only three words of English, Brokmeyer first worked as a shoe-shine boy and doing odd jobs.

He went West only to return East for a more liberal education, at Brown University, where he disputed various topics with president Wayland (*q.v.*). In 1854 he went West again, living like Thoreau in the wilderness. Living the life of a recluse in an abandoned cabin in the woods of Warren County, Missouri (near Marthasville), he spent his time studying philosophy.

Brokmeyer provided a striking picture, living in a hut, without furniture, raising pigs, and dictating out his translation of Hegel's *Phenomenology*. The *Larger Logic* of Hegel's was carefully translated by Brokmeyer, but never published, now resting in a box in the Missouri Historical Society.

Brokmeyer was the inspiration and oracle for the St. Louis Movement, including William Torrey Harris (*q.v.*), who later became United States Commissioner of Education.

Married twice (his first wife having died), Brokmeyer entered politics, rising to the position of acting Governor of the state of Missouri.

After 1880, the philosophical movement declined, Brokmeyer with it, and life became rather anticlimactic. He became once again a lonely back-woodsman, taking long hunting and fishing trips into the far West, whittling on mahogany and rosewood saplings.

In influence, he was a kind of Midwestern Socrates, serving as a hegelian midwife to the ideas of others. He died — not of drinking hemlock — July 26, 1906.

•　•　•

BUCHANAN, JOSEPH (1785-1829): Genius can be produced through education whenever society so desires, Joseph Buchanan, mentioned. He was the dynamic and versatile

ALAN W. RICHARDS

Albert Einstein

Ralph Waldo Emerson

Benjamin Franklin

Self-Portrait, c. 1866

William James

philosopher and educator so important to the development of culture in the Ohio River Valley.

Born the 24th of August, 1785, in Washington County, Virginia, he was raised in Tennessee in extreme poverty, unusual hardships, and illness. Against all odds, he entered Transylvania University. Compensating for his lacks both by skill in mathematics and scepticism of authority, he experimented with physics and chemistry (their practical applications to milling and different colored glass), then went into medicine. Writing a research paper on the subject of fever, he took it to Philadelphia where it impressed Benjamin Rush (*q.v.*). Too poor either to publish the paper or afford the cost of remaining in Philadelphia for the medical lectures, Buchanan had to walk back to Lexington, Kentucky. There he was appointed professor of medicine.

His lectures became the noted book: *Philosophy of Human Nature* (1812), teaching Materialistic monism. He emphasized matter over mind, in the style of physiological psychology.

A short time later he proposed reforming education along the lines of Pestalozzi:

> In human nature, sentiment is the only spring of action — the sole power which puts the whole man in motion, and determines in a great degree the measure of his abilities. There is nothing more essential to genius itself, than strength and durability of intellectual feeling. The success of the educator in cultivating the understanding itself must depend very much on the plastic influence and rational control which he is able to exercise over the sentiments of his pupils. By instituting an ardent perseverence of temper he may generate capacity, talents, genius.

This passage is reminiscent of Spinoza's concept of "intellectual love," suggesting that the education of the emotions, which are themselves confused ideas, is the key to the development of other ideas.

In later years, Buchanan also wrote a book designed to produce political leaders, called *The Art of Popularity* (1820). He was an ardent Jeffersonian, and opposed the rise of both Jacksonian democracy and evangelical religion. He shared the belief of other rationalists that the religion appropriate to true democracy is an enlightened, undogmatic religion like deism *(q.v.)*.

As Veblen later did, Buchanan supported himself by journalism, working at a succession of Kentucky newspapers and magazines.

Always trying to escape the confines of a limiting environment, he invented a spiral boiler which, because of its superior light weight and efficient operation, he hoped would be applied to aerial navigation.

C

CALKINS, MARY WHITON (1863-1930): Having studied philosophy at Harvard under William James, Hugo Münsterberg, and Josiah Royce, Mary Whiton Calkins completed the requirements for the Ph.D. with distinction (1896). However, the university would not grant the degree to a woman.

She taught at Wellesley and wrote *An Introduction to Psychology* (1901), *The Persistent Problems of Philosophy* (1907), and *The Good Man and the Good* (1918).

Her thought is close to that of Josiah Royce and she is critical of instrumentalism and logical atomism.

She died at her home in Newton, Massachusetts, in 1930.

•   •   •

CARNAP, RUDOLPH (1891-1970): One of the leading representatives of analytic philosophy, Rudolph Carnap was a member of the Vienna Circle.

Born in Ronsdorf, near Barmen in northwestern Germany, of deeply religious parents, he and his sister were taught by their mother. Since she had been a teacher, she received special permission from the authorities to educate them. Her method was unusual, and most effective. She taught them for only one hour a day. Her theory was that the important thing was not the quantity of material learned, but rather the ability to think for oneself. She stressed clear and interconnected knowledge of each item.

Their father died when Rudolph was only seven.

From 1910 to 1914 he studied at the Universities of Jena and Freiburg/i.B., following his own interests in deciding which lecture courses to attend and which to drop.

The outbreak of war in 1914 "was for me an incomprehensible catastrophe," Carnap remarked. He served in the military, at the front for most of the time. In 1917 he was transferred to Berlin so he could work at developing wireless telegraph and telephone for the army. He observed that the only large group opposing the war was labor. He and his friends applauded the revolutions, both in Germany and Russia, for their negative results, that is, the overthrow of authoritarian regimes. In a short time, the failures of the new systems of government to perform well was disillusioning. Politics, which had not concerned them at all before the war, now seemed a puzzle beyond comprehending.

Carnap turned to philosophy. In 1919 he began to read books by Bertrand Russell, which had the force of a revelation to him. He studied the *Principia Mathematica* and began applying symbolic notation to his own thinking:

> When I considered a concept of a proposition occurring in a scientific or philosophical discussion, I thought that I understood it clearly only if I could express it, if I wanted to, in symbolic language.

In 1921 he read Russell's book, *Our Knowledge of the External World as a Field for Scientific Method in Philosophy*:

> The one and only condition, I believe, which is necessary in order to secure for philosophy in the near future an achievement surpassing all that has hitherto been accomplished by philosophers, is the creation of a school of men with scientific training and philosophical interests, unhampered by the traditions of the past,

and not misled by the literary methods of those who copy the ancients in all except their merits.

Carnap accepted this paragraph as an appeal directed personally to him.

In the same year he received his Ph.D. from Jena. He had wanted to write a dissertation in an area bordering philosophy and physics, but was unable to get either department to sanction it. Physics said it was philosophy, and philosophy said it was physics. It was to have been an exposition of "Axiomatic Foundations of Kinematics," the construction of an axiom system for a physical theory of space and time, using as primitives two relations: (1) the coincidence C of world points of two physical elements, and (2) the time relation T between the world points of the same physical element. Instead, they allowed him to submit a doctoral dissertation entitled *Der Raum,* in which he distinguished between three meanings of space: (1) formal space, (2) intuitive space, and (3) physical space.

He began teaching in 1926 at the University of Vienna. While there, he joined the Vienna Circle. In 1929 he published *Abriss der Logistik,* based on the concepts of the *Principia,* intending to provide not only a system of symbolic logic, but also to show its application to the analysis of concepts and the construction of deductive systems. Beginning in 1930, he edited, with Hans Reichenbach, *Erkenntnis* (later *The Journal of Unified Science*).

From 1931 to 1935 he taught at the German University of Prague, in the Division of Natural Sciences. Here Einstein had taught a few years before. Tycho Brahe and Kepler, earlier in history, had worked only a few miles away. But in the thirties, politics again began to affect life. The Nazis sent assassins to murder Austrian politicians in Vienna. They tracked down a fleeing German professor, fired from his university, and murdered him in Czechoslovakia. War clouds were gathering.

Carnap came to the United States in 1935 and taught at

the University of Chicago from 1936 to 1952. There, at the school now run by Hutchins (*q.v.*), in the department at which John Dewey had once occupied a post, Carnap's comments are interesting:

> I was depressed to see that certain philosophical views which seemed to me long superseded by the development of critical thought and in some cases completely devoid of any cognitive content, were either still maintained or at least treated as deserving serious consideration.... In some philosophical discussion meetings I had the weird feeling that I was sitting among a group of medieval learned men with long beards and solemn robes. This feeling was perhaps further strengthened when I looked out of the window at the other university buildings with their medieval gothic style. I would perhaps dream that one of my colleagues raised the famous question of how many angels could dance on the point of a needle.

He became a naturalized citizen in 1941.

From 1952-1954 he was at the Institute for Advanced Study in Princeton, at the same time Einstein was also there.

In 1954, he accepted the chair of philosophy at UCLA.

His books include *Der Logische Aufbau der Welt (The Logical Structure of the World,* 1928), *The Logical Syntax of Language* (1934), *Introduction to Semantics* (1942), *Meaning and Necessity* (1947), *Logical Foundations of Probability* (1950), and *Logical Structure of the World and Pseudoproblems in Philosophy* (University of California Press, 1964).

The "pseudoproblems" of philosophy for Carnap as for the rest of the Vienna Circle are metaphysical. It is fruitless, he holds, to ask ontological questions about abstract entities. Instead we must be content with a rationally constructed linguistic and conceptual system which is judged by its usefulness to the scientist.

Carnap died in 1970.

• • •

CARUS, PAUL (1852-1919): A monist, believing mind and matter to be identical, Paul Carus pointed to the identity between the laws of nature and the laws of mind. He called himself "an atheist who loved God," a pantheist who rejected the concept of a personal God. Truth, he maintained, was independent of time, human desire, or human action.

Born in Germany, the son of a Lutheran pastor in Prussia, Paul Carus was educated at Strassburg and Tübingen. He taught at the military academy in Dresden until his liberal views brought official opposition. When he was about thirty he left for the United States.

Appointed editor of the *Open Court*, later the Open Court Publishing Company, founded by a Chicago zinc manufactured for the purpose of establishing religion and ethics on a scientific basis, Carus was an energetic author. His bibliography contains over a thousand titles. He wrote that the philosopher's brain ought to work "with the regularity of a machine." Philosophy could be reduced to a science fully as objective he believed as the other sciences.

Among his publications are: *Fundamental Problems* (1889), *Kant and Spencer: a Study of the Fallacies of Agnosticism* (1899), *The Surd of Metaphysics* (1903), and *The Foundations of Mathematics* (1908).

In 1919 he died, but his memory is kept alive by the Carus Foundation, the Carus Lectures, and the American Philosophical Association.

• • •

CHANNING, WILLIAM ELLERY (1780-1842): The "American Schleiermacher," according to Schneider, William Ellery Channing marks the turning point from the American Enlightenment to Transcendentalism. Brought up under strict Calvinism, he spent two years in Virginia as a young man, where he came under the influence of Jefferson, and read Rousseau with great interest (1798-1800). He was private tutor to the Randolph family.

Channing came to a humanitarianism which provided the meeting place for the ideals of enlightened thinkers, the heritage of puritanism, and all the emotional enthusiasm of religious revival. Summing up the past, as he did, he also became the forerunner of the future.

His *Discourse at the Ordination of the Reverend Jared Sparks* (1819) is famous for clearly expressing the principles of Unitarianism, the religious movement so important for loosening the hold of Puritanism society. His text (from I Thessalonians 5:21) read: "Prove all things; hold fast that which is good:"

> Our leading principle in interpreting Scripture is this, that the Bible is a book written for men, in the language of men, and that its meaning is to be sought in the same manner as that of other books.

Channing's view of man was in sharp contrast to Calvinism: I am convinced that virtue and benevolence are *natural* to man.

Returning (in 1823) from a trip to Europe, he wrote of society: I return with views of society which make me rejoice as I never did before in the promise held out by revealed religion of *a moral renovation* of the world. I expect less and less from revolutions, political changes, violent struggles, — from public men or measures, — in a word, from any outward modification of society. Corrupt institutions will be succeeded by others equally, if not more, corrupt, whilst the root principle lives in the heart of individuals and nations; and the only remedy is to be found in a moral change....

•　•　•

CHISHOLM, RODERICK MILTON (1916-   ): Associate editor of *Philosophy and Phenomenological Research*, R. M. Chisholm has written *Perceiving — A Philosophical*

Study (1957), *Realism and the Background of Phenomenology* (1960), and *Theory of Knowledge* (1966). From North Attleboro, Massachusetts, Chisholm attended Brown and Harvard. He has taught at The Barnes Foundation, Merion, Pennsylvania (1946), the University of Pennsylvania (1947), and Brown (since 1947).

•   •   •

CHOMSKY, NOAM (1928-   ): "It may be beyond the limits of human intelligence," Chomsky once said, "to understand how human intelligence works." It depends on whether in principle the human mind can transcend first-order statements to make meaningful second-order statements about itself, to put the matter into the context of Bertrand Russell's theory of descriptions. At any rate, Chomsky is making that attempt quite seriously.

The route he is taking is based on an analysis of grammar, specifically of the aspects all languages have in common. In this way, he intends to discover some unique characteristics of the human mind.

Chomsky disagrees with the empiricists, asserting instead that there is some fixed schematic structure within which any human knowledge has to develop. It can be initiated by experience but its form is determined by the nature of the mind.

He criticizes B. F. Skinner, America's foremost behavioral psychologist, for not explaining man's linguistic creativity. Although a person must hear sentences spoken before he can speak them, Chomsky observes, afterwards he can create an infinite number and variety of sentences that he has not previously heard. Chomsky is also critical of Skinner's educational ideas:

> Skinnerian-type training is appropiate only for industrial-type workers who need to develop complex technical skills. Is growing up and learning no more

63

than the shaping of behavior? If that's what education is all about, authoritarian figures shaping people, then maybe we don't need it.

Born December 7, 1928, Avran Noam Chomsky was raised in Philadelphia and educated at Central High School and the University of Pennsylvania (Ph.D. 1955).

His interest in linguistics began at home, as his father was a Hebrew scholar. When he was ten, he helped read the proofs on his father's edition of a thirteenth-century Hebrew grammar.

At the University of Pennsylvania, he proof-read another book, by his teacher, Zellig Harris: *Methods in Structural Linguistics.* Structural, or descriptive linguistics, is the theory that language is a system of habits acquired by training, a form of human behavior established by the individual's repsonse to the external environment.

Chomsky's criticism of this theory first appeared in *Syntactic Structures* (1957). By "transformational analysis" we can develop a "generative grammar," he believes, based on the idea that every human being has an innate capacity to use language. This capacity is activated by external stimuli but then functions autonomously. The sounds and words of a sentence are the "surface structures." The meaning is derived from "deep structures." Chomsky was never content to merely describe linguistic phenomena, but always attempted to explain them.

His books include *Current Issues in Linguistic Theory* (1964), *Aspects of the Theory of Syntax* (1965), *Cartesian Linguistics* (1966), *Topics in the Theory of Generative Grammar* (1966), *Language and Mind* (1968), and (with Halle) *Sound Patterns of English* (1968).

In all these works, the topics debated between empiricists and rationalists are directly involved, and Leibniz, among others, is examined with reference to the concept of innate ideas. (see *Aspects of the Theory of Syntax,* p. 50).

Noam Chomsky has taught at the Massachusetts Institute of Technology since 1955.

In 1965 he began to protest against the Vietnam war in earnest, and became deeply involved in many radical activities. He was a member of the steering committee of RESIST, a national anti-war movement, and he participated in the October 1967 protest march on the Pentagon. The government subpoenaed him in connection with a grand jury investigation of the unauthorized release of the Pentagon Papers by Daniel Ellsburg. Chomsky charged the government with an illegal wiretap.

He wrote "The Moral Responsibility of Intellectuals" in *American Power and the New Mandarins* (1969), a polemic work dedicated to "the brave young men who refuse to serve in a criminal war." When he was a student, Chomsky had seriously considered joining the Israeli struggle in 1947-48. His opposition to the war in Southeast Asia is part of the new concept of selective pacifism which has evolved over the course of the past decade.

In "Notes on Anarchism" (*New York Review of Books,* May 21, 1970), Chomsky praises "the doctrines and the revolutionary practices of libertarian socialism" of a century ago which could well serve as "an inspiration and a guide" in solving contemporary social problems.

However, sounding a more moderate note, he comments in his essay, "On Resistance," that Americans should appreciate their freedom to criticize the acts of their government. Violent resistance might provoke a fascistic repression by the government:

> We must not, I believe, thoughtlessly urge others to commit civil disobedience, and we must be careful not to construct situations in which young people will find themselves induced, perhaps in violation of their basic convictions, to commit civil disobedience. Resistance must be freely undertaken.

"It is the responsibility of intellectuals," declares Chomsky, "to speak the truth and to expose lies."

• • •

CLAP, THOMAS (1703-1767): The origins of American philosophy are so modest that we find ourselves reviewing as significant a work that today would not receive a passing grade as a freshman essay. Thus we come to Thomas Clap's contribution to ethical theory.

President of Yale College from 1740, he was author of *An Essay on the Nature and Foundation of Virtue and Moral Obligation* (1765). It was the third book on ethics (following Johnson and Edwards) to appear in America after 1740. The one valid contribution it made was its hesitant and clumsy demand for a more scientific foundation for the principles of conduct. Examining the basis for ethical theory, Clap wrote:

(1) Self-love cannot be the basis for ethical action. It is an absolute inversion of the order, dignity and perfection of beings. It makes a small part bigger than the whole.

(2) Benevolence is a good principle, so far as it goes. However, it is only one of the perfections which every moral agent ought to have.

(3) Moral sense (taste) may proceed wholly from self-love, so far as it exists in the mind of a mere natural and unenlightened man. It is thus not the same as conscience, which is a judgment of action as agreeable or disagreeable to the law of God. If taste were the rule there would be as many rules as there are different tastes among mankind.

(4) Reason, similarly, is insufficient as the basis for moral obligation. The term is too vague. Even if rightly understood, it must have some data or principle to act upon. As a power it can not be so excellent as to be the criterion of divine favor or to claim supreme authority.

If so, man would be his own lawgiver. It is too general to be the special criterion of moral virtue.

(5) Moral fitness is too vague a term to be a proper criterion for virtue.

(6) Conformity to the truth is a true principle if (and only if) truth means the perfections of God. If, however, it means the truth of fact, that can not determine moral action. [This particular point — at least the second half — reappears as a point of criticism in contemporary analytical ethical theory.]

(7) Right and wrong are also too vague. To set up the right as the standard for moral behavior is to set up a thing which is not God as the standard for God. If this criterion were accepted, there would be many and various ideas of ethical conduct.

(8) Obedience to the will and command of God for the purpose of promoting one's own happiness is, as we have seen, the principle of self-interest.

However, all such principles may be admitted if they are kept subordinate to the main principle of moral action.

Divine revelation alone can show us how to know the perfection of God and what intention and action conforms to those perfections.

Clap defines moral virtue as conformity to the moral perfections of God. This, he claims, is the foundation of moral obligation.

Thus Clap belongs to the large pre-revolutionary group of clergymen-educators, and his theories are notable principally for their steadfast orthodoxy.

• • •

COHEN, MORRIS RAPHAEL (1880-1947): A naturalist, Morris Raphael Cohen has been called a "structural" naturalist because of his interest in the "structural" sciences, physics and mathematics, as opposed to the "functional" naturalism or John Dewey, who was more drawn to the "functional" sciences, biology and sociology.

Cohen was born in Minsk and called a moron by the townspeople. At twelve, he was brought to the United States and educated at CCNY and Harvard, attending during its "Golden Age," when its teachers included James, Royce, Perry, and Münsterberg. He taught at CCNY for years, and was responsible for the renaissance of philosophy in American law. He wrote *Reason and Nature* (1931) and *The Faith of a Liberal* (1946). He criticized Bergson for confusing metaphysics and natural science to the detriment of both, and remarked further:

> We befuddle the issues with essentially vague and question-begging terms like religious experience, very much as the old Scottish theological realists elevated questionable dogma into a fundamental intuition of the human mind.

• • •

COLDEN, CADWALLADER (1688-1776): A New York politician, an immigrant from Scotland, Cadwallader Colden had a pronounced interest in science. This contrasts sharply with the theological backgrounds of other colonial philosophers.

Colden is noted for some rather valuable work in botany. His achievements in this area, for those who are interested, may be traced in a dictionary of American botanists.

He wrote a letter to Samuel Johnson criticizing Berkleyan idealism, a letter worth mentioning but not worth quoting.

His positive contribution to American philosophy lies more in the area of the philosophy of science. He wrote a book entitled *An Explication of the First Cause of Action in Matter and of the Cause of Gravitation* (1745).

68

Chapter I discusses the first principles of physics, primary material agents. Matter is defined as that which is both extended and impenetrable. These are the essential properties of all matter, but there may be different kinds of matter. One different property is the power of resistance. Resistance is said to be an active force. It differs from the other two kinds of matter, moving force and elastic (expansive) force. Resistance is negative in relation to both of these.

Thus, matter, he concludes, is fundamentally power, action, or force. Action without motion is not inconceivable, thinking being one example of action without motion. This conception of matter as a force prevented Colden from agreeing with Johnson (*q.v.*) that action and intelligence are identical.

Chapter II treats the cause of gravitation. Gravity is the result of the pressure of ether on two bodies. This pressure is proportional to the depth of the ether pressing on them. Since the depth of ether between the bodies is less than the pressure on their opposite sides, they are pushed together.

I leave it to the reader to judge the profundity of his work.

Colden is classed with Benjamin Franklin and David Rittenhouse, as he cooperated with them in founding the American Philosophical Society, with the idea of promoting "useful knowledge," "more useful knowledge than can be learned from books," presumably even from his own book.

When he introduced his son to philosophy, Colden wrote: "I told you before that the school learning is really a misapplication of time, in learning of things which exist nowhere but in the imagination of idle, monkish, useless men, and serves no good purpose in life." — from *An Introduction to the Study of Phylosophy,* reprinted in Blau, *American Philosophic Addresses 1700-1900,* 301.

This attack on classical education is notable. Colden wanted to obtain the unity of the sciences, a unity intended to serve the "well-being" of life, that is, whatever produces health and pleasure.

CONSCIENCE:

1. In *The Nature of True Virtue,* Jonathan Edwards observes: Some vices may become in a degree odious by the influence of self-love, through an habitual connection of ideas of contempt with it; contempt being what self-love abhors. So it may often be with drunkenness, gluttony, sottishness, cowardice, sloth, niggardliness. The idea of contempt becomes associated with the idea of such vices, both because we are used to observe that those things are commonly objects of contempt, and also find that they excite contempt, in ourselves. — Some of them appear marks of littleness, i. e., of small abilities, and weakness of mind, and insufficiency for any considerable effects among mankind. — By others, men's influence is contracted into a narrow sphere, and by such means persons become of less importance, and more insignificant among mankind. — Jonathan Edwards (1755), in Faust & Johnson, 370.

2. John Dewey: Our intelligence is bound up, so far as its materials are concerned, with the community life of which we are a part. We know what it communicates to us, and know according to the habits it forms in us. . . . So with conscience. When a child acts, those about him re-act. They shower encouragement upon him, visit him with approval, or they bestow frowns and rebuke. What others do to us when we act is as natural a consequence of our action as what the fire does to us when we plunge our hands in it. The social environment may be as artificial as you please. But its action in response to ours is natural, not artificial. In language and imagination we rehearse the responses of others just as we dramatically enact other consequences. We foreknow how others will act, and the foreknowledge is the beginning of judgment passed on action. We know with them; there is conscience. An assembly is formed within our breast which discusses and appraises proposed and perfor-

med acts. The community without becomes a forum and tribunal within, a judgment-seat of charges, assessments and exculpations. Our thoughts of our own actions are saturated with the ideas that others entertain about them, ideas which have been expressed not only in explicit instruction but still more effectively in reaction to our acts. — *Human Nature and Conduct*.

• • •

COOPER, THOMAS (1759-1839): A refugee from England, like his friend Joseph Priestly (*q.v.*), Thomas Cooper fled the social and political thought-control that threatened to stifle him. In 1794 he settled near Priestly in Northumberland, Pennsylvania.

Cooper was a materialist in philosophy and a revolutionist in political theory. He readily applied his materialistic psychology to the problems of morality and religion, to the horror of clerics. Cooper replied by colorful denunciations of the craft of priesthood.

In America, he became passionately attached to Jefferson's party. Attacking the Sedition Act, he was himself convicted under it, sentenced to six months in prison and fined $400. For the rest of his life he fought for recovery of this fine, which at last, after his death, was refunded to his heirs, with interest.

After a stormy career in politics, during which he was attacked as too conservative by radical democrats, surely the supreme irony, he returned to the solace of science, teaching chemistry at Carlisle (now Dickinson) College.

Jefferson invited him to be the "corner-stone" of the new University of Virginia, but owing to clerical opposition and some delay in the opening of the institution, Cooper was unable to serve. Jefferson was greatly disappointed.

Instead, Cooper went to another southern school, the University of South Carolina, in 1820. Serving first as professor of chemistry, later as president, he became the chief academic philosopher of the theory of states rights. He valued union much less than he prized liberty.

The *Lectures on the Elements of Political Economy* (1826) was used extensively as a text-book in America.

Cooper was a consistent, firm, effective believer in the doctrine of salvation through knowledge.

* * *

CREIGHTON, JAMES EDWIN (1861-1924): Sage Professor of Philosophy at Cornell, James Edwin Creighton was a strenuous critic of the Pragmatism of James and Dewey, as well as of neo-realism and materialism. Creighton espoused idealism greatly influenced by Hegel. *Studies in Speculative Philosophy* appeared posthumously, in 1925.

D

DAVIDSON, THOMAS (1840-1900): Born at Old Deer, Scotland, Thomas Davidson moved to Canada and the United States after he had completed his education. Teaching high school in St. Louis, he became the life-long friend of W. T. Harris (q.v.), the famed American Hegelian and United States Commissioner of Education. Davidson, however, never saw anything in Hegelianism. His own philosophy was much more individualistic. Based on the writings of Rosmini, Davidson's thought can be classified as pluralistic idealism, which he called "apeirotheism."

In later years he founded the "Bread-Winners' College" on New York City's lower East Side. A sort of Hard Hat University, it was supposed to make the best culture of the ages available to wage-earners, so they could rise to higher mental and spiritual levels.

Davidson wrote for the *Journal of Speculative Philosophy* and published such books as *Aristotle and Ancient Educational Ideals* (1892), *Education of the Greek People, and its Influence on Civilization* (1894), *Rousseau and Education According to Nature* (1898), and *A History of Education* (1900).

•   •   •

DEISM: The theory that God's transcendence is more fundamental than his immanence. Proof of God's character is not by means of miracles or revelation, but by eternal law and natural reason.

Deism was closely associated with the American Revolution, advocated by Thomas Paine (*q.v.*) and Ethan Allen, among others.

Ethan Allen (1738-1789) was a soldier commanding the Green Mountain Boys who were seeking their own state (Vermont) out of the New Hampshire Grants. The area was hotly contested by New York and New Hampshire, and in 1771 Allen was an outlaw with 20 pounds on his head. In 1784 he wrote *Reason the Only Oracle of Man; or, A Compenduous System of Natural Religion.* He opposed authority of any kind. Tradition was fallible. Faith was unreliable and unimportant. Reason was the highest gift of God. Because the world was created by God, there "can be no ultimate failure," even though humans are "the most selfish, oddest, and most cunning medley of beings of that size in the universe." This book is quite rare because most of the first edition was destroyed by fire at the printer's in Bennington. The fire was hailed as "an act of God," because of the book's "atheistic" content, so the printer attempted to finish the process himself by burning most of the remaining volumes.

•   •   •

DEW, THOMAS RODERICK (1802-1846): Dew of Dewsville is notable for his pro-slavery arguments in the *Review of the Debate in the Virginia Legislature of 1831 and 1832* [reprinted as part of *The Pro-Slavery Argument* (1852)]. A noted economist, he was chosen the first lay president of the College of William and Mary. This was at the time when there were not enough students for the clergymen to bother fighting over.

1831 was the year of the first (and only) successful slave rebellion in the United States. Instigated by Nat Turner, a house slave who saw a vision of blood descending on corn stalks in late August and naturally interpreted this remarkable sight as a divine sign for him to go to Jerusalem (which was a town a convenient distance north of Cross Keys Plantation), killing all the whites along the way. This led to some opposition on the part of those who disagreed. Stiff resistance surpressed the revolt.

The matter was hotly debated in the State Legislature a safe distance away. The fact was noted that Turner had been reading the Bible, previous to the revolt. The legislators decided that the dissatisfaction of the slaves could be cured by forbidding them to read.

Dew proposed turning Virginia into a kind of breeding-ground for slaves, producing them to sell to other states.

Thomas Roderick Dew had been well educated in the classics, and traveled in Europe for two years after gradua-tion. He was quite impressed by the German scholars' frank recognition of human inequalities.

Receiving the salary of $1000 as a professor, he decided to make hay while the sun was shining; marrying Natalia Hay. The sun went down sooner that he thought. He died on his honeymoon in Paris.

Following this romantic death, he remained in Europe for some time, returning only in 1939 to occupy a crypt in the Wren building at the College, where he has been ever since.

His books include *Lectures on the Restrictive System* (1829) *And Digest of the Laws, Customs, Manners, and Institutions of the Ancient and Modern Nations* (1853).

The renowned American authority on Dew is H. Marshall Booker, Dean of the Christopher Newport College of the College of William and Mary in Virginia.

•   •   •

DEWEY, JOHN (1859-1952): The third of the Pragmatists (after Peirce and James), John Dewey was a profound and prolific writer who deserves to stand in the front rank of the world's great thinkers.

Born in Burlington, Vermont, October 20, 1859, he graduated from the University of Vermont (A.B. 1879)

75

and taught school for two years in rural Vermont and Pennsylvania. He entered Johns Hopkins and received the Ph.D. in 1884.

He taught for the next four years at the University of Michigan, then (1888-1889) at the University of Minnesota, both rivals for the little brown jug. He returned to Michigan for five more years (1889-1894). For the next ten years (1894-1904) he taught at The University of Chicago, becoming the head of the combined departments of philosophy, psychology and education. He established and directed the Lab school there. In 1904 he went to Columbia, where he remained for twenty-six years, until his retirement in 1930, seventy years of age.

He was a guest lecturer and consultant in such countries as China, Turkey, Japan, Mexico, and the U.S.S.R.

On the celebration of his ninetieth birthday, he declared that losing faith in our fellow man means losing faith in ourselves, "and that is the unforgivable sin."

II. Works

Dewey was the author of some fifty-six books, the most significant of which are:

(1) *Psychology* (New York: Harper & Bros., 1887),

(2) *The School and Society* (Chicago: The University of Chicago Press, 1900),

(3) *Studies in Logical Theory* (Chicago: The University of Chicago Press, 1903) in which he acknowledged his debt to William James, and set forth his "instrumentalism,"

(4) *Democracy and Education* (New York: The Macmillan Co., 1916),

(5) *Reconstruction in Philosophy* (New York: Henry Holt & Co., 1920),

(6) *Human Nature and Conduct* (New York: Henry Holt & Co., 1922),

(7) *The Quest for Certainty* (Minton, Balch & Co., 1929),

(8) *Art as Experience* (Minton, Balch & Co., 1934),

(9) *A Common Faith* (New Haven: Yale University Press, 1934),

(10) *Logic: The Theory of Inquiry* (New York: Henry Holt & Co., 1938).

Certain other of his works are more topical in character, and include: *German Philosophy and Politics* (1915), *Letters from China and Japan* (1920), *Why I am Not a Communist* (1934), *The Case of Leon Trotsky: Report of Hearings on the Charges Made Against Him in the Moscow Trials* (1937), and *The Bertrand Russell Case* (1941).

III. Thought

As the foremost American Pragmatist, last of the triumvirate, Dewey's conceptions in epistemology are significant. It will be recalled that Pragmatism is the theory that truth consists in the practical effectiveness of an idea. Truth is what works, what guides us successfully. The question left unanswered by this general formulation is how to interpret the term "success." Schiller had viewed it in terms of utility. James had seen it in terms of human satisfaction. Peirce and Dewey (who preferred the term "instrumentalism") together conceived it as predictive power, verifiability, utility in inquiry.

As Dewey wrote, knowledge is not the confrontation of a subject with an object, but rather the resolution of experiential problems. As situations present themselves to the organism, they are indeterminate and problematic. Knowledge thus is the transformation of such a situation into one which is coherent and determinate.

Metaphysically, Dewey is a critical naturalist. Nature includes whatever exists, not merely what is physical or material. Everything, values included, can be understood in terms of natural knowledge. In *A Common Faith,* Dewey interprets religion in naturalistic and humanistic terms. In ethics moral principles are judged by their effectiveness in resolving human difficulties without introducing further difficulties.

Dewey's aesthetics is best expressed in *Art as Experience.* Art intensifies those features which make experience satisfying to us. It raises them above the level of more perception so that they may be enjoyed for their own sake. Dewey's theory of art is best presented by the Barnes Foundation of Pennsylvania, through its various educational enterprises.

His educational theory, which has had such a wide influence in America, characteristically opposes an externally imposed discipline. Students in a progressive classroom derive their sense of discipline from constructive work, tasks chosen by themselves. "Experience" and "learning by doing" were the slogans of the new educational theory. Dewey's pedagogic creed begins:

> I believe that all education proceeds by the participation of the individual in the social consciousness of the race. This process begins unconsciously almost at birth.... Through this unconscious education the individual gradually comes to share in the intellectual and moral resources which humanity has succeeded in getting together. He becomes an inheritor of the funded capital of civilization.

• • •

DRAKE, DURANT (1878-1933): One of the school of Critical Realists, opposing the difficulties inherent in Neo-Realism, Durant Drake of Vassar was from Hartford, Connecticut. His education was received at Harvard and

Columbia. His wife hailed from Milford, Pennsylvania, the town to which Charles S. Peirce had retired to escape his creditors. He taught at Illinois and Wesleyan of Connecticut. He wrote the *Problem of Things in Themselves* (1911), *Problems of Conduct* (1914), *Problems of Religion* (1916), *Shall We Stand by the Church?* (1920), *Essays in Critical Realism*, with others (1921), and *Invitation to Philosophy* (1933).

In his last book, he observes that:
The conclusions of science are the surest knowledge we have; and *so far as science goes,* we can trust it more confidently than any other brand of truth.... *Philosophy is the integration of knowledge, the synthesis of the sciences.*

•   •   •

DURANT, WILL (1885-   ): Historian of philosophy, Will Durant has popularized various philosophers through his best-selling books: *Philosophy and the Social Problem* (1917 — this was not best-selling, but it was his first book), *The Story of Philosophy* (1926 — really a collection of articles on some of the world's great thinkers, published first in the Haldeman-Julius series of Little Blue Books, an effort to make cultural knowledge available to the masses of working men), *Transition* (1927), *The Mansions of Philosophy* (1929 — later entitled *The Pleasures of Philosophy*), *Adventures in Genius* (1931), *On the Meaning of Life* (1932), the ten volumes of *The Story of Civilization* 1935-1967), *The Lessons of History* (1968), and *Interpretations of Life* (1970).

Born in North Adams, Massachusetts, November 5, 1885, William James Durant was educated at St. Peter's College, New Jersey, and Columbia (Ph.D. 1917). He taught Latin and French at Seton Hall, 1907-11, directed the Labor Temple School in New York City, 1914-27, taught at Columbia, 1917, and UCLA, 1935.

When he was twelve, literature came to him with the force of a revelation, beginning with a copy of *Pickwick Papers* which he borrowed from his girl friend. He saved fourteen cents, bought *David Copperfield,* and was permanently hooked on the power of literary expression. When twenty, he read Darwin and Spencer, "lost my faith and found philosophy." He conceives of philosophers as:

all who have persistently inquired into the meaning and possibilities of life, or who have tried to live in the perspective of a humane intelligence.

• • •

DWIGHT, TIMOTHY (1752-1817): The American who tried to refute David Hume in a poem, and in the bargain to "slay the dreadful Monsieur de Voltaire" *(The Triumph of Infidelity, a Poem,* 1788), Timothy Dwight was much more successful as an administrator and teacher, president of Yale from 1795 until his death twenty-two years later.

Dwight's father was the grandson of Jonathan Edwards, a giant of a man, six feet four and (by actual test) as strong as an ox. Young Timothy was a brilliant student. His young mother (seventeen at his birth) taught him early. He learned the alphabet at one lesson, and was reading the Bible easily and correctly by the age of four. At six, against the wishes of his father and without the knowledge of his schoolmaster, he would sneak into the schoolroom while the other boys were out at play, and teach himself Latin by reading their books. At that rate he would have been ready for college at eight, but the school was closed, and he had to wait until he was thirteen to enter Yale.

College taught him how to waste time, which he did by playing cards. At fifteen, however, he got hold of himself, and began studying in earnest, which for him meant rising at 4:30 in the winter and 3:30 in the summer, to read by candlelight. This ruined his eyes. He also decided to save time by not eating more than twelve mouthfuls in any one meal. This ruined his health. He recovered by a rigorous walking and riding regimen, two thousand miles in the first case and three thousand (by horseback) in the second.

When he had finished school, he continued his industrious way of life, teaching (a school for both sexes, six hours a day), preaching, writing (at least nine books, including *The Conquest of Canaan* (1785), intended to be an American *Iliad* or *Aeneid*) and running two farms.

When elected president of Yale, he was no less energetic. He would dictate to several secretaries at once, turning from one to the other without losing his train of thought. He taught the senior class rhetoric, logic, metaphysics, and ethics. He supplied the college pulpit. Called by some "Pope Dwight," more appreciative mothers taught their children to consider him second only to St. Paul.

From his administration Yale dates her modern era. He encouraged the teaching of science, started the medical school, and planned for the addition of departments of theology and law.

He rates as the prime example of all that was good in puritanism, and all that was bad in it, as well. He combined the highest in noble purposes with the lowest in intolerance and bigotry.

He died on January 11, 1817, of cancer.

II

Dwight can be said to represent the enlightened orthodoxy of the period, as Franklin and Paine represented enlightened heresy.

He believed there was no conflict between reason and revealed religion. Whatever conflicts appeared were caused, he thought, by our finite nature. Revealed truth ought to be accepted by a reasonable man until any apparent conflicts could be resolved reasonably.

Dwight, like Edwards, held that faith in the ultimate

rationality of revealed religion would save the human mind from the precipice of abstract reason.

Dwight's orthodoxy was mild, reasonable, and humane, as compared with other religious formulations of the time. Yet it can be easily appreciated that Dwight's ideas led to a kind of *ad hominem* attack upon scepticism. Scepticism refused his invitation to be meek and mild until revealed truth could be shown to be rational after all, especially when the process seemed likely to take longer than one lifetime.

EDUCATION:

1. In his letter to the trustees at Princeton, offering him the Presidency ("head of Nassau Hall"), Jonathan Edwards describes his conception of the proper duties of such an educational office:

> If I should see light to determine me to accept the place offered me, I should be willing to take upon me the work of a president, so far as it consists in the general inspection of the whole society; and to be subservient to the school, as to their order and methods of study and instruction, assisting, myself, in the immediate instruction in the arts and sciences, (as discretion should direct, and occasion serve, and the state of things require,) especially of the senior class; and added to all, should be willing to do the whole work of a professor of divinity, in public and private lectures, proposing questions to be answered, and some to be discussed in writing and free conversation, in meetings of graduates, and others, appointed in proper seasons, for these ends. It would be now out of my way, to spend time, in a constant teaching of the languages; unless it be the Hebrew tongue; which I should be willing to improve myself in, by instructing others. — Letter of Oct. 19, 1757, in Faust & Johnson, *op. cit.*, 413.

2. John Dewey:

(1). All education proceeds by the participation of the individual in the social consciousness of the race. This process begins unconsciously almost at birth, and is continually shaping the individual's powers, saturating his consciousness, forming his habits, training his ideas, and arousing his feelings and emotions. Through this unconscious education the individual gradually comes to share in the intellectual and moral resources which humanity has succeeded in getting together. He becomes an inheritor of the funded capital of civilization. The most formal and technical education in the world cannot safely depart from this general process. It can only organize it or differentiate it in some particular direction. — *My Pedagogic Creed.*

(2). Education... is a process of living and not a preparation for future living. — *Ibid.*

(3). Education is the fundamental method of social progress and reform. — *Ibid.;* also *Education Today.*

(4). While our educational leaders are talking of culture, the development of personality, etc., as the end and aim of education, the great majority of those who pass under the tuition of the school regard it only as a narrowly practical tool with which to get bread and butter enough to eke out a restricted life. — *The School and Society.*

(5). Speaking generally, education signifies the sum total of processes by which a community or social group, whether small or large, transmits its acquired power and aims with a view to securing its own continued existence and growth. — "Education," in the *Cyclopedia of Education* (ed. by P. Monroe).

(6). Education may be defined as a process of continuous reconstruction of experience with the purpose of widening and deepening its social content, while, at the same time, the individual gains control of the methods involved. — *Ibid.*

(7). The function of education is to help the growing of a helpless young animal into a happy, moral, and efficient human being. — *Schools of To-Morrow* (with Evelyn Dewey).

(8). Education is not something to be forced upon children and youth from without, but is the growth of capacities with which human beings are endowed at birth. — *Ibid.*

(9). Education which treats all children as if their impulses were those of the average of an adult society is sure to go on reproducing that same average society without even finding out whether and how it might be better. — *Ibid.*

(10). The educative process is a continuous process of growth, having as its aim at every stage an added capacity of growth. — *Democracy and Education.*

(11). Even in a savage tribe, the achievements of adults are far beyond what the immature members would be capable of if left to themselves. With the growth of civilization, the gap between the original capacities of the immature and the standards and customs of the elders increases. Mere physical growing up, mere masterly of the bare necessities of subsistence will not suffice to reproduce the life of the group. Deliberate effort and the taking of thoughtful pains are required. Beings who are born not only unaware of, but quite indifferent to, the aims and habits of the social group have to be rendered cognizant of them and actively interested. Education, and education alone, spans the gap. — *Ibid.*

(12). The best thing that can be said about any special process of education, like that of the formal school period, is that it renders its subject capable of further education: more sensitive to conditions of growth and more able to take advantage of them. Acquisition of skill, possession of knowledge, attainment of culture are not ends: they are marks of growth and means to its continuing. — *Reconstruction in Philosophy.*

(13). Those who received education are those who give it; habits already engendered deeply influence its course.... There is no possibility of complete escape from this circle. — "Body and Mind," in the *Bulletin of the N. Y. Academy of Medicine,* IV (1928).

(14). We educate for the *status quo* and when the students go forth they do not find anything so settled that it can be called anything of a static kind. — *Education and the Social Order.*

(15). The history of educational theory is marked by opposition between the idea that education is development from within and that it is a formation from without; that it is based upon natural endowments and that education is a process of overcoming natural inclinations and substituting in its place habits acquired under external pressure.... To imposition from above is opposed expression and cultivation of individuality; to external discipline is opposed free activity; to acquisition of isolated skills and techniques by drill is opposed acquisition of them as means of attaining ends which make direct vital appeal; to preparation for a more or less remote future is opposed making the most of opportunities of present life; to static aims and materials is opposed acquaintance with a changing world. — *Experience and Education.*

Thomas Jefferson

Charles Sanders Peirce

Josiah Royce

Henry Thoreau
(From the Rowse Sketch)

E

EDWARDS, JONATHAN (1703-1758): The thought of the eminent American philosopher, Jonathan Edwards, is difficult to understand because it appears in the theological idiom of the time. Despite the barbarous Calvinism that masks his thought, he was an original and profound thinker. His death at the age fifty-four was a definite loss to the American scene, as he was then at the high point of increasing powers of thought. Edwards was important as a contributor to the philosophy of religion, metaphysics, the psychology of religion, and ethics. Further, the methods used in his writings suggest some originality and importance in epistemology.

I. Life

Born at East Windsor, Connecticut, on October 5, 1703, Jonathan Edwards wrote when only eleven or twelve his observations on the flying or Balloon Spider. His father, a clergyman, had been in correspondence with some English friends who had asked for information on American spiders. Aside from various teleological and theological lessons he derived from his observations, the following selection is included here:

> Of all Insects no one is more wonderfull than the Spider especially with Respect to their sagacity and admirable way of working.... I have Plainly Discerned in those webs that were nearer to my eye and Once saw a very large spider to my surprise swimming in the air in this manner, and Others have assured me that they

often have seen spiders fly, the appearance is truly very Pretty And Pleasing and it was so pleasing as well as surprising to me that I Resolved to endeavour to Satisfy my Curiosity about it by finding Out the way and manner of their Doing of it, being also Persuaded that If I could find out how they flew I could easily find out how they made webs from tree to tree.... Another Reason why they will not fly at any other time but when a dry wind blows is because a moist wind moistens the web and makes it heavier than the air And if they had the sense to fly themselves, we should have hundreds of times more spiders and flies by the sea shore than any where else. — "Of Insects," quoted in Clarence Faust and Thomas Johnson, *Jonathan Edwards* (New York: American Book Company, 1935), p. 3 ff.

In 1716 he entered Yale College and graduated in 1720. During his college years, he wrote essays on "The Soul," "Of the Rainbow," "Of Being," and "Colours." In these works he gives evidence of an understanding of Newton and a capacity for original thinking on various scientific and philosophical subjects. During these years, he also wrote "Notes on the Mind," covering the philosophical topics of existence and perfection ("excellency"):

It is now agreed upon by every knowing philosopher, that Colours are not really in the things, no more than Pain is in a needle; but strictly no where else but in the mind. But yet I think that Colour may have an existence out of the mind, with equal reason as any thing in Body has any existence out of the mind. . . . For what else is that, which we call by the name of Body? I find Colour has the chief share in it. Coroll. 1. How impossible is it, that the world should exist from Eternity, without a Mind. Coroll. 2. Since it is so, and that absolute Nothing is such a dreadful contradiction; hence we learn the necessity of the Eternal Existence of an All-comprehending Mind; and that it is the complication of all contradictions to deny such a mind. — *Ibid.*, 28.

For the next two years, from 1720 to 1722, he studied theology in New Haven.

In August of 1722, he went as a minister to a Scotch Presbyterian church in New York which met on William Street between Liberty and Wall. The church system in Connecticut, following the teachings of Stoddard, having adopted the Saybrook Platform of 1708, was so close to the Presbyterian practice that such an appointment was possible. There was violent enmity, on the other hand, to episcopal polity. They still talked of the scandal at Yale, when Jeremy Dummer's gift of library books had been received and read by Rector Cutler and his tutors, Johnson and Browne, converting them to the episcopacy and causing their dismissal by the trustees of the school.

Jonathan Edwards' *Resolutions* and *Diary* were begun at this period: 25. Resolved; To examine carefully, and constantly, what that one thing in me is, which causes me in the least to doubt of the love of God; and to direct all my forces against it. — *Ibid.*, 40.

The manuscript of the *Diary* was lost, and survives only in Dwight's Life, which provides the text of the document. In May of 1723, he left the New York church. The church was not responding to him, so he went to Bolton, Connecticut. Spending the summer at East Windsor, he had completed arrangements at Bolton when he received an offer from Yale, took the M.A. in September, and became a Tutor on May 21, 1724.

As there was still no president at the time, Edwards was virtually in charge, in charge, that is, of one other colleague. Together they instructed the student body of sixty.

In 1725, he fell seriously ill. The next year he resigned

his academic position and became the colleague of his aging grandfather, Solomon Stoddard, in the church at Northampton, Massachusetts.

In Northampton Edwards married Sarah Pierrepont. They had eleven children, eight daughters and three sons. In 1729 he succeeded to the pastorate of the church on the death of his grandfather. He remained in this post until 1750.

During this time he was actively writing, producing such books as *God Glorified in the Work of Redemption by the Greatness of Man's Dependence upon Him in the Whole of It* (1731), *A Divine and Supernatural Light, Immediately Imparted to the Soul by the Spirit of God, Shown to be both a Scriptural, and Rational Doctrine* (1734), *A Faithful Narrative of the Surprising Work of God in the Conversion of Many Hundred Souls in Northampton, and the Neighboring Towns and Villages* (1737), *Charity and its Fruits* (1738, publ. 1851), *Discourses on Various important Subjects* (1734, publ. 1738), *Narrative of His Conversion* (1739), *The Distinguishing Marks of a Work of the Spirit*, the famous sermon preached at Enfield, Connecticut, *Sinners in the Hands of an Angry God* (1741), *Some Thoughts concerning the Present Revival of Religion in New England* (1742), *A Treatise concerning Religious Affections* (1742-43, publ. 1746), *An Humble Attempt to Promote Visible Union of God's People in Extraordinary Prayer for the Revival of Religion* (1747), *An Account of the Life of the Late Reverend Mr. David Brainerd* and *An Humble Inquiry into the Rules of the Word of God, concerning the Qualifications Requisite to a Complete Standing and Full Communion with the Visible Christian Church* (1749).

However, as voluminous as his writing was, his great work on the freedom of the will remained in the future. The occasion that presented itself to him was, oddly enough, dissension in the Northampton parish.

During his years at Northampton the Great Awakening, a widespread revival of interest in religion, had taken place. This phenomenon of 1740-41 had been intensely emotional. Indirectly, however, it was connected with growing rejection of aristocracy, "special privilege." People wanted a democratic and universally available religious salvation. "I won't worship a wig," was the comment of one of those soon to be involved in the "bad book" controversy.

The aftermath of the revival saw several suicides. One was the father of a boy active in agitating against Jonathan Edwards. The revival had left a strange taste of bitterness in the land. There was greatly increased mobility among the ministers. The old ideal of life tenure in a parish was lost.

The pews began to feel their power. Laymen began to challenge the pulpit's statements on various matters. Points of doctrine were disputed. The evangelists of the Great Awakening, beginning with George Whitefield, had encouraged laymen to preach the Gospel. Once grasped, this privilege was eagerly kept. It became a direct challenge to the aristocratic ministry. The most prominent victim of such forces was Jonathan Edwards, an active supporter of the revival in the first place.

The "bad book" controversy was what led to his dismissal. It was a case involving the moral behavior of teenagers. Some of them had gotten hold of a book of instructions used by midwives in the delivery of babies. They were passing it around to each other, reading about sex. In the New England of the time, public denunciations of watermelon stealing and "horse borrowing" were common. Sex was a much more serious threat to the public morals. The situation invited exposure.

Exposure came, from the pulpit. Yet when it did, there was a storm of local controversy. Edwards read the list of accusers and accused. He made no differentiation between them, in the course of the announcement hearings, or at least the shocked parents heard none. Parents and friends were enraged.

The document in the collection of Edwards' papers containing the names does have various markings which differentiate between the accusers and accused. Possibly Edwards did not make these differences sufficiently clear. The failing, if any, would be one of tact. However, considering the number of years he had served the town, it is hard to understand how such a small matter could become so important. The key must be found elsewhere, no doubt in the reaction against the aristocracy rising throughout the land.

Another cause of trouble was a disagreement in the parish over who should be admitted to communion. As in the case of Emerson, years later, Edwards' difficulty stemmed from his careful re-examination of the basis of the practice. Thus, Edwards attempted to restrict the number of communicants to those who intended to follow religious principles, who could agree to some such statement as the following:

> I hope I truly find in my heart a willingness to comply with all the commandments of God, which require me to give up myself wholly to him, and to serve him with my body and my spirit, and do accordingly now promise to walk in a way of obedience to all the commandments of God, as long as I live.

As this amounted to an important departure from orthodox practice in the area at that time, another storm arose. Stoddard, Edwards' grandfather, though long dead, still dominated thought in the area on this subject. He had liberalized the membership around the Lord's Table. His arguments and books on the subject were well remembered at the Northampton church and in the surrounding county.

Edwards' argument was simply that Stoddard had been mistaken. He examined all of the old arguments and demonstrated their falsehood. This elaborate procedure convinced no one. A vote of the church was taken. Two hundred thirty voted against him, twenty-three voted for, and a number abstained. The Church Record reads: "June 22, 1750. Revd. Jonathan Edwards was dismissed."

On July 1 he preached his *Farewell Sermon:*

How often have we met together in the house of God in this relation? How often have I spoken to you, instructed, counselled, warned, directed, and fed you, and administered ordinances among you, as the people which were committed to my care, and of whose precious souls I had the charge? But in all probability, this never will be again. . . . Let me be remembered in the prayers of all God's people that are of a calm spirit, and are peaceable and faithful in Israel, of whatever opinion they may be with respect to terms of church communion. And let us all remember, and never forget our future solemn meeting on that great day of the Lord; the day of infallible decision, and of the everlasting and unalterable sentence. Amen.

At 46, with a large family to support, "fitted for no other business but study," Edwards felt under an "awful frown of Heaven." It took him a year to relocate. Then the relocation was in Stockbridge, Massachusetts, a frontier town. He would be a missionary to the Indians. John Wonwanonpequunnonnt was his interpreter to the Housatonnucks.

The chief advantage of Stockbridge, so far as intellectual actvity was concerned, was that it was so isolated that there would be few visitors or other distractions. People would not drop in on the way to somewhere else.

However, distractions presented themselves in other forms. Three years after his arrival, a war broke out, in 1754. Terrified whites flocked to Edwards' house, built a hasty fort, and proceeded to eat him out of house and home, consuming eight hundred meals and drinking seven gallons and one quart of Edwards' supply of West India rum.

Edwards' health was not good during these years. He often ran a high fever and trembled violently.

The books he produced were *Misrepresentations Corrected,* and *Truth Vindicated* (1752). This was followed by his most famous and original work on the freedom of the will, *A Careful and Strict Enquiry into the Modern Prevailing Notions of that Freedom of the Will which is supposed to be Essential to Moral Agency, Vertue and Vice, Reward and Punishment, Praise and Blame* (1754). This remains his major work.

During these days, Edwards was obliged to complain about the civil mismanagement of the town. It was controlled by the Williams family, old enemies from Northampton. They were steadily enriching themselves at the expense of the Indians. They had devised the "pupil payment system," by which they were reimbursed on a per capita basis. This they planned to double by opening a second school, although the first school was badly run. The Indian boys at the school constantly complained to Edwards: not enough blankets, too little food, only salt meat and porridge, lumps of bran in the meal, some boys had no breeches, all the boys hired out to work six days a week, the Bible read but once. The Williams family had a school of slaves, and directly profited by their mistreatment.

The attitude of the state authorities in Boston was to leave well enough alone. It was hard in any case to get men to administer frontier posts. So what if they got rich in the process?

However, the protests about mismanagement were finally taken seriously when the schoolhouse was burned down. Then at last it appeared, even to Boston, that things were not going well. Edwards' enemies charged that he had himself set the fire just to embarrass them. This slander was not taken seriously. The civil administration was changed, and things did improve.

In 1755 he wrote "The Nature of True Virtue" and "Concerning the End for which God Created the World" (later published in 1765 as *Two Dissertations*). *The Great Christian Doctrine of Original Sin Defended,* which was printed in 1758, was written about this time.

Edwards' exile in Stockbridge lasted seven years. Yet when he received a call to the presidency of New Jersey College (Princeton) he was not pleased. By this time, he had adjusted to frontier life.

His son-in-law, Aaron Burr (father of the stormy vice-president), had been president of the college, but had died. The trustees voted to offer the position to Jonathan Edwards.

He replied by listing his defects. For example, he had a constitutional sluggishness which made him low-spirited and unfit for conversation. This would hamper him in the administration of the college. He was not alert enough. He was in the decline of his life. He had too little knowledge of higher mathematics. He did not know the Greek classics.

In addition, he said, he had in mind three projects to write: an answer to the prevailing errors of Arminianism, a history of the Work of Redemption, and a harmony of the Old and New Testaments. He was not inclined to give up work on his books in any event.

However, he continued, if they were still inclined to have him as president, he would set these conditions. The presidency would be primarily administrative. He would limit his teaching, contrary to the current practice, to arts and sciences for the senior class, and to "the whole work of a professor of divinity." He would not agree to teach all the languages nor all the subjects to one class.

These terms were agreeable to the college trustees, who renewed their call. Edwards thereupon accepted, and arrived at Princeton on February 16, 1758. His family would follow later.

During the preceding months, there had been a serious outbreak of smallpox in the vicinity of Princeton. Many had died. Edwards, as advised, took the vaccine. It seemed favorable enough. Then, unexpectedly:

a secondary fever set in, and by reason of a number

of pustules in his throat, the obstruction was such, that the medicines necessary to check the fever, could not be administered.

A doctor from Philadelphia was in attendance. He wrote:

He spoke to Lucy (his daughter) to the following purpose: dear Lucy, it seems to me to be the will of God that I must shortly leave you. Therefore give my kindest love to my dear wife and tell her that the uncommon union that has so long subsisted between us has been of such a nature as I trust is spiritual and therefore will continue forever. And I hope she will be supported under so great a trial and submit cheerfully to the will of God. And as to my children you are now like to be left fatherless which I hope will be an inducement to you to seek a father who will never fail you. And as to my funeral I would have it to be like unto Mr. Burr's. And any additional sum of money that might be expected to be laid out that way, I would have it disposed of to charitable uses.
On March 22, 1758, Jonathan Edwards died.

II. The Manuscripts

Quite a few of the Edwards manuscripts are, regrettably, missing. Anne Grant, his great-granddaughter, wrote:

When I was a child there was a great heap of papers on the garret floor belonging to the Edwards estate; of these many were injured by the rain from the leaky roof until they crumbled to dust, and many others were given to various persons, who, anxious to obtain some memento of the family were allowed to help themselves from the collection.

In 1865, Alexander B. Grosart wrote that he then had in his possession "Priceless and hitherto unknown materials for a worthy biography." These materials have never since come to light.

Besides carelessness, other motives have sometimes operated. For instance, the minutes of the Hampshire Association for the years 1748-1751 (the years concerning the contraversy at the Northampton church) have been cut from the record and disappeared.

Those manuscripts that do remain are concentrated (1) in the Andover-Harvard collection, in Cambridge, Massachusetts, and (2) in the Yale collection. There are some additional items of interest at Princeton. Others are at the Massachusetts Historical Society, the American Antiquarian Society, the Library of Congress, the New York Public Library, the Boston Athenaeum, the Congregational Libraries of Boston and of London, the Essex Institute, the First Church Records of Northampton, the Forbes Library, the British Museum, and the Lambeth Palace Library, London.

III. Bibliography

The best single volume, containing both biography and selections, is by Faust and Johnson: *Jonathan Edwards* (New York: American Book Company, 1935). The best single volume biography is Ola Elizabeth Winslow: *Jonathan Edwards 1703-1758* (New York: Collier Books, 1940). Perry Miller's *Jonathan Edwards* (New York: Meridian Books, Inc,. 1949) is also excellent.

The best edition of Edwards' works, in terms of care of preparation, is the series by the Yale University Press, edited by Perry Miller, Paul Ramsey, John Smith, and others: *Works of Jonathan Edwards* (New Haven: Yale University Press, 1957ff.). Conrad Cherry has a good book out: *The Theology of Jonathan Edward: A Reappraisal* (Garden City, New York: Doubleday & Co., 1966).

•　　•　　•

EINSTEIN, ALBERT (1879-1955): The greatest theoretical physicist in the history of science, Einstein spent twenty-one years in the Unites States. In the winter of 1933 he joined the newly-founded Institute for Advanced Study at Princeton, New Jersey. In 1940 he became an American citizen. In addition to his contributions to physics he wrote some significant material on the relation between science and philosophy.

I. Life

Born into a business family in Ulm, Bavaria, Germany, on the 14th of March, 1879, he spent his formative years in the city of Munich. His teachers thought him stupid.

It was his uncle who interested him in mathematics. At fourteen, he taught himself calculus. In 1894 the family moved to Milan. Einstein continued his schooling at Aarau in Switzerland.

He graduated with a major in physics and math education from Z. P. I. (Zurich Polytechnic Institute) in 1901. During that same year he became a Swiss citizen and married for the first time. He also published an article in the *Annalen der Physik* entitled *Folgerungen aus den Capillaritätserscheinungen.*

Unable to get a teaching job after graduation, he finally took a job with the Patent Office in Bern. Inspector Einstein's responsibilities were to conduct the preliminary examination of applications for patents. The job left him plenty of time to ponder the fundamental problems in physics. Physics at the time was considered a nearly perfect science. The few small problems left unsolved, such as those connected with radiation, were expected to be cleared up within a year or two. Then the science would, according to all expectations, be completely unified as a body of knowledge.

Einstein read the works of Boltzmann, Maxwell, Helmholtz, Hertz and Kirchoff. He contributed a number of articles to the *Annalen der Physik: Über die thermodynamische Theorie der Potentialdifferenz zwischen Metallen und volständig dissociierten Lösungen ihrer Salze, und über eine elektrische Methode zur Erforschung der*

Molekularkräfte Kinetische Theorie des Wärmegleichge-wichtes und des zweiten Haupsatzes der Thermodynamik (1902), *Eine Theorie der Grundlagen der Thermodynamik* (1903), and *Zur allgemeinen molekularen Theorie der Wärme* (1904).

In the year 1905 he received the Ph.D. degree from the University of Zurich. His inaugural dissertation was *Eine neue Bestimmung der Moleküldimensionen* (*A New Determination of Molecular Dimensions*).

On the basis of these preliminary studies, Einstein was in a position to publish the paper, *The Electrodynamics of Moving Bodies* (*Elektrodynamik bewegter Körper*), in *Annalen der Physik*, ser. 4, vol. 17, pp. 891-921.

This was the initial paper on special relativity. Years later, at a war bond rally in Kansas City, a manuscript copy of this article would sell for six million dollars before being deposited at the Library of Congress.

Four of Einstein's most important discoveries came at the same time: (1) the special theory of relativity, (2) the foundation of the photon theory of light, (3) the establishment of mass-energy equivalence, and (4) the theory of Brownian motion (1906: *Zur Theorie des Brownschen Bewegung*).

1907 was the year of the publication, in *Jahrbuch der Radioaktivität*, of "Über das Relativitätsprinzip und die aus demselben gezogenen Folgerungen," containing the first explicit statements of both the equivalence of inertial and gravitational mass and the equation for mass in terms of energy, $E = mc^2$.

In 1908-9 he was allowed to lecture part time at the University of Bern on "The Theory of Radiation." His class the first term was four students. The second term it was one. The sessions continued in Einstein's own rooms.

In 1909 Einstein received an appointment as associate professor of theoretical physics at the University of Zurich, at the same salary he had received at the patent office. To make ends meet, his wife, Mileva, had to take in student lodgers. His wife was rather disorganized and restless.

By 1910 they had their second son, Eduard, and later in the year moved to Prague, where Einstein joined the faculty of the German University. In Prague (where they could finally afford electric lights — it had been gas in Zurich and oil lamps in Bern) he was introduced to the mathematical machinery which helped him solve the problems of general relativity.

In 1911 he published "Über den Einfluss der Schwerkraft auf die Ausbreitung des Lichtes" ("On the Influence of Gravitation on the Propagation of Light") in *Annalen der Physik*, ser. 4, xxxv, 898-908, which deduces from the article of 1907 the consequence that light beams from stars must be bent in passing the edge of the sun's disc.

Franz Kafka and Max Brod were living in Prague at the time.

Einstein's wife was not completely happy in Bohemia, and he was irked by the regularity and limitations of regular university classroom lectures. So, in 1912, he returned to Zurich to teach at the Zurich Polytechnic Institute.

In 1913 he moved to Berlin. Max Planck, deeply impressed by him at the 1911 Solvay Congress, had secured for him the directorship of the newly formed Kaiser Wilhelm Society for the Advancement of the Sciences. They wanted his ideas more than his administrative ability. They also gave him the post of professor at the University of Berlin, with no duties except lecturing whenever he felt like it, and full membership in the Prussian Academy of Sciences with a salary of 12,000 marks. Someone had remarked that there were at the time only a dozen men in the world that really understood relativity, and that eight of them lived in Berlin.

Einstein's aim in this move was to complete the work on the general theory of relativity. One of his friends wrote with perception:

> To be able to work when a great idea is at stake, which has to be nursed to maturity during a longer period of time, a scientist must be unencumbered by cares, must

avoid all disturbing conflicts of life, must bear with all humiliations from his opponents in order to safeguard that precious something which he bears in his soul.

Or, more blunty:

The true artist will let his wife starve, his children go barefoot, his mother drudge for a living at seventy, sooner than work at anything but his art.

For his part, Einstein remarked to a friend, "The gentlemen in Berlin are gambling on me as if I were a prize hen. As for myself I don't even know whether I'm ever going to lay another egg."

They moved to Berlin on April 6, 1914. The date is important because Freundlich and his expedition were going to the Crimea to observe the solar eclipse and thus provide experimental proof — or disproof — of the truth of Einstein's theory. On August 1, Germany declared war on Russia, the First World War broke out, and the scientific party was arrested within Russia. Not only were they unable to make their observations, but they were lucky to get back home to Berlin at all.

His wife, Mileva, and the two boys went back to Zurich during the summer for a visit. She did not like Berlin. She stayed in Switzerland through Christmas. Einstein spent Christmas Eve with friends, playing his violin to them. He commented later that if he had not had the strength of mind to keep Mileva at a distance, out of sight and mind, he would have been worn out physically and morally.

1916 saw the publication of "Die Grundlage der Allgemeinen Relativitäts-theorie" ("The Foundation of the Generalized Theory of Relativity") in *Annalen der Physik*, ser. 4, xlix, 769-822. The correct generalization of the special theory of relativity, published nine years before, must include, he believed, a theory of gravity. This was provided in this paper.

At Easter, he went to Zurich to see Mileva, in what turned out to be a stormy and disastrous meeting. He resolved never to see her again, and relied on a friend to act as a go-between to make various arrangements for the children, their schooling, and so forth.

In October, Einstein learned that his old friend, Friedrich Adler, fervently anti-war, had become furious over the failure of the government to convene Parliament and put its policies to the test of public debate. He had gone to the fashionable Austrian Hotel Meissel and Schadn, and shot the Prime Minister, Count Stürgkh, to death. When in prison, waiting trial, Adler wrote a long paper on relativity theory.

Einstein suffered a breakdown. A medical friend wrote: "As his mind knows no limits, so his body follows no set rules. He sleeps until he is wakened; he stays awake until he is told to go to bed; he will go hungry until he is given something to eat; and then he eats until he is stopped." He lost fifty-six pounds in two months. It was August of 1917 before he recovered.

By 1919, he divorced Mileva and married his cousin, Elsa, who organized his private and social life with care that he not be disturbed by events or used by opportunists.

In this same year, the British sent two expeditions, one to Brazil, the other to Africa, to photograph the solar eclipse of that year, and thus to see whether experimental confirmation existed for relativity theory. On June 3 Eddington developed the plates, measured one, and found that the predicted displacement had taken place.

September 27, 1919, Lorentz sent Einstein a telegram with the good news. On October 25, Einstein attended a meeting of the Dutch Royal Academy in Amsterdam, but the confirmation was not printed in the official report. On November 6, the Royal Astronomical Society met at Burlington House in England. Alfred North Whitehead, James Jeans, and J. J. Thompson were present in the crowded hall. When the report was read, everyone there knew that the Newtonian theory of the universe was gone forever. Old certainties were replaced by new theories.

On November 7, 1919, Einstein awoke to find himself

famous. The city of Berlin was barricaded in anticipation of a clash between the army and leftist revolutionaries. A continuous stream of reporters besieged Einstein.

All over the world popular lectures on relativity were delivered. Newpaper and magazine articles were written to explain the revolution in thought. Most such efforts added to the confusion rather than anything else.

Writing of Newton, Einstein was able to make clear the relation between the two theories:

> The old theory is a special limiting case of the new one. If the gravitational forces are comparatively weak, the old Newtonian law turns out to be a good approximation to the new laws of gravitation. Thus all observations which support the classical theory also support the General Relativity theory. We regain the old theory from the higher level of the new one.

The years following were tumultuous. From 1920 to 1933 a swirl of lectures and politics formed Einstein's life. Political events within Germany were tense and tangled. The incredible inflation made life difficult. These were the days when it took a larger box to carry the money to the store than one needed to carry the groceries back home.

Anti-relativity debates provoked furious newspaper debates. Rising anti-Semitism became more and more of an issue. Einstein had several years previously become a Zionist. Many of the pseudo-scientific attacks on relativity theory were racially motivated.

Einstein's time was spent largely in extensive lecture tours through Europe and the United States. He served on a commission of the League of Nations. Political assassinations in Germany made it likely that his own life was also in danger.

In 1922 he received the Nobel Prize for his work on photo-electric effects on crystals. The money from the prize, reduced by currency regulations when transferred from country to country and further diminished by bad management was given to his first wife. She was able to buy a house with it and live modestly, disturbed by her younger son, who had become schizophrenic.

The Nobel Prize was also the occasion for a controversy with the German Civil Service over whether Einstein's nationality was German or Swiss.

He lectured in Japan, China, Palestine, and Spain. But Berlin, even in those stormy days, still supplied the kind of intellectual climate needed for him to keep on with his work.

In 1925 Bertrand Russell's *The ABC of Relativity* appeared, an extraordinarily clear exposition of the subject, written by one of the first to describe in the press the implications of the 1919 eclipse expeditions. Like Einstein, Russell was basically a pacifist.

Einstein visited Holland on occasion, staying in the villa of his friend Ehrenfest. There he found the kind of free, non-political atmosphere he missed in contemporary Berlin, and enjoyed the climate of opinion at Leiden, much as the English Puritans had, three centuries before.

Intellectually, the developments of the time concerned quantum theory, which seemed to deny the concept of cause in physical phenomena, and the gradual merging of particle and wave concepts. Schrödinger's interpretation of the de Broglie waves meant that the particle gave way to what was in effect a standing electron wave. Instead of being a wave-controlled corpuscle it became a corpuscular wave. Niels Bohr said that whether light was waves or particles depended solely upon how the observer studied it, upon which effects he was intending to observe.

Distracted by lecturing and politics, Einstein, to his sorrow, was somewhat out of touch with these new formulations in physics. At the Fifth Solvay Congress, in 1927, the "trapdoor of indeterminacy" was opened. Einstein debated with Bohr. Indeterminacy, he said, was the result of ignorance. Does God play dice? If only we had the right equipment, we could conduct an experiment which would discover all the characteristics of an electron. Bohr claimed that indeterminacy was part of nature herself. The meeting was in an uproar.

When someone remarked that Einstein himself had started this process — challenging the laws of classical mechanics — he replied that it ruins a good joke to repeat it too often.

In 1928 he had a breakdown.

1929 saw the publication of an attempt at the construction of a unified field theory by Einstein. Also, being his fiftieth birthday, the Berlin city council — after having been told who Einstein was — agreed to honor him, in a comedy of errors which saw them present him with a house, which was already occupied by tenants with a perpetual lease, then a plot of land, which legally could not be built upon, and finally the offer to buy a lot wherever he chose, an offer that was never concluded because by then it had become controversial. The result was that Einstein bought the lot on his own and built a house which, because of politics, he could not occupy for more than a few years. It took all his savings. 1929 was also the year the great world depression hit Germany.

In the summer of 1930, the Indian mystic and philosopher, Rabindranath Tagore, came to walk in the garden of his home and to talk. Tagore observed that truth and beauty were entirely dependent upon man. Einstein asked, "If there were no more human beings, then the Apollo of Belvedere would not be beautiful any more?"

"No," replied Tagore.

Einstein said that might be the case with regard to beauty, but not with regard to truth, and exclaimed, "Then I am more religious than you are!" Explaining his view, Einstein said:

> I cannot prove that scientific truth must be conceived as a truth that is valid independent of reality, but I believe it firmly. I believe, for instance, that the Pythagorean theorem in geometry states something that is approximately true, independent of the existence of

man. Anyway, if there is a *reality* independent of man, there is also a truth relative to this reality; and in the same way the negation of the first engenders a negation of the existence of the latter. . . . Our natural point of view in regard to the existence of truth apart from humanity cannot be explained or proved. But it is a belief which nobody can lack — not primitive beings even. We attribute to truth a superhuman objectivity, it is indispensable for us, this reality which is independent of our existence and our experience and our mind — though we cannot say what it means.

Einstein again visited America, especially the California Institute of Technology, and England, particularly Oxford. Political events in Germany were deteriorating rapidly under the impact of Hitler.

Finally, in 1933, he broke with Germany. He resigned from the Prussian Academy, and sought for somewhere else to live. The authorities confiscated his bank account on the grounds that it might be spent for treasonable activities, and padlocked his apartment and house. A picture of him was published with the words "Not yet hanged" printed underneath.

His two step-daughters fled to France April 12. He decried "this epidemic of hatred and violence." A German nationalist organization offered $5000 to the man who would assassinate him. "I did not know it was worth so much," he said, touching his head.

In September came news that Paul Ehrenfest, his close friend, had shot his young son, whom he only blinded, and committed suicide, the victim, Einstein later said, of "a conflict of conscience that in some form or other is spared no university teacher who has passed, say, his fiftieth year."

In the fall, Einstein sailed for the United States. Abraham Flexner, having previously secured a $5 million endowment, had begun to set up a new kind of educational institution, The Institute for Advanced Study, "a haven where scholars and scientists may regard the world and its phenomena as their laboratory without being drawn into the maelstrom of the immediate." Earlier, having mentioned to a friend the possibility of going to Princeton, Einstein had been told, "Why? Do you want to commit suicide?"

In Princeton, he carried on his research modestly, interrupted by fund-raising appearances for charitable causes. They lived at 112 Mercer Street. In 1936, Elsa died, grieving for the daughter she had lost two years before, in Paris.

The three subjects of his thought while at the Institute were (1) the search for an adequate formulation of a unified field theory, which he never found; (2) the development of the general theory of relativity so that it could accommodate cosmological developments; and (3) trying to prove inconsistencies in the quantum theory. Oppenheimer wrote that Einstein's last twenty-five years of life were a failure, but "he had a right to that failure.... He did not like the elements of indeterminacy.... He fought with the theory which he had fathered but which he hated. It was not the first time that this has happened in science."

Asked why he published one unsatisfactory formulation of a unified field theory, he replied, "To save another fool from wasting six months on the same idea."

He had been so out of touch with theoretical physics, for the reasons mentioned — political and public affairs — that he was not aware of the experimental confirmation of his formula, $E = mc^2$, by now a commonplace in the laboratory, with bodies whose energy content is variable to a degree (e.g. with radium salts).

In a letter dated August 2, 1939, suggested by Leo Szilard, Einstein wrote President Roosevelt:

it may become possible to set up nuclear chain reactions in a large mass of uranium, by which vast amounts of power and large quantities of new radium-like elements would be generated. . . . This new phenomenon would also lead to the construction of bombs, and it is conceivable — though much less certain — that extremely powerful bombs of a new type may thus be constructed.

The Manhattan Project was launched and the atomic bomb was produced. Much later, he was to say that signing this letter was "the greatest mistake" of his life.

Retiring, officially, in 1945, Einstein was interviewed by *The Reporter* in 1954, during the time of the McCarthy loyalty oaths, and said:

> If I would be a young man again and had to decide how to make my living, I would not try to become a scientist or scholar or teacher. I would rather choose to be a plumber or a peddler in the hope to find that modest degree of independence still available under present circumstances.

In 1952 he was offered the Presidency of the state of Israel, which he declined, saying:

> I know a little about nature and hardly anything about men.

On April 18, 1955, in the early hours of the morning, after one week in the hospital, Albert Einstein died. His last words were spoken in German to a nurse who did not understand that language.

II Selected Bibliography

Einstein's private papers and letters and manuscripts are being prepared for publication by the Princeton University Press. Helen Dukas, his secretary from the days in Berlin, the only person who can decipher his cryptic script, has been working diligently on the project for years.

Other key books, readily available, include: Einstein and others, *The Principle of Relativity* (New York: Dover Publications, 1923); Einstein, *Relativity, the Special and General Theory* (New York: Crown Publishers, 1961); Einstein, *The Meaning of Relativity* (Princeton: Princeton

University Press, 1922); Einstein, *Out of My Later Years* (New York: The Philosophical Library, 1950); Clark, *Einstein: the Life and Times* (New York: The World Publishing Company, 1971); Schilpp, *Albert Einstein, Philosopher-Scientist* (New York: Harper & Brothers, 1959).

• • •

ELIADE, MIRCEA (1907-   ): Mircea Eliade, at the University of Chicago since 1958, is an important thinker in the analysis or the symbol (cf. Tillich, Langer). Born in Bucharest, Rumania, March 9, 1907, he was educated at Bucharest (Ph.D. 1932), having spent three years in study at the University of Calcutta previously. He taught at Bucharest, Paris, worked in the Rumanian diplomatic corps, and came to the United States in 1956. Among his books are *The Myth of the Eternal Return* (1954), *Patterns in Comparative Religions* (1958), *Birth and Rebirth* (1958), *Myths, Dreams, and Mysteries* (1959), *Images and Symbols* (1960), *The Forge and the Crucible* (1962), *Myth and Reality* (1963), *Shamanism* (1964), and *The One and the Two* (1964).
He writes:

The chief difference between the man of the archaic and traditional societies and the man of the modern societies with their strong imprint of Judaeo-Christianity lies in the fact that the former feels himself indissolubly connected with the Cosmos and the cosmic rhythms, whereas the latter insists that he is connected only with History.

• • •

ELIOT, CHARLES WILLIAM (1834-1926): President of Harvard from 1869 to 1909, Charles William Eliot increased the faculty from 60 to 600, the student body from 1000 to

4000 during that time. One of the foremost educational reformers of his time, President Eliot developed the elective system and advocated the College Board Examination system. Democracy, he believed, consisted in social mobility, in which education would enable each man to discover and realize his own special abilities.

His books include *Educational Reform* (1898) and *American Contributions to Civilization* (1897).

• • •

EMERSON, RALPH WALDO (1803-1882): "To believe in your own thought, to believe that what is true for you in your private heart is true for all men — that is genius."

Ralph Waldo Emerson, one of the greatest American thinkers since Jonathan Edwards, firmly believed that nature and human nature were sufficient sources for thought and action. With self-reliance a man could build his own world.

Emerson was the leading figure in American Transcendentalism. A reaction against certain aspects of the Enlightenment, Transcendentalism has also been called American Romanticism. Emerson was as appalled at Hegel's system of thought as was his European contemporary Kierkegaard. Transcendentalism stressed (1) the divinity of nature, (2) the worth of man, and (3) the capacity of man to know the truth directly. It was epistemologically intuitionistic and metaphysically idealistic.

The epistemology of Transcendentalism was based on a rejection of empiricism. Empiricism cannot get beyond facts. The only knowledge worth having is certainty. Intellectual scepticism is also moral scepticism, the "pig philosophy" of Utilitarianism. Within the human mind are faculties which transcend the senses. These faculties provide intuitions which need no further validation.

The idealistic methaphysics of Transcendentalism asserted that reality lay behind the world of sense. Nature, essentially, was the expression of spirit. In this sense nature was divine, and, of course, included man.

I

"There is properly no History; only Biography" — *Essays,* "History" (1841).

The fourth of the eight children of William Emerson, Ralph Waldo was raised in genteel poverty. His father had died when Ralph was not quite eight.

Aunt Mary Moody Emerson became fanatically devoted to the upbringing of her nephews. She said, "They were born to be educated." Before he was three, Ralph was sent to Mrs. Whitwell's nursery school. Later he entered Lawson Lyon's grammar school. When he was ten, he attended the Boston Latin School.

A year later, the family was forced by the high cost of living to leave Boston for Concord. After a year's worth of village instruction, the family sent him back to Boston, where he spent two years preparing himself for college.

In August of 1817 he entered Harvard on a kind of scholarship as the "president's freshman." That meant he was a messenger boy, paid for his services by free lodging at the president's house. He also waited tables at the Commons.

"One of the benefits of a college education is to show the boy its little avail," he later wrote. He was more interested in the books that were not assigned than those that were. He did not make much of an impression on his teachers, graduating 30th in a class of 59.

After graduation he taught at his brother's finishing school for young ladies in Boston, a school held in his mother's house. Four years later he closed the school, having earned a good deal of money.

Emerson then entered seminary and prepared to follow the family tradition, serving the church. Later he was to write:

I like a church; I like a cowl;

111

I love a prophet of the soul;
And on my heart monastic aisles
Fall like sweet strains or pensive smiles;
Yet not for all his faith can see
Would I that cowlèd churchman be."

He became minister of Second Church, Boston, from 1829 to 1832. He and the congregation fell out over whether the Lord's Supper was commanded or not, Emerson holding not.

Heartily know,
When half-gods go,
The gods arrive.

In 1829 he had married Ellen Louisa Tucker, who died seventeen months later of tuberculosis. Deeply depressed and dispirited by her death, his health threatened to give way again. Thirty years old, Emerson sailed for the Mediterranean. In Europe he met John Stuart Mill, Coleridge, Carlyle, and Wordsworth.

Returning to the United States, Emerson discovered that Ellen's inheritance provided nearly as much income as had the salary from the church. He could supplement his income by supply preaching on Sundays, which he did for the next four years.

By 1835 he was giving lectures in Boston to increasingly enthusiastic listeners: on biography, English literature, the philosophy of history, human culture, human life, and the present age. These became the basis for the first series of *Essays*, published in 1841:

Nothing can bring you peace but yourself. — *Self-Reliance.*
A foolish consistency is the hobogoblin of little minds, adored by little statesmen and philosophers and divines. — *Ibid.*
All mankind love a lover. — *Love.*
The only way to have a friend is to be one. — *Friendship.*

II

He moved to Concord again, and married Lydia Jackson from Plymouth. He made new friends, among them Bronson Alcott, Henry David Thoreau, and Nathaniel Hawthorne. Sadly, death again struck close, this time claiming his two brothers, Edward (in 1834) and Charles (in 1836).

The first book he published was *Nature* (1836). Unsuccessful, except to impress those of like mind, it did contain the important Transcendental thesis:

> Why should not we enjoy an original relation to the universe?.... There are new lands, new men, new thoughts. Let us demand our own work and laws and worship.

The desire was to recover the Golden Age of Greece, to build upon the fact of American independence, so that man could think the great new thoughts that were inhibited, Emerson believed, by scholarly pursuits, quotation and translation.

Emerson was invited to deliver the end-of-August lecture at Harvard, the Phi Beta Kappa oration of 1837. In his address, *The American Scholar*, he declared:

> Meek young men grow up in libraries, believing it their duty to accept the views which Cicero, which Locke, which Bacon have given; forgetful that Cicero, Locke, and Bacon were only young men in libraries when they wrote these books....
> We will walk on our own feet; we will work with our own hands; we will speak our own minds.

Oliver Wendell Holmes called this lecture by Emerson "our intellectual Declaration of Independence."

Harvard rewarded Emerson by inviting him back the next year, this time to address the graduating class of Divinity College. However, this time he spoke his mind so clearly that he was unwelcome at Harvard for the following thirty years. He had even offended Dean Palfrey. He declared that the church of the time was dead and helpless. The church had mistakenly been content with communicating the traditions of the past, when it should have been investigating the spiritual resources available at the present. We ought to seek a new revelation proper to the times. Solitude and self-reliance should be cultivated. Salvation could only be found within the soul.

The storm of controversy aroused by these sentiments prompted Emerson to write in his Journal: "If they will not hear me lecture, I shall have leisure for my book which wants me."

Hawthorne and Emerson were in the habit of staying out of sight in the village of Concord on Sunday mornings until the "good citizens" had gotten safely to church. Then they would set out for their walk to Walden Pond.

"A preacher is a bully," Emerson remarked: "I who have preached so much, — by the help of God will never preach more."

III

Lecturing became his means of support, and Emerson widened his tours year by year. He felt self-critical about the process, saying: "Are not lectures a kind of Peter Parley's story of Uncle Plato, and a puppet show of the Eleusinian mysteries?"

In 1841 the first series of *Essays* was published: History, Self-Reliance, Compensation, Spiritual Laws, Love, Friendship, Prudence, Heroism, The Over-Soul, Circles, Intellect, and Art.

The following year brought the last and greatest tragedy of his life, the death of little Waldo, five years old: "He gave up his little innocent breath like a bird. Sorrow makes us all children again, — destroys all differences of intellect. The wisest knows nothing."

In the coming years Emerson lectured in New York,

114

Philadelphia, Baltimore, and Washington. The second series of the *Essays* was published in 1844: The Poet, Experience, Character, Manners, Gifts, Nature, Politics, Nominalist and Realist, and New England Reformers. His reputation was consolidated, so that when (in 1847) he went to lecture in England, he found that he was already famous there. The *Essays* had a popularity of their own at Oxford.

English Traits (1856) made the following perceptive observation: Art is a Jealous mistress, and, if a man have a genius for painting, poetry, music, architecture, or philosophy, he makes a bad husband, and an ill-provider.

Lecturing through the West (as far as the Mississippi river), Emerson found audiences not quite as receptive as in England. Sometimes he spoke for as little as ten dollars an evening. One audience, in Illinois, walked out of the hall after ten minutes because the speech was not funny enough.

The Conduct of life (1860) was said by Carlyle to be his best work:

The highest compact we can make with our fellow is, — "Let there be truth between us two forevermore." There is no beautifier of complexion, or form, or behavior, like the wish to scatter joy and not pain around us.

Representative Men (1850) observed:

Every hero becomes a bore at last.
Keep cool: it will be all one a hundred years hence.
Is not marriage an open question, when it is alleged, from the beginning of the world, that such as are in the institution wish to get out, and such as are out wish to get in?

In *Society and Solitude* (1870) Emerson asked:
Can anybody remember when the times were not hard and money not scarce? and he advised:

Hitch your wagon to a star.

The years turned. He commented sagely: "It is time to be old, to take in sail." In 1872 his house at Concord burned. His friends sent him on a trip to Europe, and when he returned, found that they had completely rebuilt and restored the home.

In 1876 Emerson toured the South accompanied by his daughter Ellen. At the University of Virginia, in Charlottesville, there occurred a famous scene. The size of the crowd, its noise, and the lecturer's weak voice prevented his talk from being heard. It became painfully evident that his strength was no longer equal to his will.

A few weeks after Longfellow was buried, Emerson contracted pneumonia and died on the 27th of April, 1882. He was laid to rest near Thoreau. Years before, he had written:

Great men are they who see that spiritual is stronger than any material force; that thoughts rule the world.

EPISTEMOLOGY: (John Dewey)

1. Knowledge implies reference to the self or mind. Knowing is an intellectual process, involving psychical laws. It is an activity which the self experiences. A certain individual activity has been accordingly presupposed in all the universal facts of physical science. These facts are all facts known by some mind, and hence fall, in some way, within the sphere of psychology. This science is accordingly something more than one science by the side of others: it is a central science, for its subject matter, knowledge, is involved in them all. — *Psychology*.

2. To find out how to make knowledge when it is needed is the true end of the acquisition of information in school, not the information itself. — *Schools of To-Morrow* (with Evelyn Dewey).

3. Information severed from thoughtful action is dead, a mind-crushing load. Since it simulates knowledge and thereby develops the poison of conceit, it is a most powerful

obstacle to further growth in the grace of intelligence. — *Democracy and Education.*

4. Knowledge is always a matter of the use that is made of experienced natural events. — In the *Creative Intelligence:* Essays in the Pragmatic Attitude (a Symposium).

5. Knowledge is not something separate and self-sufficient, but is involved in the process in which life is sustained and evolved. The senses lose their place as gateways of knowing to take their rightful place as stimuli to action. To an animal an affection of the eye or ear is not an idle piece of information about something indifferently going on in the world. It is an invitation and inducement to act in a needed way. It is a clue in behavior, a directive factor in adaptation of life in its surroudings. It is urgent, not cognitive in quality. — *Reconstruction in Philosophy.*

6. Knowledge is power and knowledge is achieved by sending the mind to the school of nature to learn her processes of change. — *Ibid.*

7. The reason a baby can know little and an experienced adult much when confronting the same things is not because the latter has a "mind" which the former has not, but because one has already formed habits which the other has still to acquire. The scientific man and the philosopher like the carpenter, the physician and politician know with their habits, not with their "consciousness." — *Human Nature and Conduct.*

8. Of course there has been an enormous increase in the amount of knowledge possessed by mankind, but is does not equal probably the increase in the amount of errors and half truths which have got into circulation. — *The Public and Its Problems.*

•   •   •

ETHICAL CULTURE SOCIETY: Founded in 1876 by Felix Adler (1851-1933), the Society for Ethical Culture is a religious society "which shall be practical as well as spiritual, and unhampered by sectarian religious dogmas." Adler had been born in the Rhineland and brought to the United States by his father, who was a rabbi, at the age of six. Liberal thought, largely inspired by New England Transcendentalism, led Adler to question authoritative religion, and to insist rather on a religious observance which stressed, as he said, "deed not creed." Social reform was an important goal for Adler, founding free kindergartens for children and agitating for the abolition of child labor.

ETHICS:

1. Jonathan Edwards wrote several works touching the concepts of ethics, including the famous *Freedom of the Will* and the lesser known *Nature of True Virtue*. From a strict Puritan viewpoint, his insistence upon strict adherence to the highest ideals always carried a theological sanction.

A moral Agent is a being that is capable of those actions that have a moral quality, and which can properly be denominated good or evil in a moral sense, virtuous or vicious, commendable or faulty. To moral Agency belongs a moral faculty, or sense of moral good and evil, or of such a thing as desert or worthiness, of praise or blame, reward or punishment; and a capacity which an agent has of being influenced in his actions by moral inducements or motives, exhibited to the view of understanding and reason, to engage to a conduct agreeable to the moral faculty.

The sun is very excellent and beneficial in its action and influence on the earth, in warming it, and causing it to bring forth its fruits; but it is not a moral Agent. Its action, though good, is not virtuous or meritorious. Fire that breaks out in a city, and consumes a great part of it, is very mischievous in its operation; but it is not a moral Agent. What it does is not faulty or sinful, or deserving of any punishment.

The brute creatures are not moral Agents. The actions of

118

Alfred North Whitehead

Walt Whitman

some of them are very profitable and pleasant; others are very hurtful; yet, seeing they have no moral faculty, or sense of desert, and do not act from choice guided by understanding, or with a capacity of reasoning and reflecting, but only from instinct and are not capable of being influenced by moral inducements, their actions are not properly sinful or virtuous; nor are they properly the subjects of any such moral treatment for what they do, as moral Agents are for their faults or good deeds. — *Freedom of the Will* (1754), in Faust & Johnson, 281, 282.

2. John Dewey:

(1). Morals is as much a matter of interaction of a person with his social environment as walking is an interaction of legs with a physical environment. The character of walking depends upon the strength and competency of legs. But it also depends upon whether a man is walking in a bog or on a paved street, upon whether there is a safeguarded path set aside or whether he has to walk amid dangerous vehicles. If the standard of morals is low it is because the education given by the interaction of the individual with his social environment is defective. Of what avail is it to preach unassuming simplicity and contentment of life when communal admiration goes to the man who "succeeds" — who makes himself conspicuous and envied because of command of money and other forms of power? — *Human Nature and Conduct.*

(2). Morals has to do with all activity into which alternative possibilities enter. For wherever they enter a difference between better and worse arises. Reflection upon action means uncertainty and consequent need of decision as to which course is better. — *Ibid.*

(3). All moral judgment is experimental and subject to revision. — *Ibid.*

(4). Why did morality set up rules so foreign to human nature? — *Human Nature and Conduct.*

(5). Morals may be a growing science if it is to be a science at all, not merely because all truth has not yet been appropriated by the mind of man, but because life is a moving affair in which old moral truth ceases to apply. — *Ibid.*

(6). Moral Science. Morals is the most humane of all subjects. It is that which is closest to human nature; it is ineradicably empirical, not theological nor metaphysical nor mathematical. Since it directly concerns human nature, everything that can be known of the human mind and body in physiology, medicine, anthropology, and psychology is pertinent to moral inquiry. Human nature exists and operates in an environment. And it is not "in" that environment as coins are in a box, but as a plant is in the sunlight and soil. It is of them, continuous with their energies, dependent upon their support, capable of increase only as it utilizes them, and as it·gradually rebuilds from their crude indifference an environment genially civilized. Hence physics, chemistry, history, statistics, engineering, science, are a part of disciplined moral knowledge so far as they enable us to understand the conditions and agencies through which man lives, and on account of which he forms and executes his plans. Moral science is not something with a separate province. It is physical, biological and historic knowledge placed in a human context where it will illuminate and guide the activities of men. — *Human Nature and Conduct.*

•   •   •

EVERETT, CHARLES CARROLL (1829-1900): A New England theologian, administrator of the Harvard Divinity School (one of President Eliot's earliest and most important appointments), Charles Carroll Everett anticipated Tillich in viewing philosophy as the vehicle for the study of theology. Among his important books are *The Science of Thought* (1869) and *Fichte's Science of Knowledge* (1884).

• • •

EVOLUTION: A term which denotes a process of orderly change from a simple toward a more complex state. In accurate usage it is restricted to processes which exhibit the characteristics of organic unity and growth. The three areas in which the concept is used are as follows: 1) In biology it refers primarily to the transformation of one species into another. It may also be used to designate the process of growth within a species or within a biological individual. 2) In sociology and anthropology the term denotes the modification of human institutions and ideas when this process is considered as taking place according to a law which involves orderly change from simplicity to complexity; 3) in metaphysics the term is applied to the cosmic process in those philosophies which regard the universe itself as exhibiting a pattern of growth.

F

FARBER, MARVIN (1901-   ): The American phenome-
nologist, Marvin Farber studied with Husserl at Freiburg
(1922-24 and 1926-27). A graduate of Harvard, he has taught
at the University of Pennsylvania and at the State University
of New York at Buffalo. Among his many books on phenomenology are *Husserl* (1956), *The Foundation of Phenomenology* (1943), *Phenomenology and Existence* (1967), and
Basic Issues of Philosophy (1968).

•   •   •

FEIGL, HERBERT (1902-   ): Author of such significant
works as *Readings in Philosophical Analysis* (with Sellars,
1949), *Readings in the Philosophy of Science* (with Brod-
beck, 1953), and *The Mental and the Physical* (1967),
Herbert Feigl comes from Austria-Hungary, was educated
at Munich and Vienna (Ph.D. 1927), and came to the
United States in 1930. He has taught at the University of
Minnesota since 1940.

•   •   •

FISKE, JOHN (1842-1901): Attending Harvard College,
John Fiske received the better part of his education not in
the classrooms, but in the area bookstores. He accidentally
discovered a book by Herbert Spencer, and became an
enthusiastic disciple of evolution. The school authorities
warned him not to spread his views around or they would
expel him. Although they graciously allowed him to gra-

duate (1863) they prevented him from teaching on account of his radical views.

Such pressures helped make Fiske one of the most important intellectual influences on America during the last quarter of the nineteenth century. He became a powerful and effective lecturer, the chief advocate of new ideas in the country.

His books include *Outlines of Cosmic philosophy* (1874), *Darwinism and Other Essays* (1879), *The Destiny of Man Viewed in the Light of his Origin* (1884), *The Idea of God as Affected by Modern Knowledge* (1886), and *American Political Ideas Viewed from the Standpoint of Universal History* (1885).

Opposed to exercise, he came to weigh more than three hundred pounds. He died on the 4th of July, 1901, in Gloucester, Massachusetts.

•　•　•

FLEWELLING, RALPH TYLER (1871-1960): Defender of Personalism (*q.v.*), Ralph Tyler Flewelling was born and educated in Michigan. Attending Boston University (Ph. D. 1909), he became a Personalist and taught at the University of Southern California beginning in 1917. He wrote *Personalism and the Problems of Philosophy* (1915) and *Philosophy and the War* (1918) .

•　•　•

FOLLEN, KARL T. C. (1796-1840): Important for bringing German thought to the attention of the New England transcendentalists, Karl Follen arrived in America in 1824, aged twenty-eight. He became the first teacher of German at Harvard, and soon was the leader of the liberals in Boston. Enthusiastic about German philosophy and literature, he knew the works of Kant first-hand but had little sympathy for the post-Kantian idealists. Follen also knew Hume's and Spinoza's writings.

In 1836 he left Harvard to become a Unitarian minister, but died soon afterward, in 1840.

Follen influenced to some degree all the transcendentalists from James Marsh to Channing and Emerson (*q.v.*).

● ● ●

FRANKLIN, BENJAMIN (1706-1790): Born three years after Jonathan Edwards, Franklin, sometimes called "the first civilized American," was more philosophically inclined than might be imagined. Never a technical philosopher (except in one disastrous pamphlet), he is nevertheless too important as a man of letters to be overlooked in this study.

"He snatched the lightning from the skies and the sceptre from the tyrants," said Turgot. This image of a daring man braving heaven and earth was the ideal of many European intellectuals. They were not too far from the mark in so describing Franklin's attitude toward the world.

If France admired him excessively, he admired France more. His library was heavily weighted with French books: a Latin grammar in French, a history of commerce in French, and many other books, characteristically in French.

I. Life

Franklin once complained that he had been born "at the wrong time." It seemed him that at some later time, science would have made such great progress in so many areas. He wished he could be a sort of Einstein, helping the onward progress of scientific thought.

From this we can gain an important clue to his precise importance in the history of thought. Franklin looked toward the future, a future freed from theology, a scientific future. Unlike Jonathan Edwards, who was his contemporary, he was looking away from the concepts of the past.

Gone was the reproach for sin so characteristic of the

Calvinism of the time. Whenever Franklin committed some sin — and he was capable of some gross ones, he listed it as an "Erratum," a printer's error.

When he had his brother over a barrel in Boston — the police had forbidden James to print because of his criticisms against the government for its sloth in pursuing pirates, and Ben could thus get out of his apprentice's contract — he calls the unfair advantage he pursued an Erratum. When he "attempted familiarities" with his best friend's mistress in London, that too was termed an Erratum.

Born on Milk Street in Boston, Benjamin was the tenth of seventeen children. He was the object of much career planning both by his father, Josiah, and his uncle, Benjamin, who lived with the family. For a time they wanted to make him a clergyman. Then they realized how much it would cost to send him through school and seminary, and that idea was abandoned. He was taught to read by his father, so early that he could not remember having learned it. He was tutored for some years. He learned writing, but failed arithmetic.

At ten he was taken to learn his father's business, soap and candle making. He hated cutting wicks and generally despised the whole trade. His father did not want him to run off to sea as had one of his older brothers. So he took him around the city of Boston to see what other trades he would like to learn. His brother James had just returned from London with a new printing press. Ben liked books, so he was signed on with him as an apprentice.

Ben not only learned the trade, he also carried on a program of self-education, reading such books as Plutarch's *Lives* and Cotton Mather's *Essays to Do Good*. At 13 he became a Deist after having read William Derham's *Physico-Theology* (1712) which contains the Boyle lectures refuting Deism. He also read the *Spectator* which became the model for his writing style, and Tryon's *Way to Health*, which made him a vegetarian. As you might expect he thriftily saved the money he would have spent on meat.

126

After James' business suffered, due to government repression, Benjamin left town. He was seventeen, and made for New York. He got free passage on a ship by hinting to the captain that he had "got a naughty Girl with Child."

There was no work in New York, so he went to Philadelphia. There, with amazing rapidity, he worked his way to the top. First he earned enough to live on, then went into business for himself, then became a promoter of events and a dealer in land. Writing popular material all the while, he became noted for both his private and his public activities.

Always the opportunist, he sailed for London on the promise of a letter of support from the governor. The letter never came. In London he considered starting a swimming school because he could swim three miles. Instead, he returned to Philadelphia to work in a friend's store.

In Philadelphia, business affairs proceeded exceptionally well. By 1748 he had attained financial security. Earlier, in 1730, he had entered into a common-law marriage with Deborah Read. They had two children, one of whom survived, and also brought up William, Ben's illegitimate son by an unidentified woman.

His curiosity about natural phenomena led to his exploration of electrical phenomena. His ingenuity produced a number of discoveries and inventions along the lines of his "one fluid" theory. Electricity was the most novel subject in European science at the time, so the publication of his letters describing his experiments made him famous. As a result he received honorary degrees from Harvard, Yale, William and Mary, Edinburgh and Oxford.

From 1753 to 1785 he was a public servant, representing the colonies in London and elsewhere. In 1764 he testified that the proposed Stamp Act was the wrong way to raise money from the American colonies. When the act passed after all, Franklin underestimated the violence of the American resistance to this measure. He ordered the stamps and nominated a friend for the post of stamp collector in the city of Philadelphia. When the Philadelphians heard this, they rioted around his house so that his wife had to get guns and have male relatives stay with her for protection.

Franklin, in London, redeemed his public reputation by campaigning for repeal of the act. In 1766, his part in the debate before the House of Commons was published from a transcript. When Parliament repealed the unpopular tax, he was given credit for the new turn of events.

In March of 1775, aware that there might be war, Franklin left London. The day after his arrival back in Philadelphia he was elected a delegate to the second Continental Congress.

William, his son, had been appointed royal governor of New Jersey in 1763, and had, to his father's embarrassment, remained loyal to the crown.

In 1776 Franklin was sent to France to negotiate for military aid. These secret negotiations were successful by 1778, after Burgoyne's defeat at Saratoga convinced the French that the colonists were not soon going to be crushed.

After negotiating the peace of 1783, with his fellow commissioners John Adams and John Jay, he worked on trade treaties until 1785 when, at the age of 79, he returned home.

His sister Jane burdened him with a succession of family troubles. He generously helped his relatives and, for a reward, was severely criticized by them.

In 1787 he was a member of the Constitutional Convention. By this time he was so ill — he had a large stone in his bladder and other such infirmities of age — that he had to be carried down to Independence Hall in a sedan chair by four inmates from the Walnut Street Jail.

He proposed to the Convention (1) that the head of the government should not be a President but a central committee, (2) that there be a single chamber legislature, and (3) that all public servants ought to serve without pay.

That none of these particular proposals were adopted caused him no concern at all, for he had a pragmatic view which allowed him to view everything, including political matters, as experiments, and right insofar as they were experimental. He supported the resulting constitutional document.

Bedridden for the last year of his life, he was kept from pain only by taking opium.

On April 17, 1790, he died, aged 84.

II. Works

Franklin was a prolific and varied writer, as can be seen from the following list:

(1722) "Silence Dogood" series in the *New England Courant;*

(1725) *A Dissertation on Liberty and Necessity, Pleasure and Pain,* London, written in reply to William Wollaston's book, which had so impressed the American Samuel Johnson *(q.v.)* We shall review Franklin's work in the following section;

(1729) *Modest Enquiry Into the Nature and Necessity of a Paper Currency,* the book that won him (by design) the contract printing the currency for Pennsylvania, New Jersey, Delaware, and Maryland;

(1729) editor and publisher of the *Pennsylvania Gazette;*

(1732-1757) *Poor Richard* almanacs, published annually;

(1732) a German language newspaper started but failed;

(1749) *Proposals Relating to the Education of Youth in Pennsylvania,* a learned book which quotes such authorities as Locke, Milton, George Turnbull (Chaplain to the Prince of Wales), Obediah Walker, Homer, Photius, Archimedes, Euclid, Ptolomy, Theon, Dioplantus, "all the Roman classical writers," Grotius, and various French and Italian writers. This was all in support of his curriculum for education, which consisted of:

(1) Handwriting,

(2) Drawing,

(3) Arithmetick, Accounts, Geometry and Astronomy,

(4) English,

(5) History ("Nothing, saith Mr. Locke, so delights more than history"),

(6) Geography,

(7) Chronology,

(8) Antient Customs,

(9) Morality,

(10) Oratory,

(11) Publick Religion (History), including the "excellency of the Christian Religion,"

(12) Politicks (History),

(13) Logic (the systems of Grotius and Puffendorff),

(14) Language,

(15) Universal History,

(16) Histories of Nature (Natural History, including the following sub-topics: Health, Air, Perspiration, Foods, Gardening, Planting, Grafting, and Inoculating),

(17) History of Commerce,

(18) Mechanicks.

The "great Aim and End of all Learning," which will follow from this course of study, is: "Benignity of Mind, Good Breeding, True Merit, and Ability to serve Mankind, One's Country, Friends and Family."

(1747) *Plain Truth; or, Serious Considerations on the Present State of the City of Philadelphia and Province of Pennsylvania,* written as a call to self-defence after French and Epanish privateers began invading the Delaware River;

(1751) *Experiments and Observations on Electricity,* a collection of his letters on his scientific experiments;

(1760) *The Interest of Great Britain Considered With Regard to Her Colonies, and the Acquisitions of Canada and Guadaloupe;*

(1773) "Rules by Which a Great Empire May be Reduced to a Small One," and "An Edict by the King of Prussia," both printed in the *Public Advertiser;*

(1785) "Maritime Observations;"

(1785) "The Causes and Cure of Smoky Chimneys."

III. Thought

"We are, I think, in the right road of improvement, for we are making experiments." This sentiment represents Franklin's approach to philosophy, politics, science, and the practical art of living.

The hopes he entertained for this method were quite high, as we find from a letter to an English friend:

> God grant that not only the love of liberty but a thorough knowledge of the rights of man may pervade all the nations of the earth, so that a philosopher may set his foot anywhere on its surface and say, 'This is my country.'

So far as Franklin's one explicitly philosophical essay is concerned, entitled *A Dissertation on Liberty and Necessity, Pleasure and Pain* (1725), Franklin so regretted its publication that he did his best to get it back off the market. Some copies survived, from which we quote his argument.

He argues, briefly, that whatever is, is in its nature just, since all things are by Fate. Because God is omnipotent and good, nothing can be wrong in the world. Therefore there is no real distinction between virtue and vice.

> All things exist now in a manner agreeable to His will, and in consequence of that are all equally good and therefore equally esteemed by Him.

Franklin concluded as a result of this work that his reasoning may very well be correct, but it was not useful. In fact, it might be positively harmful, especially to a rising business man. So he abandoned such speculation. Instead, he turned to what he knew was certainly useful, advice to a young apprentice on how to succeed. He listed the necessary virtues as:

(1) Veracity
(2) Fidelity

(3) Temperance
(4) Silence
(5) Frugality
(6) Industry.

There are not enough, however, without more sound advice: don't complain about the food; choose good company; don't brag; don't swear; don't "make amusement your business," for "there is no recreation like business;" work hard; don't over-extend; don't ever sue anyone (the lawyers get all the money you would recover anyway); choose the right kind of servants; be kind to your apprentices when you have some; choose a wife with great care; be a good father. If you want to do something on your time off, be sure to check with your boss. He may have some suggestions about what you should do, and, of course, you wouldn't want to displease him.

We see what a world of difference there was between Franklin and the theological aristocracy of the colonial past. Gone is theology. Its place is taken by business, science, and experimental politics. It is man's world, and Franklin is its son.

FREEDOM:

1. Jonathan Edwards:

To talk of liberty or the contrary, as belonging to the *very will itself*, is not to speak good sense.

2. John Dewey:

(1). Freedom is the "release of capacity from whatever hems it in." — *Reconstruction in Philosophy*.

(2). We are free in the degree in which we act knowing what we are about. The identification of freedom with "freedom of the will" locates contingency in the wrong place. — *The Quest for Certainty*.

(3). We are free not because of what we statically are, but in so far as we are becoming different from what we have been. — *Philosophy and Civilization.*

(4). Freedom is not something that can be handed to men as a gift from outside, whether by old-fashioned dynastic benevolent despotism or by new-fashioned dictatorship, whether of the proletarian or of the fascist order. It is something which can be had only as individuals participate in winning, it, and this fact, rather than some particular political mechanism, is the essence of democratic liberalism. — *Liberalism and Social Action.*

(5). In ultimate analysis, freedom is important because it is a condition both of realization of the potentialities of an individual and of social progress. Without light, a people perishes. Without freedom, light grows dim and darkness comes to reign. Without freedom, old truths become so stale and worn that they cease to be truths and become mere dictates of external authority. Without freedom, search for new truths and the disclosure of new paths in which humanity may walk more assuredly and justly come to an end. Freedom which is liberation for the individual, is the ultimate assurance of the movement of society toward more humane and noble ends. He who would put the freedom of others in bond, especially freedom of inquiry and communication, creates conditions which finally imperil his own freedom and that of his off-spring. Eternal vigilance is the price of the conservation and extension of freedom, and the schools should be the ceaseless guardians and creators of this vigilance. — "Academic Freedom," in *Intelligence in the Modern World* (ed. by J. Ratner).

(6). What is freedom and why is it prized? Is desire for freedom inherent in human nature or is it a product of special circumstances? Is it wanted as an end or as a means of getting other things? Does its possession entail responsibilities, and are these responsibilities so onerous that the mass of men will readily surrender liberty for the sake of greater ease? Is the struggle for liberty so arduous that most men are easily distracted from the endeavor to achieve and maintain it? Does freedom in itself and in the things it brings with it seem as important as security of livelihood; as food, shelter, clothing, or even as having a good time; Did man ever care as much for it as we in this country have been taught to believe? Is there any truth in the old notion that the driving force in political history has been the effort of the common man to achieve freedom? Was our own struggle for political independence in any genuine sense animated by desire for freedom, or were there a number of discomforts that our ancestors wanted to get rid of, things having nothing in common save that they were felt to be troublesome? — *Freedom and Culture.*

(7). Men may be brought by long habit to hug their chains. — *Ibid.*

(8). If we want individuals to be free we must see to it that suitable conditions exist. — *Ibid.*

(9). Everything that bars freedom and fullness of communication sets up barriers that divide human beings into sets and cliques, into antagonistic sects and factions, and thereby undermines the democratic way of life. — "Creative Democracy," in *The Philosopher of the Common Man:* Essays in Honor of John Dewey (a Symposium, ed. by W. H. Kilpatrick).

(10). The democratic idea of freedom is not the right of each individual to do as he pleases, even if it be qualified by adding "provided he does not interfere with the same freedom on the part of others." While the idea is not always, not often enough, expressed in words, the basic freedom is that of freedom of mind and of whatever degree of freedom of action and experience is necessary to produce freedom of intelligence. The modes of freedom guaranteed by the Bill of Rights are of this nature: Freedom of belief and conscience, of expression of opinion, of assembly for discussion and conference, of the press as an organ of communication. They are guaranteed because without them individuals are not free to develop and society is deprived of what they might contribute. — *Problems of Men.*

G

GEORGE, HENRY (1839-1897): A great social philosopher, admired by John Dewey, influential in England and Germany, Henry George devoted his attention to the solution of one problem: why are the rich so rich and the poor so poor? George's entire life was spent in a sort of field study of poverty, beginning in the little brick house in Philadelphia where he was born (on the east side of 10th St., south of Pine). He found high school boring, and dropped out at fourteen, becoming an errand boy for two dollars a week. He went to sea, then worked as a typesetter (like Ben Franklin), strikebreaker, and store clerk.

In San Francisco, George married Annie Fox despite the fact that he was in debt and out of work. When their second child was born, the doctor told George that both mother and child were starving. None of his jobs brought in enough money, so he stopped the first well-dressed man he met on the street and asked him for five dollars. If the man had not been moved by his story, he said, he was prepared to knock him down and rob him.

Finally, working as a newspaperman, he began to think and write about the "shocking contrast between monstrous wealth and debasing want." His theory was that the prosperity of California was due to the fact that the "natural wealth of the country was not yet monopolized — that great opportunities were open to all."

The reason, he concluded, why progress has poverty as its twin, was that "with the growth in population, land grows in value, and the men who work it must pay more for the privilege. I turned back, amidst quiet thought, to the perception that then came to me and has been with me ever since."

To solve the problem, George advocated the "single tax," one tax levied only upon the land value, not upon either wages or industry. *Our Land and Land Policy* (1871) and *Progress and Poverty* (1879) were two of his influential books, followed by *An Open Letter to the Pope* (1891) and *A Perplexed Philosopher* (1892).

He died on October 29, 1897, while campaigning for the position of mayor of New York City.

He was firmly convinced that republican institutions would break down under the inequitable distribution of wealth.

• • •

GIBRAN, KAHLIL (1883-1931): Mystical writer and artist, Kahlil Gibran's aphorisms and parables dealt with the problems of life in a way full of insight and imagination. A native of Bechari, Lebanon, Gibran lived for some time in the United States, which he first visited when he was twelve.

Educated in a Syrian College and at an art school in Paris, he wrote his earlier works in Arabic, his later in English. *The Prophet* (1923) dealt with man's relation to his fellow-man; *The Garden of the Prophet* (1933) with man and nature; and *The Death of the Prophet* with man and God.

Among his many other moving works is *Tears and Laughter* (1949).

He died on April 10, 1931, at the age of forty-eight, in St. Vincent's Hospital, New York.

GOODMAN, NELSON (1906-   ): The distinguished
American philosopher Nelson Goodman was born in Somer-
ville, Massachusetts, on August 7, 1906. He went to Harvard,
ran an art gallery in Boston (1929-42), and went back to
Harvard (Ph.D. 1941). He has taught at Tufts, the Univer-
sity of Pennsylvania, Brandeis, and Harvard (from 1967).
He has written *The Structure of Appearance* (1951), *Fact,
Fiction, and Forecast* (1955), and *Languages of Art* (1968).

H

HAMPSHIRE, STUART (1914-   ): In 1963 Stuart
Newton Hampshire came to the United States to teach
at Princeton. Born in Healing, England, he was educated
at Oxford, where he lectured from 1936-40. After serving
five years with the British Army, he returned to teach at
the University College, London (1947-50), and Oxford
(1950-55). Research fellow at All Souls College (1955-60),
he then was appointed philosophy of mind and logic at
the University of London (1960-63). Stuart Hampshire
has written *Spinoza* (1951), *Thought and Action* (1959),
and *Freedom of the Individual* (1965).

• • •

HARPER, WILLIAM RAINEY (1856-1906): Engaged in
selling Hebrew lessons at the same time John D. Rockefel-
ler was selling oil, the two men merged their educational
interests in 1892 with the founding of The University of
Chicago. Providing (as did Harvard and Columbia) one
of the three main patterns of higher education for the
country, the institution was divided into three parts: the
University proper, the University extension work, and the
University publication work. Harper's aim was to establish
a great research institution whose knowledge would educate
everyone everywhere, through the second two divisions.

The University proper was divided into two parts: the
academic college, general education for the first two years,
and the university college, consisting of the last two and
providing specialized education. The theme of the Univer-

sity would be research and the training of research workers. For instance, in outlining the task of the Division of Biology and Medicine, Harper said:

> I do not have in mind an institution of charity, or an institution which shall devote itself merely to the education of a man who shall be an ordinary physician; but rather an institution which shall occupy a place beside the two or three such institutions that already exist in our country... one in which honor and distinction will be found for those only who make contributions to the cause of medical science... (who make discoveries) from time to time so potent in their meaning as to stir the whole civilized world.

Among his works is a volume entitled *The Trend in Higher Education* (1905). When the University opened it had a library of more than 200,000 volumes, bought in Berlin. Harper characteristically believed that "it seems a great pity to wait for growth when we might be born full-fledged."

The faculty at the school included A. A. Michelson, the first American to win the Nobel Prize in science, Albion Small the sociologist, and later John Dewey (*q.v.*).

When dying of cancer, less than fifty years of age, William Rainey Harper remarked on his last day that he was much less worried now than when he had accepted the presidency of the University.

• • •

HARRIS, WILLIAM TORREY (1835-1909): "Philosophy can bake no bread," read the motto on the *Journal of Speculative Philosophy*, "but it can give us God, Freedom, and Immortality." William Torrey Harris, a philosopher of great energy and skill, founded the *Journal* to serve as the organ of the St. Louis Movement, American Hegelianism.

The *Journal* can boast among its discoveries William James, John Dewey, Josiah Royce, Howison and Peirce.

W. T. Harris was from Connecticut. He attended various local schools, all of which were distasteful. Finally he went to Yale (following A. D. White), which he considered equally bad. He dropped out in the middle of his junior year, remarkable for a man who later became United States Commissioner of Education.

During 1957 he taught school in St. Louis, where he had a series of successes, rising to the post of superintendent of schools. He celebrated his success by marrying Sarah T. Bugbee.

Harris had become acquainted with Brokmeyer *(q.v.)*. He was the secretary to whom Brokmeyer dictated his translation of Hegel's *Phenomenology*. On another occasion he saved Brokmeyer's life, finding him alone in a hut suffering from an intense fever.

In 1880 he left St. Louis to work on behalf of the Concord School of Philosophy. Following nine years at this endeavor, he accepted appointment as United States Commissioner of Education, a post which he held until 1906. He worked hard to place education on a sound psychological basis.

Harris' life and career show the definite connection between the idealism studied in the comparative obscurity of St. Louis and the spread of those ideas and ideals to all the nation's schools.

The books written by Harris, who was an exceptionally prolific author, include the *Introduction to the Study of Philosophy* (1889), *Hegel's Logic, a Book on the Genesis of the Categories of the Mind* (1890), and *The Psychologic Foundations of Education* (1898).

Said to have presented Hegel more clearly in English than did Hegel himself in German, Harris was widely read during his lifetime, yet is hardly read at all, today. He died November 5, 1909, in Providence.

The definitive work on Harris was written by Professor Kurt F. Leidecker, of Mary Washington College of the

University of Virginia, entitled: *Yankee Teacher, the Life of William Torrey Harris* (New York: The Philosophical Library, 1946).

• • •

HAZARD, ROWLAND GIBSON (1801-1888): He had just completed a refutation of Jonathan Edwards' theme on the will when the entire manuscript was lost in the wreck of a Mississippi steamboat. Refusing to accept this accident as the manifestation of divine displeasure, he wrote the book again. This time, a Civil War being in progress, Providence was occupied elsewhere. It did not destroy the book a second time. Thus in 1864 *Freedom of Mind in Willing; or Every Being That Wills a Creative First Cause* appeared. William Ellery Channing had put him up to writing it, and John Stuart Mill liked it.

When he was not writing books or losing them in the Mississippi River, Hazard was engaged in the wool trade. This he had inherited from his father, whose interests had been broader than wool (extending to peace, marrying Mary Peace in Charleston, S.C.).

• • •

HEDGE, LEVI (1766-1844): The first professor of Philosophy at Harvard, Levi Hedge was also known for his "eminent umbrella," vast, heavy, and difficult to furl. He wrote *Elements of Logick, or a Summary of the General Principles and Different Modes of Reasoning*, including a chapter on the calculation of chances, which might be subtitled, "How to Hedge your Bet." The book is remarkably clear, simple, and practical. He used to instruct his classes by saying:

It took me fourteen years, with the assistance of the adult members of my family, to write this book, and

144

I am sure that you cannot do better than to employ the precise words of the learned author.

• • •

HEMPEL, CARL GUSTAV (1905-   ): A key thinker in the philosophy of science, Carl Gustav Hempel was born in Germany and educated at Göttingen, Heidelberg, Berlin, and Vienna. In 1937 he came to the United States as part of that extraordinary intellectual migration forced by German politics. He was research associate at The University of Chicago, 1937-38, teacher at CCNY, 1939-40, Queens College, 1940-48, Yale, 1948-55, and Princeton from 1956. He wrote *Der Typusbegriff in Lichte der neuen Logik* (with Oppenheim, 1936), *Fundamentals of Concept Formation in Empirical Science* (1952), *Aspects of Scientific Explanation and Other Essays in the Philosophy of Science* (1956), and *Philosophy of Natural Science* (1966).

• • •

HOCKING, WILLIAM ERNEST (1873-1966): The distinguished Harvard idealist, William Ernest Hocking stood in the tradition of W. T. Harris and Josiah Royce. Born in Cleveland, he was educated at Harvard, three degrees in a row. He spent a year at Berlin and Heidelberg as a Harvard fellow. Back in the United States, he taught philosophy at the University of California, Yale, and Harvard. His books are: *The Meaning of God in Human Experience* (1912), *Human Nature and its Remaking* (1918), and *Morale and its Enemies* (1918). He was president of the American Philosophical Association 1926 and 1927.

Hocking believed that philosophy must be idealistic because the pursuit of meaning is the search for values. Mind is the creative principle. It is the primary certitude of experience.

•   •   •

HOFFER, ERIC (1902-   ): "Eric Hoffer's philosophy," remarks one critic, "is a good example of the danger of being self-taught."

Hoffer himself would not claim to be a philosopher:

I tried to read philosophical works but, like Einstein, I felt I was swallowing something I didn't have in my mouth. I did read some Nietzsche.

Nevertheless, his observations on life and American destiny have had the force of a powerful thinker, and he represents the philosophical spirit for many people in this land.

Born in New York City July 25th, 1902, Eric Hoffer was the only son of an immigrant couple. When he was seven his mother died. Later that year he went blind. Because of his blindness he had no formal schooling.

At fifteen, his eyesight returned. He was seized with an enormous hunger for the printed word. He read for ten or twelve hours a day, afraid that his sight would go again.

In 1920 his father, who had been a cabinet-maker, died. Hoffer had to fend for himself. California being the poor man's paradise, in his eyes, he boarded a bus and went there. His money ran out after a while and he nearly starved. Finally he began taking odd jobs.

Life on Skid Row ended when he became a migrant worker. All through the thirties he worked the crops from El Centro to Nevada City. In 1942 he joined the longshoremen's union, and has worked the docks ever since.

His books include: *The True Believer* (1951), *The Ordeal of Change* (1963), *The Passionate State of Mind and Other Aphorisms* (1955), *Working and Thinking on the Waterfront* (1969), and *First Things, Last Things* (1971).

One of his persistent themes is that

America is the only mass civilization there ever was. The masses eloped with history to America and we have been living in common-law marriage with it.

In his faith in the common man, Hoffer is sounding the same theme as Walt Whitman and Abraham Lincoln.

Along with this belief in the common man goes a distrust of the educated class:

Intellectuals are more corrupted by power than any other human type.

• • •

HOLT, EDWIN BISSELL (1873-1946): The American psychologist who introduced the work of Bok (1915) and Kappers (1917), developing the theory of the reflex-circle, that the response to one stimulus is the stimulus for the next response. Unmarried, he attended Harvard and Columbia and then taught at Harvard. He wrote *The Concept of Consciousness* (1914).

• • •

HOOK, SIDNEY (1902-   ): A left-wing disciple of Dewey's, Sidney Hook was early influenced by Marxism as he found in it important parallels with Pragmatism. However, he became disenchanted with communism as he observed its actual practice, and is now a leading opponent of the Leninist-Stalinist wing of Marxism:

What Marx understood by Communism was profoundly different from the system of political despotism and terror, of *gleichgeschalte* culture and economy, which prevails in the Soviet Union. Marx was a democratic socialist, a secular humanist, and a fighter for human freedom.

Born in New York City December 20, 1902, Hook was educated at CCNY (under Cohen) and Columbia (under Dewey), receiving his Ph.D. in 1927. He taught in the

147

New York City public schools, at Columbia's summer session, and at the Washington Square College of NYU.

He is the author of many books, including *The Metaphysics of Pragmatism* (1927), *From Hegel to Marx* (1936), *Reason, Social Myths and Democracy* (1940), *The Hero in History* (1943), *Education for Modern Man* (1946), *The Paradoxes of Freedom* (1962), and *The Place of Religion in a Free Society* (1968).

He is an empiricist because "empiricism is more likely to be critical, socially, than intuitionism." He insists on the fact that "every philosopher has a set of value judgments." His philosophical work illustrates his own firmly held set of such judgments.

• • •

HOPKINS, MARK (1802-1887): The ideal of every budget-conscious legislator, the name of Mark Hopkins promises to end the need for university buildings. Simple but inexpensive logs will do, one end reserved for the student and the other for Mark Hopkins. His immortal fame as a teacher was due to none other than James A. Garfield, then working as President of the United States. At a dinner for Williams alumni in New York Garfield remarked that his ideal of a college would be fully met by a log in the woods with a student at one end and Mark Hopkins at the other.

Hopkins, president of Williams College, believed that the resources of a college and library were not needed for good education:

Moral science appeals directly to the consciousness of the hearer. No learning is needed; no science, no apparatus, no information from distant countries.

He wrote *An Outline Study of Man* 1873) and *Lectures on Moral Science* (1862), commenting:

When the Lectures were first written, the text-book here, and generally in our colleges, was Paley. Not agreeing with him, and failing to carry out fully the doctrine of ends, I adopted that of an ultimate right, as taught by Kant and Coleridge, making that the end.

If Mark Hopkins fails, perhaps the log could say a few words.

• • •

HOWISON, GEORGE HOLMES (1834-1916): A personal idealist who opposed absolutism which seemed to deny free will, George Holmes Howison managed to be a forerunner of both William James and Borden Parker Bowne (*qq.v.*). A member during his earlier years of the St. Louis Movement and an associate of Brokmeyer and Harris (*qq.v.*), Howison taught at M. I. T., Harvard, and the University of California. His main work was *The Limits of Evolution and Other Essays Illustrating the Metaphysical Theory of Personal Idealism* (1901).

• • •

HUMANISM [Lat. *humanus*, Human]: Ger. *Humanismus;* Fr. *humanisme;* Ital. *umanesimo, umanismo.* (I) Any system of thought, belief, or action which centres about human or mundane things to the exclusion of the divine (of. the *New English Dict.*, sub verbo).

(2) The spirit, ideals, and doctrines of the Humanists — the scholars who, in the age of the RENAISSANCE (q.v.), devoted themselves to the study of the classical literatures and the culture of the ancient world.

• • •

HUTCHINS, ROBERT MAYNARD (1899-   ): Tremendously innovative as president (and chancellor) of The

University of Chicago (1929-1951), Robert Maynard Hutchins was the most creative force in American higher education in the first half of the twentieth century. He remarked that:

We have confused science with information, ideas with facts, and knowledge with miscellaneous data.

Believing that students ought to come to college "to think," he designed a curriculum requiring all students to be proficient in four fields: biological, physical, and social sciences, and the humanities. In this way he sought to avoid graduating "uneducated specialists." They would receive the degree as soon as they could pass the final achievement examination prepared by the board of examiners.

Born in Brooklyn, the son of a Presbyterian minister, Hutchins was educated at Oberlin, but interrupted his education to serve in the ambulance corps during World War I. He was decorated with the Italian *Croce di Guerra*. Returning, he went to Yale, graduating in 1921. He graduated from the Law School in 1925, began teaching, and became a full professor in 1927. For a year he served as acting Dean of the Law School, and the next year as Dean.

In 1929 he was invited to become president of The University of Chicago at the age of thirty.

Many of his educational reforms were so controversial that some of the faculty resigned, including George Mead (*q.v.*).

His main books include *No Friendly Voice* (1936), *The Higher Learning in America* (1936), *Education for Freedom* (1943), *The Conflict in Education in a Democratic Society* (1953), *The University of Utopia* (1953), *Some Observations on American Education* (1956), *The Great Conversation* (1951), and *The Learning Society* (1968).

I

INGERSOLL, ROBERT GREEN (1833-1899): Son of a Congregational minister and a strikingly beautiful mother, Robert Green Ingersoll became first a lawyer, then a colonel in the Civil War, then a noted lecturer, speaking on controversial subjects, slavery, suicide, marriage and divorce, capital punishment, and world unity. Since he attacked the institutional church for its superstition and hypocrisy and cowardice he was called an atheist, although he never was. He wrote:

An honest God is the noblest work of man.

His creed was:

Justice is the only worship.
Love is the only priest.
Ignorance is the only slavery.
Happiness is the only good.
The time to be happy is now.
The place to be happy is here.
The way to be happy is to make others so.

J

JAMES, HENRY (1811-1882): A brilliant writer, Henry James the Elder produced a radical critique of liberalism, denouncing Unitarianism, democracy, and capitalism. Cursed from youth by inherited wealth, he continually felt the injustice of his own favored position in society. He atoned for it by denouncing society and by devoting his life to the education of his two sons, one of whom was William James (*q.v.*).

Henry James attended Princeton Theological Seminary for a while, but grew weary of "the endless task of conciliating a stonyhearted Deity":

> The scheme postulates God as a being of such essential malignity . . . as to require that His thirst of blood once aroused by the sin of His own subject and helpless creatures, should be slaked only in one of two ways either . . . by the substantive reduction of these creatures themselves to eternal misery; or else . . . by the substitution in their place of an exquisitely innocent victim . . . Judged of by either alternative this scheme . . . reduces the Divine name indeed below the level of the lowest diabolism.

Although he became a personal friend of Emerson, James did not like his philosophy any the better, rejecting self-reliance as only another name for pride and sin.

He saw the Civil War as an effort to rid the land of forced and arbitrary inequalities among men, to raise the lot of the common man, after which, democracy having done its task, it will "shrivel up and disappear." That is, the state would wither away.

His wife died in Cambridge, Massachusetts, on the 29th of January, 1882, and he died December 18th of the same year.

• • •

JAMES, WILLIAM (1842-1910): The great popularizer of pragmatism (*q.v.*), which he preferred to call "radical empiricism," William James was the first American philosopher to be taken seriously in Europe, and is the only one represented in the *Great Books of the Western World*.

I. Life

The eldest son of Henry James, senior, William was born in New York City on the 11th of January, 1842. Named for his grandfather, an Irish immigrant who made his fortune and left enough for his heirs to become financially independent, William was very close to his younger brother, Henry, born only fifteen months after he was.

Except for these two and their father, the rest of the Presbyterian James family was notably undistinguished.

Henry, Sr., was attracted to the theology of Swedenborg with its radical mysticism. As a boy, he had been severely burned, necessitating the amputation of one leg above the knee. He was always restless, moving from New York to Europe and back to America.

The children were schooled irregularly in London, Paris, Boulogne-sur-Mer, Geneva, and Bonn. Even such schooling as this led William to scorn the routine of schools and colleges. At home, allowed to follow his own interests, he drew pictures for hour after hour, and browsed at random in his father's library.

His father had attended Princeton Theological Seminary and was preparing to enter the ministry, but instead

154

developed an "antipathy to all ecclesiasticisms which he expressed with abounding scorn and irony throughout all his later years." He was most anxious for his sons to "*be* something, something unconnected with specific doing, something free and uncommitted."

When he was eighteen, the family was living in Newport, Rhode Island, and William took up the study of painting under William Hunt and John LaFarge. Within a year he tired of it and entered the Lawrence scientific school of Harvard University. He studied, successively, chemistry, anatomy, and medicine.

In 1865, he joined Louis Agassiz on a trip to the Amazon. While there, the duties irked him: "If there is anything I hate, it is collecting." His health failed.

Returning to the Harvard Medical School for a term, he went to Germany and attended the lectures of Helmholtz and others. He began reading everything he could find on the subject of philosophy. This uncertainty over a vocation was reflected in a severe mental depression.

When he returned home, late in 1868, he was quite ill. He had had thoughts of suicide.

By June of 1869, he received the M.D. degree from Harvard Medical School, but was too ill to begin practice. For the next three years he lived as a semi-invalid at his father's house, doing nothing but reading.

He was finally liberated from his phobic panic by reading Renouvier on the freedom of the will, contrary to the deterministic universe of Mill, Bain and Spencer. He declared: "My first act of free will shall be to believe in free will." He opposed the notion of the "block universe," in this instance for entirely personal reasons.

In 1872 he was appointed an instructor in physiology at Harvard College. Work was good therapy for him. By 1875 he had set up the first laboratory for experimental psychology in America, physiological psychology. Having accomplished this, he soon exhausted his own desire to work in the lab.

Married in 1878, at 36, to Alice Gibbens of Cambridge, Mass., life seemed better. He had purpose and energy. Neurasthenia practically disappeared. In that year he signed a contract with Henry Holt and Company to produce a textbook in psychology within two years.

Twelve years later, the book appeared, *The Principles of Psychology* in two ponderous volumes. It took two more years to distill a textbook from this work. However, it was both definitive and original. Functional psychology was its viewpoint. Biology was the basis for mental activities, which were instruments in the struggle for survival.

Once he had completed his book, James lost interest in psychology, which he then called "a nasty little subject; all one cares to know lies outside it."

However, the publication of the book brought a great number of invitations to lecture around the country. Many of these lectures were printed as *The Will to Believe and Other Essays in Popular Philosophy* (1897), *Human Immortality* (1898), and *Talks to Teachers on Psychology and to Students on Some of Life's Ideals* (1899).

James' approach in these matters differed in that it was empirical and experimental. The nature of God, if it could be found, was to be sought in religious experience. Belief and action should be examined in the search for free will and determinism.

He concluded, on the basis of such investigations, that immortality was not proved; that religious experience established the existence of God, but as a plurality of saving powers of the same basic quality as the human personality itself; that freedom is to be found in a certain looseness in the course of events, such that the future is not inevitably determined by past history and present form.

James enjoyed a religious experience in 1898 during a vacation climb in the Adirondack mountains: "It seemed as if the Gods of all the nature-mythologies were holding an indescribable meeting in my breast with the moral Gods of the inner life."

A similar trip to the Adirondacks the following summer was physically disastrous. He lost his way, and the sustained effort and exposure injured his heart. The next two years were needed to recover.

At last, in 1901-2, he was able to give the Gifford Lectures at the University of Edinburgh, which he had been invited to deliver several years before. These were *The Varieties of Religious Experience* (1902), widely acclaimed for their rich concreteness and scientific approach to religious phenomena.

Belatedly, as he said, he now turned explicitly to philosophical topics, lamenting that he had built only one side of the arch. Some thirty years before, he had met Charles S. Peirce (*q.v.*), the founder of a method of thinking termed pragmatism. Now James interpreted this epistemology in a series of lectures published as *Pragmatism: A New Name for Old Ways of Thinking* (1907).

These were the years, under the influence of Charles Eliot and the driving ambition of A. Lawrence Lowell, that Harvard was changing from a sleepy provincial college to a great university.

Criticisms of his theory were answered in *The Meaning of Truth* (1909). His studies entitled "Does Consciousness Exist," and "The Thing and its Relations" were published posthumously (1912) as *Essays in Radical Empiricism*. A more popular treatment of the same essential themes was *A Pluralistic Universe* (1909).

Some Problems in Philosophy (1911) was the last collection of his thoughts, a collection that also appeared posthumously.

James had lectured, quite late in his career, at the newly-opened Stanford University, and while there (1906) had also witnessed the San Francisco earthquake.

Finally, physical discomfort became too great even for his remarkable capacity for endurance. He and his wife sailed to Europe to try the cure at Nauheim.

There, he allowed himself too strenuous a schedule, talking

with interested people, and the fatigue made him worse.

Returning to America, he went with his brother up to their summer home at Chocorua, New Hampshire. There, on August 27th, 1910, he died, two days after having arrived.

• • •

JEFFERSON, THOMAS (1743-1826): Exemplar of the American Enlightenment, the nearest America has come to a universal man, Thomas Jefferson excelled in political theory, architecture, invention and music. Chronologically, his life spans the interval between Jonathan Edwards and Ralph Waldo Emerson.

Born at Shadwell, Virginia, April 13th, 1743, his father had made himself wealthy and prestigious. When Thomas was only thirteen his father unexpectedly died. Three years later the sixteen-year-old Jefferson went down to the College of William and Mary planning to learn Greek, Latin, and mathematics. Instead he learned science, literature, and law. The great influences on his life at that time were Dr. William Small (q.v.) and George Wythe. They introduced him to the social and political life of the capital city.

Admitted to the bar in 1767, he was elected to the House of Burgesses in 1769, serving until 1779. There he fell in with the group of young men persistently challenging British authority.

At twenty-nine, he took time out to marry. Martha Wayles Skelton bore him six children, only two of whom survived infancy.

In 1774 the English Parliament attempted to punish the colonies by passing a series of coercive acts designed to demonstrate England's power over America. The port of Boston was closed. Representative government in Massachusetts was virtually abolished. British troops were given the power to move into private houses in any of the thirteen colonies.

A Continental Congress was called, which Jefferson was

unable to attend. Instead, he wrote his *Summary View of the Rights of British America,* arguing for the equality of colonial legislatures and Parliament, under, of course, the delegated powers of the Crown. Because of this, Jefferson became the most eloquent and effective spokesman for resistance.

I

The Committee of Five appointed to draw up a draft Declaration of Independence delegated the task to him in June of 1776. He wrote (quoting from Jefferson's original draft, before the changes made by Franklin and Adams):

We hold these truths to be sacred and undeniable; that all men are created equal and independent, that from that equal creation they derive rights inherent and inalienable, among which are the preservation of life, and liberty, and the pursuit of happiness; that to secure these ends, governments are instituted among men, deriving their just powers from the consent of the governed; that whenever any form of government shall become destructive of these ends, it is the right of the people to alter or to abolish it, and to institute new government, laying its foundation on such principles and organising its powers in such form as to them seem most likely to effect their safety and happiness.

Prudence indeed will dictate that governments long established should not be changed for light and transient causes: and accordingly all experience hath shewn that mankind are more disposed to suffer while evils are sufferable, than to right themselves by abolishing the forms to which they are accustomed.

But when a long train of abuses and usurpations, begun at a distinguished period, and pursuing invariably the same object, evinces a design to subject them to arbitrary power, it is their right, it is their duty, to

159

throw off such government and to provide new guards for their future security.

II

This was the first of his great accomplishments, the Declaration of American Independence. His second (in his own eyes) was the Statute of Virginia for religious freedom.

Having returned to Virginia, Jefferson spent the next several years trying to reform the laws of the state in accordance with the best in scientific, sociological, and psychological theory. This was the same basic enterprise which occupied Jeremy Bentham at the time, in England.

The intensely practical nature of American thought is evident, as Jefferson applied his ideas directly and immediately to present-day conditions. The resistance of tradition in Virginia, however, prevented the realization of most of Jefferson's best efforts. The most important victory was the Statute for Religious Freedom (quotation from Jefferson's original draft of the bill):

Well aware that the opinions and belief of men depend not on their own will, but follow involuntarily the evidence proposed to their minds; that Almighty God hath created the mind free; and manifested his supreme will that free it shall remain by making it altogether insusceptible of restraint; that all attempts to influence it by temporal punishment, or burthens, or by civil incapacitations, tend only to beget habits of hypocrisy and meanness, and are a departure from the plan of the holy author of our religion, who being lord both of body and mind, yet chose not to propagate it by coercions on either, as was in his Almighty power to do; but to extend it by its influence on reason alone; that the impious presumption of legislature and ruler, civil as well as ecclesiastical, who, being themselves but fallible and uninspired men, have assumed dominion over the faith

160

of others, setting up their own opinions and modes of thinking as the only true and infallible, and as such endeavoring to impose them on others, hath established and maintained false religions over the greatest part of the world and through all time: That to compel a man to furnish contributions of money for the propagation of opinions which he disbelieves and abhors, is sinful and tyrannical.

Jefferson went on to write that "the opinions of men are not the object of civil government, nor under its jurisdiction. To suffer the civil magistrate to intrude his powers into the field of opinion and to restrain the profession or propagation of principles on supposition of their ill tendency is a dangerous fallacy, which at once destroys all religious liberty."

Later (1800) he was to write his famous lines to Benjamin Rush; "I have sworn upon the altar of God eternal hostility against every form of tyranny over the mind of man."

From 1779 to 1781 Jefferson served as governor of Virginia. These were bad years to hold that office. The revolutionary war made all life precarious. The legislature, supporting a rebellion against one king, was afraid of allowing another to develop in the Governor's Palace. Jefferson passed his time making a sketch of the layout of rooms in the mansion at Williamsburg. The legislature refused to allow him enough power to defend the commonwealth against British troops, who promptly occupied the capital. The state government simply ceased to function as the officials fled.

Jefferson was blamed for this humiliation by Patrick Henry who, at the time, was enjoying liberty rather more than death. A formal inquiry was convened. Even though it excused Jefferson from blame, and complimented him on his conduct he was not overjoyed. He retired to his family and property.

His wife died. They had been married only ten years. He never remarried.

His public life from this point on is quite well known: member of Congress (1783), Minister to France (1785-1789), Secretary of State (1790-1794), Vice President (1796-1800), and President (1800-1808).

Jefferson's rise to these political heights was helped by the split which had developed between John Adams and Alexander Hamilton within the Federalist Party. Both believed in the natural depravity of man, but Adams believed it good reason to limit sharply the power of government, while Hamilton believed that man was basically evil except when elected to public office. Adams was a conservative in the tradition of Hume and Burke, Hamilton in the tradition of Machiavelli and Hobbes.

Jefferson, on the other hand, feared the possible renewal of the oppressions of monarchy. He wrote to Madison (in 1787):

I prefer dangerous liberty to tranquil servitude. Even this evil is productive of good. It prevents the degeneracy of government, and nourishes a general attention to the public affairs. I hold it, that a little rebellion, now and then, is a good thing, and as necessary in the political world as storms in the physical. Unsuccessful rebellions, indeed, generally establish the encroachments on the rights of the people, which have produced them. An observation of this truth should render honest republican governors so mild in their punishment of rebellions, as not to discourage them too much. It is a medicine necessary for the sound health of government.

Jefferson as President was popular and effective until his last year in office. He had chosen the Embargo Act as preferable to war with either England or Napoleonic France, both of whom were raiding American ships. The individual coercion which the Act involved was great, and Jefferson at last signed its repeal four days before leaving office.

Writing to a friend Jefferson said: "Never did a prisoner, released from his chains, feel such relief as I shall on shaking off the shackles of power. Nature intended me for tranquil pursuits of science, by rendering them my supreme delight."

III

His retirement to Monticello set the stage for his third great achievement, the founding of the University of Virginia. In 1813 Central College was established in Charlottesville. Peter Carr, Jefferson's nephew, was President of the Board of Trustees. Jefferson wrote him a letter outlining some ideas on education, which he considered indispensable to a working democracy. His plan was printed in the Richmond *Enquirer*. Soon after, the Legislature approved it and appropriated $600,000. In 1819 the University of Virginia was founded. Jefferson at the time was in his seventies.

Let us quote from his letter:

It is highly interesting to our country, and it is the duty of its functionaries, to provide that every citizen in it should receive an education proportioned to the condition and pursuits of his life.

More specifically:

All the branches, then, of useful science, ought to be taught in the general scools, to a competent degree.... These are, I. Language; II. Mathematics; III. Philosophy.

I. Language. In the first department, I would arrange a distinct science. 1, Languages and History, ancient and modern; 2, Grammar; 3, Belles Lettres (poetry, comsition, and criticism); 4, Rhetoric and Oratory; 5, A scool for the deaf, dumb and blind. History is here associated with languages, not as a kindred subject, but on the principle of economy, because both may be attained by the same course of reading, if books are selected with that view.

II. Mathematics. In the department of Mathematics, I should give place distinctly: 1. Mathematics pure (1, Numbers, and 2, Measure in the abstract; that of numbers comprehending Arithmetic, Algebra and Fluxions; that of Measure (under the general appellation of Geometry), comprehending Trigonometry, plane and spherical, conic sections, and transcendental curves); 2, Physico-Mathematics (which treat of physical subjects by the aid of mathematical calculation. These are Mechanics, Statics, Hydrostatics, Hydrodynamics, Navigation, Astronomy, Geography, Optics, Pneumatics, Acoustics); 3, Physics (or Natural Philosophy not entering the limits of Chemistry, treating of natural substances, their properties, mutual relations and action. They particularly examine the subjects of motion, action, magnetism, electricity, galvanism, light, meteorology, etc.; 4, Chemistry; 5, Natural History, to wit: Mineralogy; 6, Botany; and 7, Zoology; 8, Anatomy; 9, the Theory of Medicine.

III. Philosophy. In the Philosophical department, I should distinguish: 1, Ideology; 2, Ethics; 3, the law of Nature and Nations; 4, Government; 5, Political Economy.

This was the substance of Jefferson's plan, with the exception of the profesional schools. It is worth noting that he had a definite American preference for useful knowledge, practical subjects, and a practical cast to theoretical subjects.

Jefferson was the implacable foe of ignorance and of religious superstition. They were, he believed, the two foundations of despotism. In 1816 he wrote:

My opinion is that there would never have been an infidel, if there had never been a priest. The artificial structure they have built on the purest of all moral systems for the purpose of deriving from it pence and power revolts those who think for themselves and who read in that system only what is really there.

In his last letter, written two weeks before he died (1826), he again touched the same basic theme, that the American Revolution had been the signal step in the enlightenment of mankind and its deliverance from superstition:

May it be to the world, what I believe it will be (to some parts sooner, to others later, but finally to all), the signal of arousing men to burst the chains under which monkish ignorance and superstition had persuaded them to bind themselves, and to assume the blessings and security of self-government. That form which we have substituted, restores the free right to the unbounded exercise of reason and freedom of opinion. All eyes are opened, or opening, to the rights of man. The general spread of the light of science has already laid open to every view the palpable truth, that the mass of mankind has not been born with saddles on their backs, nor a favored few booted and spurred, ready to ride them legitimately, by the grace of God.

On the fourth of July, 1826, the fiftieth anniversary of the Declaration or Independence, Jefferson died. John Adams, strangely enough, died the same day.

"Can one generation bind another, and all others, in succession forever?" he had written two years earlier. "I think not. The creator has made the earth for the living, not the dead."

•   •   •

JOHNSON, SAMUEL (1696-1772): The American Samuel Johnson is commonly mentioned as the first American philosopher worthy of serious attention. This is true if you steadfastly overlook such European contemporaries as Hume, Berkeley, Locke, Newton, and Spinoza. With them aside, Johnson was surely a profound thinker. Johnson did know Berkeley personally. It is as a kind of small footnote to Berkeley that he is best considered. Berkeley at the time was residing in America. After all, he had to know someone.

An example of Samuel Johnson's thought often quoted is from his book on physics:

Q. Why do not the Peripatetics (Aristotelians) follow this method (Ramist logic, thought at the time to be a tremendous improvement over Aristotelian logical theory)?
A. The Peripatetics do not follow this method because they do not follow Moses but Aristotle; and learn their philosophy not from the sacred pages, but from the heathen Aristotle, and because they do not run through the whole course of the nature of things, but deal only with certain parts of physics as for example, the highest heaven and the angels, whose nature is nowhere considered. — Quoted in Miller, *The New England Mind*, 105.

The improvement of physics texts by the addition of a chapter on angels, while definitely original, does not appear particularly profound to the contemporary mind.

That part of Johson's psychological theory which most impresses modern readers, his belief in the freedom of the will, is due less to his originality than to his church party affiliation. Johnson's most daring act of conscience was to prefer the Anglican to the (Calvinist) Congregational church.

I. Life

Born in Guilford, Connecticut, Samuel Johnson was educated at the Collegiate School of Saybrook. This school is better known as Yale. He took the Master of Arts degree at New Haven in 1717.

The course of study consisted of Cicero, Virgil, the New Testament in Greek, a little science, some scholastic philosophy, and a great deal of Calvinistic theology. The students were sternly cautioned against reading the new books by Descartes, Locke, and Newton lest their theology be corrupted. The school library contained mostly books brought over from the mother country sixty years before.

For the next five years he worked at three jobs. He was tutor back home, tutor back at the College, where he rashly introduced the very books he had been warned against reading, and a Congregational minister at West Haven.

In 1722, the event occurred that scandalized the whole of New England. Johnson deserted Congregationalism for the Anglican church. New England was easily scandalized at the time. He sailed for England to take orders, and spent a short time at both Oxford and Cambridge. He returned the next year as Anglican missionary to the town or Stratford. For thirty years he remained at that post. Stratford was in great need of an Anglican missionary.

Bishop Berkeley spent two years in America while waiting for the establishment of a college in Bermuda for the education of American Indians. The college never materialized. During this time Johnson visited Berkeley and wrote him letters on a number of occasions. The letters contain several requests for clarification and reveal a few points of difference between them. Berkeley's usual reply in this correspondence was to say that he wrote his philosophical works when he was much younger and obviously had made some mistakes, but that the points made by Johnson do not seem to affect the central argument of the book. Both men considered Berkeleyan idealism to be a wonderful defense

167

against unbelief and, in this exchange of letters, treated it as such.

After Berkeley returned to England, he was easily influenced by his friend Johnson to interest himself in the college at New Haven. The gift of his library and estate to the school was of tremendous value for its advancement.

In 1723 Johnson published the *Introduction to the Study of Philosophy*. This Baconesque work divides the objects of knowledge into three sections: (1) the general nature of reality (being), (2) the physical (natural) world of bodies, and (3) the moral world of relationships (both human and divine). The philosophical influences in this work are Locke and Wollaston (*The Religion of Nature Delineated*, 1722). Study was recommended to the student as the indispensable means to happiness. Happiness, as with Aristotle, was the true end and object of human life.

One influence *not* found in this work is that of Berkeley, surprisingly enough. Johnson wrote that there is a state of affairs, "existence," which is to be distinguished from our knowledge of it. Furthermore, the subject matter of logic is the organization of Knowledge, similar to Hobbes' declaration that logic is the right use of words. Johnson did not say, as did Berkeley, that logic is an instrument of discovery.

In 1746, using the pseudonym "Aristocles," Johnson published *A System of Morality* (Boston). Man, he wrote, is the center of the scheme of things. Objects, such as natural bodies, are either good or bad according to how they are used by individual men for the common welfare. Men are good or bad in the same way. In addition, men possess a kind of value which is more than a mere means to an end. The happiness of man is a good in itself. Thus it is the measure of all other goods.

At this point in his ethical theory, Johnson appears as a kind of footnote to Wollaston. He did, however, reject Wollaston's view that reason should be the guide to our happiness. Rather, Johnson declared, that guide should be revealed religion.

From 1744-1747, Johnson engaged in an interesting published debate with Jonathan Dickinson on the question of the freedom of the will. Johnson inclined toward the Arminian extreme, that is, he defended freedom against determinism. He asked what kind of a God would make a world without providing for the happiness of men? Surely, as God is good, he wishes us to enjoy ourselves. Therefore we must be free to choose the good and reject the evil.

While his sons were in college, he wrote a work for their assistance, the *Manual of Logic and Metaphysics*.

Intending to unify the theory of nature and the philosophy of history, Johnson defined nature as the art (*techne*) of God:

1. Art is the representing and directing *eupraxia* (well-doing).
2. An idea is the matter of art.
3. An idea is the pattern of a thing.
4. An idea is representing and by means of the representation directing *eupraxia* in action.
5. On which the form of art is based.
6. The object and end of an idea is *eupraxia*.
7. A thing is an object in so far as it is engaged in being represented.
8. An end, in so far as it directs by means of representing.
9. *Eupraxia* is the orderly procedure or action of an agent in acting.

An interesting point of contact may be noted with William Ames (*q.v.*) whose first and seventh logical propositions we quote here:

1. An art is the putting of a thing into existence and operation by rule to fulfil its purpose.
7. The *image* is that representation which exists either in the thought of a rational creature or in that delineation of it which is put in a book consisting of the most

perfect instructions to be had for the *eupraxia* of the given thing.

Johnson's last two works were published together under the title of *Elementa Philosophica*, by Benjamin Franklin's press in 1752. Used as a text in Franklin's Academy, the book did not sell as well as had been hoped. Franklin offered to absorb the deficit, and in 1754 a second edition was published, this time in London.

In the first part of the book (*Noetica*) Johnson declared that the source of knowledge is threefold: (1) *ab extra* (by the use of the senses), (2) *ab intra* (by imagination and memory), and (3) the "intellectual light" (conception).

Ab extra knowledge is gained by the use of the senses. The mind is passive, receiving impressions of natural objects through color and shape and other sensations. These ideas, Johnson said, are not merely pictures of things, but are the real things, at least that with which we are concerned in this division: things of the sensible kind. That is, the order and connection of our ideas is the same as the order and connection of ideas in the Divine mind.

Ab intra knowledge is gained by the consciousness. The inner perception of imagination and memory gives us ideas of objects not present: "mere creatures of our mind, or chimeras."

Intellectual light refers to the knowledge of the pure intellect. This is the conception of abstract (or spiritual) objects, the relations between them, the various mental processes, and the complex ideas resulting. These are not "ideas," but "notions," whether simple (as perception, consciousness, volition, affection, action, etc.) or complex (as spirit, soul, god, cause, effect, proportion, justice, charity, etc.).

In the second part of the book (*Ethica*), Johnson provides a kind of Berkeleyan ethical theory. Berkeley himself did not develop such a theory, and Johnson's is not universally agreed to be a pure example of what Berkeley would have written. Nevertheless, there are important points to be made for the similarity of outlook. The *Ethica* is divided into two sections: (1) theoretical ethics, and (2) practical duties.

Theoretical ethical theory, according to Johnson, deals with three questions: (1) What am I? (2) How came I to be what I am? and (3) For what end was I made and have my being?

(1) What am I?

Such a strange mixture is human nature! Such a various creature is man! Such his noble abilities and excellencies on the one hand, such his imperfections and wretchedness on the other.

From hence I not only know that I have a being, but also that when I am in tolerable circumstances, and do well, I have a great enjoyment of that being; that it is very dear to me, and that I am, above all things, concerned to preserve and continue it, and to make it as comfortable and happy as ever I can.

(2) How came I to be what I am?

Johnson provides an orthodox statement of the providence of an omnipotent and benevolent God. Whatever evils there are in the world are the result of disobedience to his will. Beyond that:

But if, after all, there should be some untoward appearances in the conduct of providence that we cannot clearly account for, they ought not to be admitted as any just objections against what hath been antecedently demonstrated; especially since we should be very vain indeed, to think ourselves qualified to be competent judges of the deep things of God.

(3) For what end was I made and have my being?

But now to return: since I am convinced, from the above method of reasoning that my well-being and happinesses must have been God's end in giving me my being and that it must be a happiness suitable to that nature which

171

He hath given me, in the whole of it; I must be persuaded, that since, besides an animal and sensitive, He hath moreover given me a rational, active and social nature, as my superior and peculiar character, it is plain He must have designed me, not merely for a sensual and animal, but chiefly for a rational, active and social happiness.

The practical duties that follow upon such theoretical considerations are divided into three parts: (1) duties to myself, (2) duties to God, and (3) duties to others.

Johnson's definition of moral philosophy is as follows:

The knowledge of the moral world, the world of spirit or free intelligent agents, and the general laws of the moral behavior, together with all that practical conduct thereon depending that is necessary to promote our true happiness, both in our present and future state.

Or, again:

Ethics is the art of living happily by the right knowledge of ourselves and the practice of virtue our happiness being the end and virtue the means to that end.

Benjamin Franklin, as might be guessed from what has been said before, was tremendously impressed by Samuel Johnson. He invited him (unsuccessfully) to be the head of the Academy (later called the College of Philadelphia, now the University of Pennsylvania).

During the years from 1744 to 1753, Johnson carried on a significant correspondence with Cadwallader Colden *(q.v.)*.

Respected throughout the colonies as an expert on education, he set forth his educational theory in the *Elementa Philosophica*, the Preface, Introduction, and sixth chapter of the first section. He recommended the use of short drafts to help the students direct and methodize their thoughts. He also developed a sort of psychology of learning.

In 1754 he became the first president of King's College, in New York (Columbia). He remained its head until 1763.

He retired to Stratford, where he remained until his death in 1772.

K

KAUFMANN, WALTER (1921-   ): An extraordinarily productive scholar, Walter Kaufmann to date has twenty-six titles to his name. His studies of Nietzsche and Existentialism are standards in the field. He has been a member of the faculty at Princeton since 1947.

Born in Freiburg, Germany, Kaufmann was raised a Lutheran:

> When I found that I could not believe in the Trinity, and especially not that Jesus was God, I decided to become a Jew. I was only eleven, and my parents felt that I was too young to make such a far-reaching choice. I persisted, and the matter was discussed for months. During that time, Hitler came to power and now I was told that in view of the persecution my decision might entail I should certainly wait until I was older. I insisted that one could not change one's mind for a reason like that. I did not realize until a little later that all of my grandparents had been Jewish; and none of us knew that this, and not one's own religion, would determine the Nazi's classification.

He came to America and entered Williams College in February, 1939. His parents, with great difficulty, managed to reach London two months later, and they spent the war years there.

Kaufmann won a scholarship to Harvard in the Spring of 1941, and studied philosophy there. Serving with the Army from 1944-46, he returned to complete his dissertation in 1947.

Among his many excellent books, we may mention the following: *Nietzsche* (1950), *Existentialism from Dostoevsky to Sartre* (1956), *Critique of Religion and Philosophy* (1958), *Religion from Tolstoy to Camus* (1961), *The Faith of a Heretic* (1961), *Hegel* (1965), and *Tragedy and Philosophy* (1968).

• • •

KOCH, ADRIENNE (1912-1971): Historian of America's formative years, Adrienne Koch's thesis was that the Founding Fathers of the country were not merely politicians brought to power in a time of revolutionary upheaval, but rather "philosopher-statesmen." She was noted for her books: *The Philosophy of Thomas Jefferson* (1943), *Jefferson and Madison: The Great Collaboration* (1950), *The American Enlightenment: The Shaping of the American Experiment and a Free Society* (1965), and *Philosophy for a Time of Crisis* (1959). She wrote:

> We need not waste time over the infantilism that advises 'all power to the people,' destroy what now exists, permit 'love' to take over and build a new utopian society. History and experience afford fairly plain lessons here. Utopian idealism accompanying violent revolution leads to total control. The avoidance of this syndrome by the American Revolution is perhaps its most precious lesson.

Born in New York City, Adrienne Koch was educated at NYU and Columbia. She taught at NYU, Tulane, the University of California at Berkeley, the University of Michigan, and the University of Maryland.

KRISTELLER, PAUL (1905-   ): Born in Berlin, educated in Heidelberg, Berlin, Freiburg, Marburg, and the University of Pisa, Paul Oskar Kristeller is a noted authority on the thought of the Renaissance. He came to America in 1939 and has taught since that time at Columbia.

L

LAMONT, CORLISS (1902-   ): The fiery and controversial humanist, Corliss Lamont was the author of the trenchant and vivid argument against immortality, entitled *The Illusion of Immortality* (1935).

Born in Englewood, New Jersey, he was educated at Phillips Exeter Academy, Harvard (1924), Oxford, and Columbia (Ph.D. 1932). He taught at Columbia College, the New School for Social Research, Cornell, and Harvard. Director of the A.C.L.U., 1932-1954, candidate for the U.S. Senate on the ticket of the American Labor Party, 1952, Lamont was indicated for contempt of Congress, a charge dismissed by an appeals court in 1956.

He has written *Issues of Immortality* (1932), *You Might Like Socialism: A Way of Life for Modern Man* (1939), *The Peoples of the Soviet Union* (1946), *A Humanist Funeral Service* (1947), and *The Philosophy of Humanism* (1957).

•   •   •

LANGER, SUSANNE K. (1895-   ): One of the greatest living American philosophers, born in New York City on the 20th of December, 1895, Susanne Langer is famed for her perceptive analytic work, which has not prevented her from developing a comprehensive philosophical position of her own.

She was educated at Radcliffe College, graduating in 1920 with an A.B., 1924 with an A.M., and two years later

175

with a Ph.D. During 1921-22 she was a student at the University of Vienna.

Married to William L. Langer in 1921, she is the mother of two sons, Leonard and Bertrand. Twenty-one years later she was divorced.

Serving as a tutor in philosophy at Radcliffe from 1927 to 1942, she taught at the University of Deleware (1943), Columbia (1945-50), N.Y.U. (1945), the New School for Social Research, Northwestern, Ohio U., U. Washington, and the University of Michigan. From 1954-1962 she was professor of philosophy at Connecticut College.

Her publications include *The Practice of Philosophy* (1930), *Philosophy in a New Key* (1942), *An Introduction to Symbolic Logic* (1953), *Feeling and Form* (1953), *Problems of Art* (1957), *Philosophical Sketches* (1962), and *Mind: an Essay on Human Feeling, Volume I* (1967).

She is now professor emeritus and research scholar with offices in Connecticut College, New London, Connecticut.

She has written that:

Modern theory of knowledge, leading naturally to a critique of science, represents the best philosophical work of our time.

One of her concerns is to investigate the logic of signs and symbols (which, she later remarks, she would change to signals and symbols, retaining the word "sign" in a generic sense, to cover both), a field which also interests Tillich greatly. She notes that she thinks of:

symbolism as the characteristically human element in cognition, and the great departure from animal mentality which symbolic expression and understanding have effected.

In later works she asks the "fundamental question," "Why must artistic form, to be expressive of feeling, always be so-called 'living form'?" Aristotle had said that organic form was the most important feature of any composition. Her question is, "Why?"

In pursuit of her answer, she attempts to unify the insights from biology, biochemistry, psychology, philosophy and esthetics. At the end, she promises another essay to investigate what in actuality happened in the shift from animal to human estate, the great shift that initiated the development of mind.

Her viewpoint throughout her life has been this:

> A philosophical theory is not called upon to furnish "irrefutable proofs," but concepts that give rise to insight and discovery. One can sometimes prove the consistency of concepts, and inconsistency can always be logically demonstrated; but one cannot prove the excellence of a concept, even if it be logically impeccable, except pragmatically, by operating with it successfully.

•   •   •

LeCONTE, JOSEPH (1823-1901): Pupil of Agassiz and teacher of Royce, Joseph LeConte was enthusiastic about evolutionary theory, which he regarded not merely as a plausible inference from biological and geological data, but as an axiomatic principle of science:

> Evolution is *absolutely certain.*.. evolution as a law of derivation of forms from previous forms. . . . The nexus between *successive events in time* (causation) is far more certain than the nexus between *coexistent objects in space* (gravitation). The former *is a necessary truth,* the latter is usually classed as a contingent truth.

Born in Liberty County, Georgia, taught by Alexander Hamilton Stephens *(q.v.),* he kept relatively aloof from politics during the Civil War. Afterwards, he and his brother applied for positions at the newly-formed University of

California at Berkeley, in 1866. In 1869 they were accepted and remained there for the rest of their days.

Among his books are *Evolution and its Relation to Religious Thought* (1888) and "What is Life?" in *Science* (1901).

An enthusiastic outdoorsman, LeConte died, as he might have wished, while on a trip with the Sierra Club into the Yosemite.

•　•　•

LEWIS, CLARENCE IRVING (1883-1964): A "conceptualistic pragmatist," C. I. Lewis criticizes both rationalism and empiricism for attempting to separate mind from experience. Standing in the pragmatist tradition, Lewis particularly admired Peirce. Born in Stoneham, Massachusetts, he graduated from Harvard and taught there from 1921 to 1953. He wrote *Mind and the World-Order* (1929).

•　•　•

LIEBER, FRANCIS (1800-1872): When Senator Sumner was caned at his desk in the Senate Chamber by the congressman from South Carolina, Preston Brooks, May 22nd, 1856, the professor of history and political economy at South Carolina College (now the University of South Carolina) was horrified. "Now they collect money here to reward Mr. Brooks by Some Pieces of plate! It is to hide one's face. . . . Sometimes nations go on so that nothing but a war will make a period of reason possible. And so I think it is now with the South and North."

Although twenty years a professor at South Carolina, Lieber cut his ties and sought a position in the North. With difficulty he obtained an appointment to Columbia.

His eldest son fought in the Confederate army, while his two others fought for the Union. In 1862 the two armies approached each other on the Virginia penninsula. After the Battle of Williamsburg, he wrote: "O'Riley... was expressing his joy that his son had received 'no scratch'... when a man sitting near him said: Why here is the name of your son, pointing to a list of 'Killed.' The poor man stared, read, and his face and hands moved convulsively. It was heart rending." In a double irony, Lieber learned some months later that his first son had himself been mortally wounded at Williamsburg, and had died deliriously raving against his father and the North.

Francis Lieber, sometimes called the American Schleiermacher (there seem to have been several American Schleiermachers — Channing (q.v.) was another) was born in Berlin (March 18, 1800) and lived the life of an adventurer until, fleeing the Prussian secret police, he came to Boston in 1827.

He was noted for his work in social and political theory. *Manual of Political Ethics* (1838-9), *Legal and Political Hermeneutics* (1839), and *On Civil Liberty and Self-Government* (1853) were among his most famous works. He also edited the *Encyclopaedia Americana* (1829-33).

He often repeated the principle: "No right without its duties, no duty without its rights."

The natural rights of man, he believed, should not be considered in the primitive state, but in man's present highly civilized condition. Social institutions were the invincible protectors of civil liberty, which he defined as the protection or check against undue interference (whether from other individuals, the masses, or government).

Society can best be maintained by "mild laws, firm judges, and calm punishments."

Lieber poured his own personal experiences into his works. As a young boy he had witnessed Napoleon's occupation of his home city (Berlin) after the Prussian defeats at Jena and Auerstedt. As a youth he had fought at Waterloo, on the winning side. His wound there had almost taken his life.

His passionate patriotism did not prevent the overly-suspicious Prussian secret police from hounding him, convinced without cause of his disloyalty. They had discovered in his diary the entry: "All day murder lazy." That must mean, they insisted, that he was plotting the assassination of his superiors. He was detained for questioning again and again. He was denied (because of police pressure) the right to study at a University. He acquired his education with the greatest difficulty.

In 1821, hearing of the Greek revolution, Lieber sailed to help them fight for independence. He and his friends were robbed by the very Greeks they had come to help. Finding the revolutionaries cowardly and crooked, Lieber very nearly starved to death before he could get back to Italy, where he appealed for help to the Prussian consulate.

Fortunately, the diplomat there was kindly. Lieber made a lasting friend in him, Niebuhr, the historian. Still, despite his powerful aid, Lieber upon his return was shadowed by the Prussian police. At last life in Germany became too difficult. He fled to England and then to the United States.

After a long period in academic life, he aided the government during the Civil War by writing *Guerilla Parties Considered with Reference to the Laws and Usages of War* (1862), and *A Code for the Government of Armies*, issued by the War Department as *General Orders No. 100. 100* (1863), which became the basis for the Hague Conventions of 1899 and 1907.

He died October 2, 1872, while listening to his wife read.

A brilliant biography has been written by Frank Freidel: *Frances Lieber, Nineteenth-Century Liberal* (Baton Rouge: Louisiana State University Press, 1947).

The most important manuscript collections are in the Huntington Library at San Marino, California, and at the Johns Hopkins University.

•   •   •

LINCOLN, ABRAHAM (1809-1865): Eric Hoffer maintains that the American masses are the most skilled and competent population the world has ever known. The life of Abraham Lincoln seems designed to prove the truth of this statement. Lincoln came from the ranks of the common man.

The son of an illiterate father, a drifter, Abraham began life with no advantages whatever. His mother died while he was still a young boy. His total attendance at school did not exceed one year. Abraham was an easy-going backwoods youth. He worked hard on the farm and used his leisure time to read: the Bible, *Robinson Crusoe, Pilgrim's Progress, Aesop's Fables,* a *History of the United States,* Parson Weems' *Life of Washington,* and the *Kentucky Preceptor.*

When on his own, rather than becoming a "river man," as he had planned, he read law. He then practiced as a country lawyer, working diligently, until he progressed to arguing more complicated cases before the higher courts.

His political party (Whig) disintegrated at an opportune moment, for him, wiping out his past history of failure at politics. Lincoln's skill as a speaker (the Lincoln-Douglas debates) and his good-tempered moderation brought him to the attention of the new Republican Party. After the front-runners deadlocked, he received the presidential nomination. The campaign strategy was to stay out of the way while the Democratic factions wrecked each other. It worked, and Lincoln was elected.

When Lincoln assumed the Presidency he was almost totally without practical administrative experience. The qualities which saw him through were his political acumen and his steadfast good will. Moderate during a time of extremes and conciliatory even in the midst of a violent war, he was a magnanimous leader who refused to allow personal feelings to interfere with the goal, preserving the Union.

His message to Congress on the 4th of July, 1861, declared:

this issue embraces more than the fate of these United States. It presents to the whole family of man the question whether a constitutional republic or democracy — a government of the people by the same people— — can or cannot maintain its territorial integrity against its own domestic foes. ... It forces us to ask: "Is there, in all republics, this inherent and fatal weakness?" "Must a government, of necessity, be too strong for the liberties of its own people, or too weak to maintain its own existence?"

Lincoln saw the struggle to prevent disunion as:

essentially a people's contest. On the side of the Union it is a struggle for maintaining in the world that form and substance of government whose leading object is to elevate the condition of men — to lift artificial weights from all shoulders; to clear the paths of laudable pursuit for all; to afford all an unfettered start, and a fair chance in the race of life.

This, Lincoln believed, was true government, government strong enough to defend itself against dissolution. Weak government encouraged the opposite of democracy, that is, "this mobocratic spirit which all must admit is now abroad in the land" (spoken in 1837).

In his first public speech (1832) Lincoln had appealed to the intelligence and good judgment of the people, as he continued to do:

My case is thrown exclusively upon the independent voters of the country; and, if elected, they will have conferred a favor upon me for which I shall be unremitting in my labors to compensate. But, if the good people in their wisdom shall see fit to keep me in the background, I have been too familiar with disappointments to be very much chagrined.

• • •

LONERGAN, BERNARD (1904-   ): An influential Roman Catholic philosopher, Bernard Joseph Francis Lonergan is the leading exponent of Transcendental Thomism, the attempt to interpret St. Thomas in the light of modern philosophical developments. *Insight; A Study of Human Understanding* (1957) is his epistemological masterpiece. The starting-point, he maintains, must be the psychological process which precedes and transcends the formulation of concepts in words.

Born in Buckingham, Quebec, Canada, he was educated at Loyola in Montreal and the University of London. He received his doctorate from the Gregorian University in Rome.

He has taught at various Jesuit seminaries in Montreal and Toronto. In 1953 he taught at the Gregorian University in Rome. One of his early students was Michael Novak, the prominent American Catholic lay theologian.

In 1965, Lonergan had to have one lung removed because of lung cancer. Since then he has been assigned to light duties at Regis College, Willowdale, Ontario, Canada. *Collection* was published in 1967, and *The Subject* in 1968.

Novak, while appreciating his philosophical contributions, criticizes him for a lack of "an adequate political consciousness" and "adequate theoretical understanding of action and experience."

•   •   •

LOVEJOY, ARTHUR ONCKEN (1873-1962): One of the Critical Realists, Arthur O. Lovejoy was born in Berlin, educated in California, Harvard, and Paris. He taught at Johns Hopkins and wrote *The Revolt Against Dualism, The Great Chain of Being* (1936), and *Essays in the History of Ideas*. He notes that the most indubitable fact of experience is that experience itself is limited by time.

M

MALCOLM, NORMAN (1911-   ): Norman Adrian Malcolm is the author of three influential books: *Ludwig Wittgenstein: A Memoir* (1958), *Dreaming* (1959), and *Knowledge and Certainty* (1963). Born in Selden, Kansas, he was educated at the University of Nebraska, Harvard (Ph.D. 1940), and Cambridge, England (1938-40). He has taught at Princeton and, since 1947, at Cornell.

•   •   •

MANDELBAUM, MAURICE H. (1908-   ): Author of *The Phenomenology of Moral Experience* (1955) and co-editor of *Phenomenology and Existentialism* (1967), Maurice Mandelbaum is a native of Chicago and a graduate of Dartmouth and Yale. He has taught at Dartmouth, Swarthmore, and Johns Hopkins.

•   •   •

MARCUSE, HERBERT (1898-   ): Asked his opinion of Herbert Marcuse, Sidney Hook (*q.v.*) replied, "Marcuse is a jackass! Aside from being a poor philosopher." Quine (*q.v.*) was slightly more charitable in his condemnation, saying: "I'm against him! Aren't you?"

The man who inspires these sentiments across the continent is currently the ideological leader of the new left. His doctrine that every political and social system, regardless of its type, needs to be overthrown, is more radical than orthodox communism, which teaches, after all, that once it is reached there is no more need for revolt.

He is also famous for his most widely-known student, Angela Davis.

Born in Berlin on the 19th of July, 1898, Herbert Marcuse was the privileged son of an upper-class Jewish family. He attended the Universities of Berlin and Freiburg.

Serving in the Army during the First World War, he was stationed in Berlin when the German Revolution broke out. He became a member of a Soldiers' Council, his first revolutionary experience. The revolution was quickly betrayed and he was disillusioned with orthodox left-wing politics.

In Freiburg he received his Ph.D. in 1922. Like Sartre, he became one of the assistants to Martin Heidegger. He spent the next ten years doing post-graduate research in philosophy at the university.

With Theodor Adorno and Max Horkheimer he founded the Frankfurt Institute of Social Research. However, in 1933, Hitler came to power, and the democratic government failed. The Nazis swiftly reorganized education, centralizing control of faculty and requiring loyalty oaths and racial tests. The Frankfurt School of Social Research was a special target of Nazi threats and denunciations.

In 1933, therefore, Marcuse fled Germany, in the same year as Einstein and Tillich. He went to Geneva, as a research fellow for one year.

In 1934, he came to the United States, where he became a lecturer at Columbia. He became a naturalized citizen in 1940. For a while he lived in Los Angeles with a group of liberal and radical German emigrés which included Brecht and Thomas Mann.

During the Second World War, he worked for the Office of Strategic Services and the State Department. After the war he became chief of the Office of Intelligence Research, where he prepared intelligence reports for such agencies as the C. I. A.

Having thus become an expert in the Russian language and Soviet affairs, Marcuse lectured at Columbia in 1951, and was loosely connected with the Russian Institute. In 1952 he did the same for Harvard.

In 1953 he received his first formal university appointment from President Abram Sachar of Brandeis. He taught politics and philosophy. Twelve years later, after a series of disputes with Sachar, he left.

In 1965 he moved to the University of California at San Diego, where he still lives. In 1969 political pressures, led by the local newspaper, forced his retirement from academic life. He has received serious death threats.

"If somebody really believes that my opinions can seriously endanger society," he has remarked, "then he and society must be very badly off indeed."

His first wife, Sophie, died in 1951, and he married Inge Werner in 1955, the widow of his friend, Franz Neumann. He has a grown son, Peter, by his first marriage and two stepsons by the second.

His books include *Reason and Revolution* (1941), a review of Hegel's thought on the subject, *Eros and Civilization, a Philosophical Inquiry into Freud* (1955), a presentation of the erotic aspect of all social and political repression, arguing that there is no real distinction between psychology and social and political philosophy.

One-Dimensional Man: Studies in the Ideology of Advanced Industrial Society followed (1964). This is his most popular book. Domination, he declares, appears in its most advanced form not as any of the traditional political forms, but rather as administration. The managers are the priests of repression.

The "sewer system" of television and mass media systematically "moronizes" individuals and lulls them into accepting social controls that are no longer necessary for the preservation of society or the well-being of man. There is no real reason, according to Marcuse, for continuing to accept monogamous marriage or public control over exclusively private affairs between individuals.

Workers will not, as in communist theory, change things, says Marcuse. They are too caught up in the status quo. Students and minority groups will be the only ones to effectively challenge the established social order.

A Critique of Pure Tolerance appeared in 1965. He contributed one essay to this book, "Repressive Tolerance," maintaining that some social evils can only be overcome by the abandonment of democratic processes.

Negations (1968) is a collection of essays from Marcuse's days in Germany in the early 30's.

An Essay on Liberation (1969) was written in celebration of the student insurrection in France in June of 1968. Marcuse especially applauded their motto of permanent challenge to the social order:

> The young militants know or sense that what is at stake is simply their life, the life of human beings which has become a plaything in the hands of generals, politicians, and managers.

Counterrevolution and Revolt (1972) is his proposal that a new cultural sensibility can become the connecting tissue between politics aimed at changing the world and the drive for personal liberation.

•　　•　　•

MARSH, JAMES (1794-1842): Born in Vermont, James Marsh was destined for life on the farm. Instead he became president of the University of Vermont. There he liberalized the entrance requirements, allowed the students more freedom, and based discipline not on obedience to rules, but on personal influence.

In 1829 he edited Coleridge's *Aids to Reflection*, looking for a modification of Calvinism which would "satisfy the heart as well as the head." He distinguished between the reason and the understanding, commending "a philosophy that is religious, and a religion that is philosophical." The understanding is discursive or demonstrative, appropriate to science. The reason is meditation for inspiration, insight, or wisdom. This use of reason was called "spiritual."

"Experimental religion," he wrote, "is not, therefore, so properly a species of knowledge, as a form of being."

This edition created a ferment among young intellectuals. Among them was Emerson (q.v.), who was deeply impressed by these ideas.

• • •

MARVIN, WALTER T. (1872-1944): One of the New Realists (along with R. B. Perry, Edwin B. Holt, W. P. Montague, Walter B. Pitkin, and E. G. Spaulding), Walter T. Marvin was born in New York and educated at Columbia (1893) and Bonn (1898). The six realists provided a refutation of idealism, and insisted that things are not significantly changed by our knowing them. Co-author of *The New Realism* (1912), the group provided a sort of bridge to critical realism, practiced by such thinkers as Lovejoy and Santayana. Walter T. Marvin taught for years at Rutgers.

• • •

MAYHEW, JONATHAN (1720-1766): "The opening gun of the revolution," according to John Adams, was the sermon by Jonathan Mayhew entitled *A Discourse Concerning Unlimited Submission and Non-Resistance to the Higher Powers; with some reflections on the resistance made to King Charles I... in which the mysterious doctrine of that Prince's saintship and martyrdom is unriddled* (1750).

West Church in Boston was the pulpit from which Mayhew shocked the city by frankly discussing political issues. He applauded the execution of King Charles I of

England during the English civil war. He refuted the doctrines of the divine right of kings and political absolutism. He argued for the right to revolution, and based his argument on natural religion.

Mayhew combined Locke and Milton on social theory, and Cudworth, Clarke and Hutcheson on ethical theory. *Seven Sermons upon the Following Subjects: viz., The Difference between Truth and Falsehood, Right and Wrong; The Natural Ability of Man for Discerning These Differences; The Right and Duty of Private Judgment; The Love of God; The Love of Our Neighbor, etc.* was published in Boston in 1749. Those were the days of long titles.

Mayhew was inclined toward Deism and Arianism. He argued that salvation was the result, not of free grace, but of successful moral struggle. The radical character of such an argument is scarcely appreciable now, but seemed quite subversive in that day.

True religion must include the love of liberty and the hatred of all tyranny and oppression, he held. Thus, if a government fails to govern justly, it should be overthrown by the people.

● ● ●

McCOSH, JAMES (1811-1894): Born by the River Doon, near the Bay of Ayr, James McCosh became a famous Scottish realist and was rewarded for his diligence by being allowed to die in Princeton.

Invited in 1868 to became president of the College of New Jersey (Princeton) on the basis of his international reputation as a scholar, McCosh discovered the school in critical financial condition and with few students. The South had formerly been its chief recruiting ground, a state of affairs which had been shattered by the war. McCosh proved to be a tremendously effective administrator, improving the college in every way.

His most important books are the *Examination of Mr. J. S. Mill's Philosophy; Being a Defence of Fundamental Truth* (1866), stating the principles of Intuitional philosophy as opposed to pure Empiricism, *The Scottish Philosophy, Biographical, Expository, Critical, from Hutcheson to Hamilton* (1875), *Realistic Philosophy Defended in a Philosophic Series* (1887), and *Psychology* (1886, 1887).

When he came to America, McCosh changed his emphasis from common sense to realism, from "intuitions of the mind" to "first and fundamental truths."

American philosophy, he wrote, should be based on practical observation and invention, opposed to either idealism or agnosticism.

• • •

McDOUGALL, WILLIAM (1871-1938): A magnificently arrogant psychologist, William McDougall was born and educated in England. He studied the wild headhunters of Borneo and got married. He spent his honeymoon in Göttingen studying experimental psychology.

Influenced by William James, McDougall described human action in terms of basic instincts which were inherited. A primary emotion was attached to each instinct: for example, disgust to repulsion and fear to flight. *Psychology, the Study of Behavior* (1912) conceived of behavior as voluntaristic, quite opposed to the deterministic behaviorism of J. B. Watson which was becoming popular in America.

The Group Mind appeared in 1920, the same year he was called to teach at Harvard. He published *Is America Safe for Democracy?* in 1921, arguing the superiority of the Nordic race on the basis of hereditary differences in mental capacity. Hostility to McDougall assumed monumental proportions.

In 1927 he accepted a post at Duke University, actively supporting J. B. Rhine's work on ESP.

His last books were *Modern Materialism and Emergent Evolution* (1929) *and The Energies of Men* (1932).

He died of cancer at Durham, North Carolina, a sad and disappointed man.

• • •

McGILL, V. J. (1897-   ): Modern American materialist, V. J. McGill studied at Harvard (Ph.D. 1925), Cambridge, and Freiburg. He taught at Hunter College and has been associated with the Institute for Philosophical Research. Former editor of *Science and Society,* he has interests in Marxism and psychology, and was co-editor of *Philosophy for the Future* (1949).

• • •

MEAD, GEORGE HERBERT (1863-1931): In the Pragmatist school, George Herbert Mead contributed to the development of "The Chicago School," enthusiastically embracing John Dewey's philosophical formulations. Mead was born in South Hadley, Massachusetts, and was educated at Oberlin (where his father was a teacher) and Harvard. He went on to Berlin, where he married a Castle from Hawaii, Helen Castle, a student whom he had met at Oberlin. Back in the United States, he taught at The University of Michigan and at The University of Chicago. He would have liked to have gone to Columbia, as did Dewey, but he died too soon.

All his books are posthumous: *The Philosophy of the Present* (1932), *Mind, Self & Society from the Standpoint of a Social Behaviorist* (1934), *Movements of Thought in the Nineteenth Century* (1936), and *the Philosophy of the Act* (1938).

His article, "The Philosophies of Royce, James, and Dewey in Their American Setting," in the *International*

Journal of Ethics is an excellent statement of the thought and relationship of these thinkers.

Mead rejected the idea of isolated, atomic individuals. The important consideration, he wrote, was the social nature of the self. All thought and all characteristically human forms of social activity are aspects of the same fundamental process, the development of communication. Thinking and knowing are actions of the organism living in an environment. The organism regulates its relations to the objective conditions of life by means of the nervous system, of which the brain is a part.

His influence during his lifetime, aside from the many conversations he had with John Dewey, came chiefly from the course on Social Psychology which he taught at Chicago.

•   •   •

MONTAGUE, WILLIAM PEPPERELL (1873-1953): Brought up in one of Norman Rockwell's small New England towns, William Pepperell Montague found it ugly. Impressed by religion, he was repelled by its practice.

He went to Harvard and was strongly influenced by Royce. Later he taught at Columbia. One of the American Neo-Realists, he wrote:

That the world is a spirit, and that we are; and that perhaps we share even the immortality of a life that contains and sustains us, is a creed almost too happy and too good to be true. And yet I do believe that if not true it is something very like the truth.

•   •   •

MULFORD, ELISHA (1833-1885): The famous Bluntschli, Stahl and Trendelenburg scholar, Elisha Mulford was even better known as the man who gave fresh impetus to Hegelian

193

idealism through his religious expression of the ideals of democracy. He wrote *The Nation* (1870), reviewing the theories of the state from Plato to Rousseau, maintaining that the nation was an organism, a personality which responded with its total life to ethical ideals. The state was not an economic society, or a legal entity, or a historical accident.

In 1880 he published *The Republic of God,* contrasting the kingdom of God with the republic of God, fusing religious language and emotion with democratic nationalism. Religious incentive was given to secular reform. This version of Hegelian philosophy became a passionate faith for many academic idealists.

• • •

MÜNSTERBERG, HUGO (1863-1916): A psychologist, like Karl Jaspers and William James, Hugo Münsterberg was born in Danzig, Germany and persuaded by President Eliot to teach at Harvard beginning in 1897. A leader in the field or applied psychology, his interests gradually widened until he developed a philosophy similar to Fichtean idealism. He believed in freedom when considering mental phenomena from the viewpoint of values, but was a strict determinist when considering mental behavior as correlated with physiological processes. He was thus a forerunner of modern behaviorism.

His books include *The Eternal Values* (1909), *Psychology and Social Sanity* (1914), and *Psychology, General and Applied* (1914).

Violently criticized for daring to support the cause of Germany during the First World War, he died on the lecture platform at Radcliffe before he had completed the opening sentence of his talk.

N

NAGEL, ERNEST (1901-   ): Ernest Nagel is a logician and philosopher of science who has been strongly influenced by pragmatism, naturalism, logical positivism, and analysis. Born in Czechoslovakia, he was brought to the United States in 1911. Educated at CCNY (under Morris Cohen) and Columbia (under Dewey), Nagel taught at CCNY and Columbia. His books include *Logic Without Metaphysics* (1957), *Gödel's Proof* (1958), and *The Structure of Science* (1960).

•   •   •

PAINE, THOMAS (1737-1809): A talented, tormented man, Tom Paine the Englishman reached his height pamphleteering for the American Revolution and his depth working for the French Revolution. In the end he lost most of his American friends by writing a letter critical of George Washington.

Perpetually restless, he could not find rest even in death. Buried first in New Rochelle, his bones were dug up by a man who intended to re-inter them in England under a suitable monument. Instead they were bought, along with the coffin, by a furniture dealer, and lost forever.

Tom Paine was born in Thetford, Norfolk, England, on the 29th of January, 1737. His father was a poor Quaker corset maker who was unhappily married. His mother, Frances, was the Anglican daughter of an attorney. He attended school until he was thirteen, when, because of the family's poverty, he was forced to become an apprentice corset maker. He had no further formal education. His enemies would later delight by pointing out cases of bad grammar in his writings.

He left home at nineteen. He signed on as a privateer on the ship *King of Prussia*. For the next twenty years he drifted from one job to another: corset maker, school teacher, grocer, tobacco merchant, excise tax collector. He failed to make good at any of them. He married, but his wife, Mary, died within a year. After eleven years he married again, but within three years separated from his wife, Elizabeth.

When the excisemen agitated for more pay, Paine was one of the most active. He wrote *The Case of the Officers of the Excise* (1772). The chief result of this activity was that he was fired.

Out of a job in London, Paine had the great good fortune to meet Benjamin Franklin, who was having troubles of his own. Franklin was very impressed, and provided letters of introduction for this "ingenious, worthy young man." So equipped, Paine sailed for America. The year was 1774.

Seldom has the right man arrived at a more crucial time. Paine's personal frustrations matched exactly the frustrations of the Americans. Bitter against the British government for his own failures, Paine saw that the same British government was hindering the free development of America.

The pen was his voice. He talked himself into a job as editor of *The Pennsylvania Magazine* after arriving in Philadelphia on November 30.

A year later he left to write fiery appeals for revolution. His old boss, Robert Aitken, refused to print such radical pieces. Benjamin Rush (*q.v.*), however, arranged for the first printing of the now famous *Common Sense written by an Englishman* (1776):

Some writers have so confounded society with government, as to leave little or no distinction between them; whereas they are not only different, but have different origins. Society is produced by our wants, and government by our wickedness; the former promotes our happiness *positively* by uniting our affections, the latter *negatively* by restraining our vices.... Society in every state is a blessing, but Government, even in its best state, is but a necessary evil; in its worst state an intolerable one.

In a manner which recalls Plato's passage in the *Republic*, Paine gives an account of the natural origin of society. His analysis heats up when he comes to a critical analysis of all the troubles caused by the British government.

Three hundred thousand copies of *Common Sense* were sold! It was, proportionately, the most extraordinary best-seller in American history. Paine believed firmly in the common man. It was evident to all, he thought, that a continent could not belong to an island. That was only common sense.

"It was the cause of America that made me an author," he said in *The Crisis Papers*, the famous pamphlets which became crucial for morale during the course of the revolutionary war:

These are the times that try men's souls: The summer soldier and the sunshine patriot will, in this crisis, shrink from the service of his country; but he that stands it NOW, deserves the love and thanks of man and woman. Tyranny, like hell, is not easily conquered.

Once the American revolution had been won, Paine turned his attention to his homeland, agitating for an English revolution in the *Rights of Man* (1791; Part II in 1792). The natural rights of man, he maintained, are (1) liberty, (2) property, (3) security, and (4) resistance to oppression. He detailed the kind of government — or rather restraint of government — which would guarantee these rights.

Paine poured out all his desires for revenge against the system which had denied him growth, education, and security. In part II of the *Rights of Man,* he recommended social and economic legislation on behalf of the poor — welfare and full employment:

> Hunger is not among the postponeable wants, and a day, even a few hours, in such a condition is often the crisis of a life of ruin.

Public housing, state-supported work, meals and lodging on a temporary basis when necessary, aid to dependent children, free public education, medical help and pensions for the elderly, donations to parents and newly-weds, death benefits for working men, jobs for the poor in the cities of London and Westminster — these were among Paine's specific legislative proposals. These laws should replace "the poor laws, those instruments of civil torture." He proposed that the money for such measures come from the salary currently paid to support the Duke of Richmond.

Accused of treason, Paine fled England for France. There he enjoyed himself and, along with Washington, Hamilton, Madison and others, was made a French citizen. Unlike the others Paine made the mistake of taking this honor seriously. He was elected to the Assembly in 1792. The Assembly was one of the most dangerous places to be in France at the time, due to its rapidly changing character. This month's radicals were next month's reactionaries. When the Terror came, Paine was caught in the net.

From prison, in danger of death, he blamed first the American ambassador, Morris, and at last General Washington for not trying to secure his release.

During those confused and unhappy days Paine wrote his great work, *The Age of Reason* (1794; Part II, 1796). He was accused of atheism for it, a false charge. The book advocated deism. He wrote:

> I believe in one God, and no more; and I hope for happiness beyond this life.... My own mind is my own church.

In a manner similar to Hume's, some forty years earlier, Paine argued against the testimony of miracles:

It appears that Thomas did not believe the resurrection; and, as they say, would not believe without having occular and manual demonstration himself. *So neither will I,* and the reason is equally as good for me, and for every other person, as for Thomas.

The basic argument of the book proceeded from a definition of knowledge: knowledge is clear, distinct, mathematical and scientific. He then demonstrated that man's knowledge of the God of the Christian tradition was not this sort of knowledge.

Of the Bible he said:

Whenever we read the obscene stories, the voluptuous debaucheries, the cruel and torturous executions, the unrelenting vindictiveness. with which more than half the Bible is filled, it would be more consistent that we called it the word of a demon, than the word of God. It is a history of wickedness, that has served to corrupt and brutalize mankind; and, for my own part, I sincerely detest it, as I detest every thing that is cruel.

At last Paine was released, and in October, 1802, he returned to America. The last few years of his life were marked by poverty, poor health, and social ostracism. His health had been hurt by his French imprisonment. He took to drinking. Several strokes paralyzed him by degrees.

Madame de Bonneville, the wife of a friend, and her three children were sent to Paine by her husband to escape the dangers of Napoleon. Paine was supposed to be well off. Selfish and overbearing, she constantly complained and bullied the old man. At length, she moved to New York City, to live at his expense.

The people of New Rochelle, where his land was, had been Tory sympathizers during the war. They did not treat the old revolutionary kindly. Children taunted him, encouraged by their parents, justifying their cruelty by his "atheism."

Afraid to be alone in his illness, Paine employed a man named Derrick. Devoutly religious, he expressed his faith by stealing and burning his employer's manuscripts. When he was finally fired, he returned with a large-bore buckshot-loaded musket which he fired through the window. He missed Paine.

After he moved to New York, Paine's health worsened. The site of his deathbed became the focus for a kind of pilgrimage. Every sort of religious person came, hoping to hear Paine denounce *The Age of Reason* on his deathbed. They were disappointed.

He died June 8, 1809. Seven people attended his funeral: Madame de Bonneville, her three children, two blacks, and a Quaker preacher. He was buried — at first — on a corner of his own farm in New Rochelle. Ten years later his bones were dug up and sent to England, part of a scheme to exhibit them in various cities. As mentioned earlier, his last remains simply disappeared.

Thus lived and died Tom Paine. Though he was denied an epitaph, we might choose two from his writings: "The ragged relic and the antiquated precedent, the monk and the monarch, will molder together." Or, with Jefferson; "government is for the living, and not for the dead."

P

PALMER, ELIHU (1764-1806): A leader in the organization of deistical societies, Palmer was born in Canterbury,
Connecticut. Educated at Dartmouth College, he graduated
in 1787. An outspoken free-thinker, he was driven out of
several churches and towns during the next four years.

The principles he advocated, considered so dangerous as
to compel him to flee to escape violence, were the following:

1. That the universe proclaims the existence of one
supreme Deity, worthy of the adoration of intelligent
beings.
2. That man is possessed of moral and intellectual faculties sufficient for the improvement of his nature, and the
acquisition of happiness.
3. That the religion of nature is the only universal
religion; that it grows out of the moral relations of
intelligent beings, and that it stands connected with
the progressive improvement and common welfare of
the human race.
4. That it is essential to the true interest of man, that
he love truth and practise virtue. — (from the *Principles of the Deistical Society of the State of New York*).

It can readily be recognized that such ideas were certainly
subversive and ought to be suppressed at all costs.

Palmer then turned to the practice of law to support himself. Shortly afterwards, in a plague of yellow fever, he lost
his wife and became blind.

Finally he went to New York where he worked organizing
societies of deists, believing the American Revolution to
have been the beginning of a new era for man.

• • •

PARKER, THEODORE (1810-1860): Theodore Parker's grandfather had been the captain of the minute-men at Lexington. His father occupied himself with other things, producing Theodore as the youngest of eleven children. Something of a child prodigy, he discovered at the age of four the voice of conscience, which clearly and loudly said to him: "It is wrong."

Learning to speak for himself, he mastered twenty languages. Despite the obstacle of poverty, he obtained a good education and became a Unitarian clergyman.

Continuing to think even while in church, he was invited by his fellow ministers to resign. His antislavery lectures made him the second most hated man in New England, trailing only Garrison (who held the top spot) by a few percentage points. His biographers blame him for not being more cheerful, suggesting that this lack may have been made up if only he had played more ball games as a youth.

In one of his lectures, he defined Transcendentalism in these terms:

> The problem of transcendental philosophy is no less than this, to revise the experience of mankind and try its teaching by the nature of mankind); to test ethics by conscience, science by reason; to try the creeds of the churches, the constitutions of the states by the constitution of the universe; to reverse what is wrong, supply what is wanting, and command the just.

He explicitly rejects empiricism ("the sensational school"). in favor of rationalism ("the transcendental school"). The importance of his enterprise, he explains, is based on the consideration that "a school in metaphysics soon becomes a school in physics, in politics, ethics, religion."

This is the philosophy of sensationalism; such its

doctrine in physics, politics, ethics, religion. It leads to boundless uncertainty. Berkeley resolves the universe into subjective ideas; no sensationalist knows a law in physics to be universal. Hobbes and Bentham and Condillac in politics know of no right but might; Priestly denies the spirituality of man, Collins and Edwards his liberty; Dodwell affirms the materiality of the soul, and the mortality of all men not baptized; Mandeville directly, and others indirectly, deny all natural distinction between virtue and vice; Archdeacon Paley knows no motive but expediency.

Parker then summarizes the views of Transcendentalism:

I. In physics it starts with the maxim that the senses acquaint us actually with body, and therefrom the mind gives us the idea of substance, answering to an objective reality. Thus is the certainty of the material world made sure of....

II. In politics, transcendentalism starts not from experience alone, but from consciousness; not merely from human history, but also from human nature.... The ideal justice of conscience is juster than the empirical and contingent justice actually exercised at Washington or at Athens, as the ideal circle is rounder than one the stone-cutter scratches on his rough seal....

III. In ethics. Transcendentalism affirms that man has moral faculties which lead him to justice and right, and by his own nature can find out what is right and just, and can know it and be certain of it....

IV. In religion. Transcendentalism admits a religious faculty, element, or nature in man, as it admits a moral, intellectual and sensational faculty — that man by nature is a religious being as well as moral, intellectual, sensational.

Parker died in Florence on May 10, 1860, and was buried in the Protestant cemetery outside the Pinto Gate.

• • •

PEIRCE, CHARLES SANDERS ("SANTIAGO"): (1839-1914): The most original and versatile of American philosophers, Charles Sanders Peirce can be judged by his contributions to Pragmatism, which he founded, logic, and the philosophy of science.

Pragmatism (*q.v.*) can be defined as the doctrine that truth is to be found by considering the practical consequences of a proposition. That is, the meaning of a statement is held to be wholly in its practical application. In Peirce's own words:

> Consider what effects, that might conceivably have practical bearings, we conceive the object of our conception to have. Then, our conception of these effects is the whole of our conception of the object.

Peirce was born in Cambridge, Massachusetts. His father was a mathematician at Harvard, an inspiring and unconventional teacher. He taught his son concentration by playing card games with him lasting all night, severely criticizing every mistake. In later years, Peirce had learned this art of concentration so well that he could write far into the night despite illness and pain.

His father never told his son the result or solution of a problem. Instead, he showed him puzzles, card tricks, chess problems and code languages, encouraging him to work out the solutions himself.

Graduating from Harvard in 1859, the one thing his father had not taught him, he later observed, was moral self-control, and, he continued, he would suffer "unspeakably" for this lack.

He worked for the U. S. Coast Survey for thirty years (1861-91), illustrating the high regard our country holds for philosophers. He did do some lecturing on logic and the philosophy of science at Harvard, 1864-5 and 1869-71.

From 1879-84 he taught logic at Johns Hopkins, the nation's first graduate school. There he was overshadowed by such immortal intellectual giants as G. Stanley Hall, lecturing on the "new psychology," and George S. Morris, on the consolations of Hegelian idealism. The high point in Peirce's teaching career came when a dozen students thronged into his class on logic. Usually he lectured to a class of four.

During these years Peirce had the bad judgment to divorce Harriet, a good New England girl, grand-daughter of a Bishop, and marry a French girl, Juliette Froissy. Friends and relatives were partly estranged by this action, and his academic standing was adversely affected.

Having the persistence of a wasp in a bottle, as he said of himself, he continued his philosophic research, retiring to a remote place, Milford, Pennsylvania. There he wrote industriously, two thousand words a day, and fell more deeply into debt. By 1907 he was practically penniless. He built an attic study himself, designed so that he could pull up the ladder and escape the annoyances of his creditors.

He had applied to Harvard for a teaching post, but had been refused. He had been involved in the controversy between Josiah Royce and F. E. Abbot, demanding that Royce be made to apologize for his intemperate attack upon Abbot. Despite the strong support of William James, President Eliot would not hear of it.

The last five years of his life were occupied with a losing fight with cancer. He had to take a grain of morphine daily to ward off the pain. Still he kept writing, without a publisher or disciple, unknown to the public. When he died April 19, 1914, his wife did not have enough money to bury him. She sold all his unpublished papers to Harvard for $500. They have proven to be a fruitful source for publication ever since.

In his famed article, "How to Make Our Ideas clear," published in the *Popular Science Monthly* (1878), Peirce has a lucid statement of his motivation in clarifying concepts:

> It is terrible to see how a single unclear idea, a single formula without meaning, lurking in a young man's head, will sometimes act like an obstruction of inert matter in an artery hindering the nutrition of the brain, and condemning its victim to pine away in the fullness of his intellectual vigor and in the midst of intellectual plenty.

• • •

PENN, WILLIAM (1644-1718): Included among American philosophers because of his extensive pamphleteering activities for liberty, Penn was granted the opportunity to found a commonwealth of his own because of his father's services for the Crown. Penn authored more than one hundred different works.

Born on the 14th of October, 1644, in England, Penn was educated in the classics at Chigwell School, and entered Oxford in 1660. There he was "sent down" as a sophomore for his nonconformity. He traveled the continent, studying for two years in France, at the University of Saumus. When he returned to England he studied law at Lincoln's Inn.

His father, Admiral Sir William Penn, sent him to Ireland to manage the family estates. In Ireland, he became a Quaker. He was jailed the following year, caught in a raid on the Quaker meeting at Cork. His father was shocked, threatened to disinherit him, but in the end was reconciled to his son's radical ways.

For the next few years he wrote extensively: *Truth Exalted* (1668), *The Sandy Foundation Shaken* (1668), *Innocency With Her Open Face* (1669).

When sentenced to the Tower of London, he used it as an opportunity to write *No Cross, No Crown* (1669), a work highly praised: "True Godliness don't (sic) turn Men out of the World, but enables them to live better in it, and excites their Endeavours to mend it."

Another of his works, *The Great Case of Liberty of Conscience* (1670), is the best argument for tolerance to appear in Restoration England.

A dramatic incident in Penn's own life followed. The authorities had padloked the meetinghouse on Gracechurch Street in London. Penn and his friend, William Mead, spoke on the street to the assembled crowd. They were both arrested and brought to trial at Old Bailey. The procedure in the case is recorded by Penn in *The Peoples Antient and Just Liberties Asserted in the Tryal of William Penn* (1670).

The trial began ominously. As the two prisoners were brought in with their hats off, the judge demanded to know which guard had removed the prisoner's hats.

"No one, sir," replied the guards.

"Then put their hats back on at once." It was done.

"Bring them forward to the bench."

The judge smiled wryly and continued: "You have your hats on. That is a sign of disrespect to the court. I fine you both for contempt of court."

As the trial progressed the judge interrupted to ask the defendant whether he had or had not been at the meeting. Penn forcefully reminded the judge of his legal right to avoid self-incrimination.

When the jury returned the verdict, they found Penn guilty and Mead not guilty. The judge was furious. He shouted at the jury that he would not allow such a verdict, that they had better bring in a verdict finding both guilty. Until they did, he declared, he would lock the jury up without food or tobacco.

This case, jailing the jury, became noted in English legal history as "Bushnell's case" (Bushnell was the foreman of the jury). When finally settled by a higher court, it established the independence of the jury. The ruling was that a judge may attempt to instruct the jury, but he "cannot lead it by the nose."

Penn wrote of those days that:

Liberty of Conscience is counted a Pretence for Rebellion; and Religious Assemblies, Routs and Riots; and the Defenders of both, are by them reputed Factious and Dis-affected.

Vigorously protesting the illegal proceedings and arbitrary arraignments, he said:

they "break open our Locks, rob our Houses, raze their Foundations, imprison our Persons, and finallly (sic) deny us Justice to our relief; as if they then acted most like Christian men, when they were most barbarous."

In 1670 Penn's father died. Young William had become a good friend of King Charles II, and of his brother, James. To settle the large debt owed by the Crown to Admiral Penn, the King granted all the land west of the Delaware River to William Penn. Later the King added the three "lower counties" (now Delaware).

William meant to conduct a "holy experiment" in his new lands. He granted complete toleration to every opinion or religion.

Arranging for the administration of his new commonwealth, Penn wrote an amending clause into the constitution, the first ever to appear in a written constitution.

In 1672 he married. They had eight children, of whom four survived infancy.

For the next decade he was active in English politics. Forty pamphlets were written during this period. In *A Just Rebuke to One and Twenty Learned and Reverend Divines (so called)*, he notes:

> The Cause of the God of Truth hath rarely wanted the Endeavours of men of greatest Power and Literature in almost every Age to slander it, nor the constant Adherers to it, Contumelious Treatment for their Integrity: No Virtue hath been so conspicuous, no Quality so Great, no Relation so Near, as to protect them from the Fury of blind Tradition and prejudic'd Education.

In 1682, finally, he sailed for his possessions in the New World. There, at Coaquannoc (Philadelphia), he became acquainted first-hand with the customs of the Leni-Lenape Indians.

That such anthropology was practiced during the early colonial period is worth remembering. Penn observed the customs of the tribes quite extensively:

> Justice they have is Pecuniary: In case of any Wrong or Evil Fact, be it Murther it self, they Attone by Feasts and Presents of their Wampon.... If Drunk, they forgite it, saying, It was the Drink, and not the Man, that abused them.

The next few years were to witness the reversal of Penn's fortunes. The Glorious Revolution in England overthrew the Catholic succession to the throne and established a Protestant one; Penn was viewed with suspicion, for he had been a friend of the Catholics.

Under William and Mary, his colony was taken away in 1693-4. He had to live in hiding to avoid arrest. During this time, he wrote more than otherwise possible.

An Essay Towards the Present and Future Peace of Europe (1693) proposes a united nations for Europe, to settle disputes between nations before they resort to warfare.

Some Fruits of Solitude (1693), published in 1807, contains his thoughts on many subjects of philosophic interest:

508. Words are for others, not for ourselves: nor for God. who hears not as bodies do, but as spirits should. — p. 95.
1. A right moralist is a great and good man; but, for that reason, he is rarely to be found. — p. 104.
69. Always remenber to bound thy thoughts to the present occasion. — p. 118.
1. It is admirable to consider how many millions of people come into and go out of the world, ignorant of themselves, and of the world they have lived in. — p. 1.

On the subject of Education:

4. We are in pain to make them scholars, but not men; to talk, rather than to know; which is true canting. — p. 2.
6. We press their memory too soon, and puzzle, strain, and load them with words and rules to know grammar and rhetorick, and a strange tongue or two, that it is ten to one may never be useful to them; leaving their natural genius to mechanical, and physical or natural knowledge uncultivated and neglected; which would be of exceeding use and pleasure to them through the whole course of their lives. — p. 3.

On the subject of Poverty:

287. God sends the poor to try us; as well as he tries them by being such: and he that refuses them a little, out of the great deal that God has given him, lays up poverty in store for his own posterity. — p. 158.

Around this time, possibly, the *Fruits of a Father's Love* was written, published with no date:

Truth, because it tells Man the Truth of his Condition, and redeems him from the Errors of his Ways; that as Darkness, Death, Sin, and Error are the same, so Light, Spirit, Grace and Truth are the same. – p. 7.

One interesting feature of Penn's writing is the fact that he, like many others in the colonial period, was quite well versed in the classics generally. Though his thought was cast in a theological mold, it can be easily translated into more general concepts. This is indicated by an interesting passage from the end of this last work:

"I have chosen to speak in the Language of the Scripture, which is that of the Holy Ghost, the Spirit of Truth and Wisdom.... (But it is also) Pythagoras's great Light and Salt of Ages; Anaxagoras's divine Mind; Socrates's good Spirit; Timaeus's unbegotten Principle, and Author of all Light; Hieron's God in Man; Plato's eternal, ineffable and perfect Principle of Truth; Zeno's Maker and Father of all; and Plotin's Root of the Soul...." – p. 77, 78.

The printer omits this from the Extract of 1831, notably altering the sense of the original.

During 1696, Penn wrote of a plan of union for all the American colonies. In the same year, his first wife having died, he married again. Seven children, of whom five survived infancy, were born of this marriage.

Finally political events returned to normal, and he received back his colony. However, things were going so poorly there that he had to go and take charge of matters himself. The citizens were not paying the rents due the proprietor. They were quarreling among themselves about the form of self-government. Therefore, in 1701 the single-chamber assembly was instituted as the legislative instrument of government. Within two years, matters were well in hand, and Penn could return to England. He never saw the American shore again.

Matters in England were even worse, if that were possible. Penn's steward, Philip Ford, had cheated him on such an enormous scale that Penn was forced to spend nine months in a debtor's prison.

By this time he was so depressed about the results of the "holy experiment" that he made plans to surrender his rights to Pennsylvania to the crown. Only a paralytic stroke prevented this.

Penn lingered on, helpless, until his death on July 30th, 1718. He was buried at Jordans, Buckinghamshire.

In a pamphlet printed in 1698, Penn had written:

Heaven is a Quiet Place; there are no Quarrels there, and Religion is a Holy and Peaceable Thing, and Excites to Piety and Charity, and not to Genealogies, Strife and Debates.

In this same work, *A Defence of a Paper, Entituled, Gospel-Truths, Against the Exceptions of the Bishop of Cork's Testimony*, the doctrine of the inner light was stated clearly:

The Bishop is still at a loss what to make of this Light, and what we should be at; for, says he, You will not allow it to be either the natural Rational Faculty, or common Innate Notions, or natural Conscience, or Conscience Illuminated, by the preaching of the Gospel, and the Operation of the Holy Ghost thereby. We say we would have it to be what the Scriptures say it to be, viz...
Every Mans Light; the Light of Every Mind and Understanding. — p. 48.

•   •   •

PERRY, RALPH BARTON (1876-1957): A Realist, Ralph Barton Perry develops a theory of value in which the ideal is a community of cooperative interests organized against cosmic neutrality. The basis of value is found in the organism's attraction to or repulsion from an object. Born in Vermont, Perry attended Princeton and Harvard. He taught at Williams, Smith, and Harvard.

Among his many books are *The Approach to Philosophy* (1905), *The New Realism* (1912), and *The Free Man and the Soldier* (1916). His most famous work is the monumental two-volume *Thought and Character of William James* (1935).

Perry wrote:

A value acquires existence when an interest is generated, regardless of any knowledge about it. A value will cease to exist when its own sustaining interest is destroyed or altered; but it does not cease to exist simply because it is cognitively excommunicated.

•   •   •

PITKIN, WALTER B. (1878-1935): A member of the Neo-Realist school, Pitkin of Columbia carried on an interesting debate with William James in the pages of the *Journal of Philosophy* (1907). He is also noted for *Life Begins at Forty*. He did not say when philosophy begins.

•   •   •

PORTER, NOAH (1811-1892): The most widely read philosopher of his time, Noah Porter wrote *The Human Intellect* (1868), a text-book on "mental philosophy" (psychology). This qualified him to become president of Yale, where he became a champion in opposing change. The ideal education, he believed, must be based on Greek and Latin, compulsory attendance, required courses rather than electives, and the de-emphasis of science. Schools of higher education ought to be "distinctively and earnestly Christian."

The high point in his life was reached when he was offered the position of minister to Great Britain by President Rutherford B. Hayes. The excitement proved too much, and he died a decade or two later.

The Elements of Intellectual Science (1871), an abridgement of his earlier textbook, and *The Elements of Moral Science* (1885) were two of his other books. He adhered to faculty psychology, but also seriously studied the British empiricists Mill and Spencer.

• • •

PRAGMATISM: [Gr. *Pragmatikos,* versed in affairs]: Ger. *pragmatisch, Pragmatismus;* Fr. *pragmatique, pragmatisme;* Ital. *prammatico, prammatismo.*

1. C. S. Peirce:

The opinion that metaphysics is to be largely cleared up by the application of the following maxim for attaining clearness of apprehension: 'Consider what effects, that might conceivably have practical bearings, we conceive the object of our conception to have. Then, our conception of these effects is the whole of our conception of the object.'

2. William James:

The doctrine that the whole 'meaning' of a conception expresses itself in practical consequences, consequences either in the shape of conduct to be recommended, or in that of experiences to be expected, if the conception be true; which consequences would be different if it were untrue, and must be different from the consequences by which the meaning of other conceptions is in turn expressed. If a second conception should not appear to have other consequences, then it must really be only the first conception under a different name. In methodology it is certain that to trace and compare their respective consequences is an admirable way of establishing the differing meanings of different conceptions.

3. John Dewey:

(1). I... affirm that the term "pragmatic" means only the rule of referring all thinking, all reflective considerations, to consequences for final meaning and test. — *Essays in Experimental Logic.*

(2). Pragmatism as attitude represents what Mr. Peirce has happily termed "the laboratory habit of mind" extended into every arena where inquiry may fruitfully be carried on. — *Ibid.*

4. Peirce (again):

This maxim was first proposed by C. S. Peirce in the *Popular Science Monthly* for January, 1878 (xii. 287); and he explained how it was to be applied to the doctrine of reality. The writer was led to the maxim by reflection upon Kant's *Critic of the Pure Reason.* Substantially the same way of dealing with ontology seems to have been practised by the Stoics. The writer subsequently saw that the principle might easily be misapplied, so as to sweep away the whole doctrine of incommensurables, and, in fact, the whole Weierstrassian way of regarding the calculus. In 1896 William James published his *Will to Believe,* and later his *Philos. Conceptions and Pract. Results,* which pushed this method to such extremes as must tend to give us pause. The doctrine appears to assume that the end of man is action — a stoical axiom which, to the present writer at the age of sixty, does not recommend itself so forcibly as it did at thirty. If it be admitted, on the contrary, that action wants an end, and that that end must be something of a general description, then the spirit of the maxim itself, which is that

215

we must look to the upshot of our concepts in order rightly to apprehend them, would direct us towards something different from practical facts, namely, to general ideas, as the true interpreters of our thought. Nevertheless, the maxim has approved itself to the writer, after many years of trial, as of great utility in leading to a relatively high grade of clearness of thought. He would venture to suggest that it should always be put into practice with conscientious thoroughness, but that, when that has been done, and not before, a still higher grade of clearness of thought can be attained by remembering that the only ultimate good which the practical facts to which it directs attention can subserve is to further the development of concrete reasonableness; so that the meaning of the concept does not lie in any individual reactions at all, but in the manner in which those reactions contribute to that development. Indeed, in the article of 1878, above referred to, the writer practised better than he preached; for he applied the stoical maxim most unstoically, in such a sense as to insist upon the reality of the objects of general ideas in their generality.

A widely current opinion during the last quarter of a century has been that reasonableness is not a good in itself, but only for the sake of something else. Whether it be so or not seems to be a synthetical question, not to be settled by an appeal to the principle of contradiction — as if a reason for reasonableness were absurd. Almost everybody will now agree that the ultimate good lies in the evolutionary process in some way. If so, it is not in individual reactions in their segregation, but in something general or continuous. Synechism is founded on the notion that the coalescence, the becoming continuous, the becoming governed by laws, the becoming instinct with general ideas, are but phases of one and the same process of the growth of reasonableness. This is first shown to be true with mathematical exactitude in the field of logic, and is thence inferred to hold good metaphysically. It is not opposed to pragmatism in the manner in which C. S. Peirce applied it, but includes that procedure as a step.

•   •   •

PRATT, JAMES BISSETT (1875-1944): One of the seven American Critical Realists (together with Durant Drake of Vassar, Arthur Lovejoy of Johns Hopkins, Arthur Rogers of Yale, Roy Wood Sellars of Michigan, Santayana, and C. A. Strong), James Bissett Pratt gave evidence of a highly original mind. Some of his articles are entitled, "Is Idealism Realism?" and "Truth and Its Verification." He also wrote *Why Religions Die.*

Born in Elmira, New York, he was educated at Williams, Harvard, Columbia, and Berlin. He taught at Williams and later was interested in Eastern religions, presumably applying the canons of his critical realism to Indian mysticism.

•   •   •

PRIESTLY, JOSEPH (1733-1804): Experimental chemist and ordained minister, Joseph Priestly fled England to escape religious and political persecution. In 1791 an angry mob attacked and burned his Birmingham house.

In chemistry Priestly is noted for isolating nine new "kinds of air," gasses: among them "de-phlogisticated air" (oxygen), "mephitic air" (carbon dioxide), "marine acid air" (hydrochloric acid), and "nitric air" (nitrous oxide). He discovered carbon monoxide after coming to America, which may be significant.

Interested in education, he proposed a radical new curriculum design which featured the teaching of modern history (as well as ancient) and practical instruction in the sciences. Priestly's ideas influenced Jefferson, who asked him for advice in setting up the new University of Virginia.

In theology he was the leading advocate of Unitarianism in the United States.

Capable of intense concentration, which accounted for his remarkable productivity in scientific investigation, he followed some of Franklin's advice, "early to bed and early to rise." This at least made him healthy and wise. Three hours daily were spent exercising or playing games, the rest were given over to reading and writing. Much of his writing was done in the evening "in the parlour before the fire," with his wife and children conversing around him. He could both talk and write at the same time without interrupting his train of thought.

I. Life

Born March 13, 1733, Joseph Priestly was the eldest son of Jonas, a dyer and dresser of woolen cloth, and Mary, a farmer's daughter. His education was most haphazard. He was first taught the Westminster Catechism, at seven. Then, after his mother died, his education was directed by his Calvinistic aunt. At twelve, he was sent to the local grammar school at Batley. His home up to then had been "Fieldhead," a wayside farm house six miles from Leeds, Yorkshire. At Batley he learned Latin, Greek, and Hebrew. Ill health caused him to miss three years of school. During this time he taught himself French, Italian, Dutch, Chaldee, Syriac, and Arabic. He also studied spiders, like Jonathan Edwards. He concentrated, however, not on how spiders fly, but on how long they could live in a sealed bottle.

When eighteen, he entered the academy at Daventry. This was a liberal and dissenting academy, and he studied there for three years.

At twenty-two, Priestly became a minister at Needham Market, Surrey. Three things interfered with his success: free thinking, stammering, and bachelorhood. He moved on to Nantwich, Cheshire, to a parish of "travelling Scotchmen," and supported himself by founding and running a private school.

He next became tutor at Warrington academy. He began to write, encouraged by cultivated and liberal friends: *The Rudiments of English Grammar* (1761). He married and had four children. Next he produced *An Essay on a Course of Liberal Education for Civil and Active Life* (1765) and *A Chart of Biography* (1765), works so impressive that he received the LL.D. from Edinburgh University.

In 1767, his wife's failing health and his own small salary made it necessary to "go home" to Leeds. He took charge of the Mill Hill congregation, and next published the *History and Present State of Electricity* (1767), *Essay on the First Principles of Government* (1768) and *The History and Present State of Discoveries Relating to Vision, Light and Colours* (1772).

In 1772, Priestly became the librarian for Lord Shelburne, a position he held for eight years. *Experiments and Observations on Different Kinds of Air*, three volumes, appeared 1774-77. Bitterly accused of atheism when the *Disquisition Relating to Matter and Spirit* was published in 1777, he maintained that man was not two substances, body and soul, but only one. He continued this concept in *A Free Discussion of the Doctrines of Materialism* (1778). Although the homogeneity of man is a doctrine found in church creeds and Scripture, that did not give pause to those looking for a new victim to persecute.

In 1780 he moved to Birmingham, as minister of the New Meeting. *An History of the Corruptions of Christianity* was published in 1782. Although this book did not win anything like the Nobel Prize, it did have the honor of being burned by the hangman of Dort, who was not able to secure a personal appearance by the author.

The first of the four volumes of *A General History of the Christian Church* was issued in 1790. Priestly was conspicuously sympathetic with the French Revolution. In its defense, he wrote the *Letters to the Right Honourable Edmund Burke* (1791).

By way of appreciation, a mob held a meeting at Priestly's house on Bastille Day, 1791, destroying his house, burning his books and personal effects. Priestly spent some time in seclusion, following this public recognition.

In 1792 he was made an honorary citizen of France and pastor of Hackney. Burke, however, thought he had not suffered enough for disagreeing with him, and Priestly's position became altogether insecure.

Therefore, in 1794, at the age of 61 (near Whitehead's age when he came to the United States), Priestly and his wife set sail for America. He received a tumultuous welcome. When he arrived he was called upon by the Governor of New York and the Bishop. He was welcomed by the Democrats, the Republican Natives of Great Britain and Ireland, and Tammany Hall.

When the welcomes were over, he realized that he had received no tangible offers. He moved on to Philadelphia, where he was again acclaimed. David Rittenhouse, among others, gave him a splendid testimonial. Philadelphia, however, proved too distracting for him. By July he decided to join his son at Northumberland, Pennsylvania. There he built a house and laboratory and spent the rest of his life.

He died on February 6, 1804. There was an eight-month-old baby in Boston, named Ralph Waldo Emerson.

II. Thought

Priestly represents an interesting combination of religious, philosophical, scientific and political interests. During the Renaissance, he would have been called a universal man. At it was, he was lucky to keep alive in the face of persistent opposition. A kind of democratic universal man, he forced a place for himself in the world of thought, a place not provided by birth or money. At the time, the church offered enough income to make a life of thought possible. Once, however, the church's doctrines were challenged as Priestly challenged them, someone was sure to make life insecure again.

For what they are worth — one commentator says he ought to have stayed with scientific production — his theological treatises were written in the United States: *Unitarianism Explained and Defended* (1796), *A Comparison of the Institutions of Moses with Those of the Hindoos and Other Ancient Nations* (1799), *Socrates and Jesus Compared* (1803), *Notes on All the Books of Scripture* (1803-4), *The Doctrines of Heathen Philosophy Compared with Those of Revelation* (1804), *A General View of the Arguments for the Unity of God; and against the Divinity and Pre-existence of Christ* (first issued in 1793, revised and re-issued 1812).

His last book (he was writing up to an hour before his death) was *The Doctrine of Phlogiston Established* (1803). Like ether, in the nineteenth century, phlogiston in the eighteenth was an important concept in scientific theory. It was the theory that when some substance burned, phlogiston was released. The function of air was to carry away phlogiston as it was liberated. There was some disagreement as to whether phlogiston was an immaterial principle or a physical substance (possessing, for example, the property of negative weight). An interesting parallel in the twentieth century is the discussion on the property of gravity, some suggesting that neutrinos might be the substance of gravity, neutrinos having no charge and no mass.

Q

QUINE, WILLARD VAN ORMAN (1908-   ): While sipping beer at the APA smoker in December of 1971, Willard Van Orman Quine said that the thing he most wanted to be remembered for was his combination of logic with science. Reminiscing about Carnap, he said he was a great thinker, although he disagreed with him on most major issues in recent years. What did he think of Tillich? "He liked paradoxes." Of Marcuse? "I'm against him! Aren't you?"

Born in Akron, Ohio, June 25, 1908, Quine was educated at Oberlin (1930) and Harvard (Ph.D. 1932). He has taught at Harvard from 1936 on, and lectured in Brazil, Oxford, and Tokyo. In 1956-7 he was a member of the Institute for Advanced Study at Princeton. Among his many books are *A System of Logistic* (1934), *Mathematical Logic* (1940), *Elementary Logic* (1941), *Methods of Logic* (1950), *From a Logical Point of View* (1953), *Word and Object* (1960), *Set Theory and Its Logic* (1963), *The Ways of Paradox* (1966), *Philosophy of Logic* (1969), and, with Ullian, *The Web of Belief* (1970).

R

RAND, AYN (1905-   ): A popular author and lecturer, Ayn Rand recommends a philosophy termed "Objectivism," and frankly refers to "the virtue of selfishness." Born in St. Petersburg, Russia, she graduated from the University of Leningrad in 1924 and came to the United States two years later. She married Frank O'Connor in 1929. She worked as a screen writer for several years, writing three plays before the popular works, *The Fountainhead* (1943) and *Atlas Shrugged* (1957). During the sixties she lectured in the universities, including Yale, Princeton, Columbia, Johns Hopkins, Harvard, and MIT. Her other works include *For the New Intellectual* (1961), *The Virtue of Selfishness* (1965), *Capitalism: the Unknown Ideal* (1966), and *Introduction to Objectivist Epistemology* (1967).

An excellent analysis of Ayn Rand's philosophy has been produced by William F. O'Neill, *With Charity Toward None* (New York: Philosophical Library, 1971).

According to Miss Rand, man needs a

frame of reference, a comprehensive view of existence, no matter how rudimentary... a sense of being *right*, a moral justification of his actions, which means: a philosophical code of values.

She recommends a new radical capitalism, and summarizes objectivist philosophy as follows:

1. Metaphysics: Objective Reality
2. Epistemology: Reason
3. Ethics: Self-interest
4. Politics: Capitalism

She writes of intellectuals with the same scorn as does Eric Hoffer.

● ● ●

RANDALL, JOHN HERMAN, JR. (1899-   ): Wearer of the mantle of Dewey, John Herman Randall, Jr. showed a pronounced interest in the history of philosophy. Born in Grand Rapids, Michigan, he was educated at Columbia (Ph.D. 1923). From 1925 on, he taught at Columia. He has written, among many works, *The Problem of Group Responsibility* (1922), *The Making of the Modern Mind* (1926), *The Career of Philosophy in Modern Times* (1962, 1965), and *How Philosophy Uses its Past* (1963). The College Outline Series book, *Philosophy, an Introduction,* which he co-authored with Justus Buchler, shows what a great change has taken place in American thought and teaching practice since 1942, when it first appeared. It includes a "Quick Reference Table to Standard Textbooks" in philosophy. Most of the books are not in use anywhere, and many of them have never even been read by graduate students (e.g., Brightman, Hocking, Mead, etc.).

● ● ●

RAUCH, FREDERICK AUGUSTUS (1806-1841): An enthusiastic Hegelian, Frederick Augustus Rauch was the first to carry the "good news" of Hegelianism to America as he fled the Prussian political police.

A young professor at Heidelberg, his "crime" had been to voice public sympathy for the new political fraternities which the government was trying to suppress. In 1831 he fled to America.

In Eastern Pennsylvania he taught in various positions, founding Marshall College in 1836 and laying the ground-work for the influential "Mercersburg theology."

In 1840 he published his most significant work: *Psy-*

226

chology or a View of the Human Soul, including Anthropology. It was written:

> to give the science of man a direct bearing upon other sciences, and especially upon religion and theology.... The present work is, as far as the author knows, the first attempt to unite *German* and *American* mental philosophy.

In his Hegelian idealism, Rauch maintained that reason was the faculty of intelligence in an intelligible world. Pure reason is one in man and nature. The finite understanding, on the one hand, proceeds inductively from sensations and perceptions. However, the mind may also be acquainted with such non-sensory realities as classes, laws, and relations. In knowing them, we know the genuine nature of reality itself. The reason and the understanding differ with respect to the nature of their object, but not especially in the nature of their method.

Rauch thus escaped the nominalism into which New England Transcendentalists fell, but had difficulty defending himself against the charge of pantheism.

● ● ●

ROGERS, ARTHUR K. (1868-1936): Professor of philosophy and education at Butler College, Indianapolis, A. K. Rogers is known for his books on the past course of American philosophy, including *A Brief Introduction to Modern Philosophy* (1899), *The Religious Conception of the World* (1907), and *British and American Philosophy since 1800* (1922).

● ● ●

ROGERS, WILLIAM BARTON (1804-1882): Enjoying a meteoric rise from state inspector of gas meters to founder of the Massachusetts Institute of Technology, both in the same year (1861), William Barton Rogers exhibited the true empirical spirit. Building on the scientific concepts of the American Enlightenment, following the achievements of Franklin and Jefferson, Rogers illustrates the progress of an enlightened scientist during the development of the nineteenth century. This progress was from institution to institution.

Beginning at the College of William and Mary, where his father had taught natural philosophy before him, Rogers (like Jefferson before him) left the atmosphere of a school predominantly dedicated to the classics and joined the faculty of a school more interested in practical, useful knowledge, the University of Virginia. Later, even this location proved too confining. "Longing for an atmosphere of more stimulating power," he moved to Boston, where he established an institution devoted to pure science (and, in the American spirit, to technology).

Born on Pearl Harbor day, 137 years before the event, he married a Savage from Boston (Emma Savage). He died on May 30 while granting diplomas to the graduating class.

• • •

ROSENSTOCK-HUESSY, EUGEN (1888-   ): Suggested by Richard H. Popkin of CUNY as one of the eminent European philosophers living in America, Rosenstock-Huessy was born in Berlin and educated at Zurich, Berlin, and Heidelberg. He taught on the law faculty at Leipzig 1912-1919, was editor of the *Daimler Werkzeitung* for a year, and was first head of the Academy of Labor at Frankfurt-am-Main, 1921-1922. Later he taught the history of law and sociology at the University of Breslau, 1923-1933. During 1933, the year Hitler came to power, Rosenstock-Huessy came to lecture at Harvard. From 1935 to 1957 he taught at Dartmouth College. He has written *Out of Revolution, Autobiography of Western Man* (1938), *The Christian Future* (1946), *The Multiformity of Man* (1949), *Biblionomics* (1959), *Die Sprache des Menschengeschlechts* (2 volumes, 1963-65), and *Judaism Despite Christianity* (1968). He now lives at Four Wells, Norwich, Vermont.

• • •

ROYCE, JOSIAH (1855-1916): As his father joined the Gold Rush to the West, Josiah Royce joined a kind of Idea-Rush to the East. The trip East was as perilous as the trip West had been. Royce gained his position at Harvard (in 1882) only as a one-year substitute for William James.

Born in Grass Valley, Nevada County, California, he received his early education from his mother, who organized and taught a school for the neighborhood in her own home. He attended the University of California, taught by Joseph LeConte (*q.v.*) among others. After he graduated in 1875, his excellent scholarship helped earn him the chance to study in Europe, at Göttingen and Leipzg, where he heard the lectures of Lotze, Wundt, and Windelband. This experience gave his thought its decidedly spiritualistic and idealistic impress.

In 1878 he graduated from the new Johns Hopkins University. He spent the next four years at the University of California, where he was an instructor in English. Here he prepared a *Primer of Logical Analysis for the Use for Composition Students* (1881).

After he began teaching at Harvard, he started to produce his greatest books. The first of them was *The Religious Aspect of Philosophy* (1885). He begins with a practical problem: the moral problem of pessimism. The pessimism he refers to is that of Schopenhauer, which turns out to be moral despair that no particular ideal ought to be accepted by every rational soul. However, Royce remarks, "the truth of the matter is concealed in the doubt." That is, the pessimist has assumed that all particular ideals ought to be harmonized. Empirical pessimism is only possible because an absolute ideal has already been assumed. Thus the moral problem of pessimism and the logical problem of judgment are closely related.

The famous "Absolute" is the universal knower who affirms all judgments and experiences all objects, thus is uniquely qualified to bring together both judgments and their objects. The metaphysical implications of this formulation are idealistic and monistic, idealistic because all reality is essentially the idea of a mind, and monistic because there is one mind to which all others are related as parts to a whole. This Absolute is the ultimate being of metaphysics, the object of worship and the standard of value.

The second of Royce's major philosophical works was *The Conception of God* (1897). In this work he defends himself against Howison's attack upon his monism. Howison objected that Royce failed to provide for the autonomy of the moral individual, and thus was inconsistent. Royce replied by stating that while the principle of individuality is based on choice or preference, the Absolute is also an individual, consisting ultimately in a sheer act of will. Absolute will is divided out among individuals, each of whom wills independently within his own province.

Royce's third work was the most widely read: *The Spirit of Modern Philosophy* (1892). He argues for the inadequacy of positivism and evolutionary theory. Science, he believes, has its limits. The world of description should be subordinate to the world of appreciation.

His fourth and most important work was *The World and the Individual* (1900-01), the Gifford Lectures at the University of Aberdeen. He argues against mysticism, realism, and "critical rationalism" (empiricism and materialism). His own position is an unqualified idealism, affirming that reality belongs exclusively to the conscious life of an all-embracing mind. Those parts of nature we consider unconscious, he remarks, may belong to minds whose "time-rate is slower or faster than those which our consciousness is adapted to read or to appreciate."

A significant development within Royce's thought may be traced at this point. In his first major work, he used the term "thought" to designate the processes of the Absolute. In the second, he used the term "will" to cover the same thing. In the fourth, the term is "purpose." Thus thought, he maintains, is essentially purposive. Further, surprisingly enough, the key to its nature is founded in ambiguity, in the double meaning of ideas. The "internal meaning" of an idea consists in the universals or ideal possibilities, *what* is judged. The "external meaning" consists in the particular object to which it refers, what is judged *about*. The object lies behind the idea, but is embraced within mind as the experience to which the idea points as its own fulfillment.

This is all little more than a restatement of German idealism. A critical problem arose at about the same point it was encountered by F. H. Bradley, the British idealist. Working with the same dialectic that troubled Royce, Bradley contended that the Infinite is purely ideal and abstract, not to be found in existence. Royce had been glorying in the infinite. To him it was not a predicament, but the ground for certainty. Now if it were non-existent, it would hardly provide certainty. The problem was faced at a situation involving infinite regress. Royce was greatly disturbed.

At this point, Charles S. Peirce (*q.v*) took pity on Royce, which was more than happened in reverse, and provided him with a key piece of advice. He advised him to study mathematical logic. It would clarify the problem and tighten up the philosophical system. As Royce did, he discovered the mathematical idea of an infinite series and the community of interpretation, which became important features of his thought. On this basis he disputed Bradley's point that the infinite was a sign of irrationality in existence. Instead, he wrote, it is the sign of "perfect order," in the sense of a well-ordered series. Infinity consists not in endlessness, but in the structure of the set, in which the members interpret each other in the light of the whole. The members never coalesce into unity, but are clearly related to each other in terms of mutual support.

Thus Royce transferred his argument from traditional epistemology to the ground of language, the social use of symbols. This provided a novel restatement of idealistic philosophy. Knowledge is social. If reality is to exhibit the same structure, it too must be social.

After the death of William James (1910) and about the same time he lost his originality, Royce became the most influential American philosopher of his day. In 1908 he had published *The Philosophy of Loyalty* (1908) advocating salvation of the individual through loyalty to a cause, ultimately by "loyalty to loyalty." In *The Hope of the Great Communtiy* (1916) he recommends solution of the world's economic problems by the extension of insurance policies to cover such things as insurance against war.

He supported the cause of the Allies during the First World War, and died on September the 14th, 1916.

•   •   •

RUNES, DAGOBERT D. (1902-   ): Born in Zastavna, Rumania, on the 6th of January, 1902, Dagobert D. Runes received his Ph.D. degree from the University of Vienna in 1924, when the famed Vienna Circle was actively developing Analytic Philosophy.

Two years after graduation, in 1926, he came to America, where he worked for the next five years as a free lance writer. The year 1927 saw the publication of *Der Wahre Jesus (The True Jesus)*.

From 1931 to 1934 he served as director of the Institute for Advanced Education in New York City. Until 1936 he was editor of *Modern Thinker*.

In 1940 he became editor-in-chief of the Philosophical Library and a member of the board of directors. The following years have seen the publication of such books as *Jordan Lieder* (1948) and *Letters to My Son* (1949). Albert

Schweitzer's comments on the latter book are: *"Letters to My Son* has given me great delight. We both travel on the same path, to bring to mankind a deeply ethical, deeply spiritual consciousness, with the purpose of leading the people back from the mentality of indifference in which they are living, to a new and higher manner of thinking."

His *Dictionary of Philosophy* has been for a generation a standard text in philosophy classes throughout the English speaking world.

Dr. Runes' keen interest in Spinoza led to the publication (1951) of the *Spinoza dictionary* to which Albert Einstein wrote the Preface.

Of God, the Devil and the Jews (1952) was followed by *The Soviet Impact on Society* (1953). He opposes communism and all it stands for, considering communism akin to fascism, both opportunistic hand-maidens of oligarchic authority.

The years to follow saw the publication of *Letters to My Daughter* (1954), *On the Nature of Man* (1956), *A Book of Contemplation* (1957), and the *Pictorial History of Philosophy* (1959). This last work was unique, and was widely translated into other languages. Its illustrations picture the philosophers, the places where they lived, and social and cultural events of the time vividly.

These publications were followed by the *Dictionary of Thought* (second edition, 1965), *The Art of Thinking* (1961), *Letters to My Teacher* (1961), *Lost Legends of Israel* (1961), *Despotism: A Pictorial History of Tyranny* (1963), *The Disinherited and the Law* (1964), *Crosscuts Through History* (1965), *The Jew and the Cross* (1965), *The War Against the Jews* (1968), *Philosophy for Everyman* (1968), and *Handbook of Reason* (1972).

Still going strong, Dr. Runes has seen his books translated into Spanish, Italian, Portuguese, German, French and Hebrew. "Tell me what you read," he says, "and I'll tell you what you are."

•　•　•

RUSH, BENJAMIN (1745 o.s.-1813): Born at Byberry on Christmas Eve, Benjamin Rush was a medical doctor who made Philadelphia into the medical center of the United States for the first half of the nineteenth century. Important as a practitioner of the empirical method, he mistakenly overemphasized the importance of the hypothesis to the neglect of its confirmation It remained for one of his many enemies to point out the correlation between "bleeding" — Rush's great new discovery for the cure of disease, sometimes amounting to the "depletion" of as much as four-fifths of all the blood in the body — and the death rate in patients so treated.

Rush was a public-spirited man, writing voluminously on such subjects as slavery, prison reform, the abolition of capital punishment (which, two hundred years later, was still being hotly debated in Philadelphia), temperance, improved education for girls, more freedom for students, and a national university.

He arranged for the first publication of Thomas Paine's *Common Sense.*

Essays, Literary, Moral and Philosophical (1798) is the collection of most of his articles on social reform.

He believed in the influence of physical causes upon the moral faculty:

There is an indissoluble union between moral, political and physical happiness; and if it be true, that elective and representative governments are most favourable to individual, as well as national prosperity, it follows of course that they are most favourable to animal life.

Experimental science, piety and an enthusiasm for humanitarian reforms were combined by Rush and his many students.

• • •

RUSSELL, BERTRAND (1872-1970): Bertrand Russell was without doubt one of the world's great philosophers, but he was really not an American philosopher in any real sense of the word. He was trapped in the United States during the course of the Second World War during what was to have been a limited stay at American universities. His experiences here were far from pleasant.

He lectured at The University of Chicago, where he felt they were happy to see him leave. He went to Southern California, and prepared to accept an appointment to the College of the City of New York in 1940 when the controversy erupted over his fitness to teach. A taxpayer sued to protect her daughter's morals from the old man who in 1929 had written *Marriage and Morals* and was now about to teach mathematical logic in a men's college where her daughter could not go anyway. Surprisingly, the New York courts nullified his appointment, thus proving that Athens has no monopoly over the persecution of philosophers.

Most of Russell's friends assumed that, since he was an earl, he had plenty of money. The fact of the matter was that he could not draw on his money, due to currency regulations in England at the time. He had a difficult time making ends meet.

He was bailed out of his predicament by Albert Barnes, who invited him to teach at the Barnes Foundation, Merion, Pennsylvania. There, Russell lived in a small farm house and wrote the manuscript of *A History of Western Philosophy* (1946), which would prove to be a best seller. Meanwhile, difficulties arose between Russell and Barnes, and Russell was fired again.

Russell at last returned to England, where he was no doubt happier. The reader is referred to other sources for a complete telling of Russell's tremendous and voluminous contributions to world philosophy.

S

SANTAYANA, GEORGE (1863-1952): George Santayana did not consider himself an American philosopher, but nearly everybody else did. Born in Avila, Spain, on December 16, 1863, of temperamentally incompatible parents, he was brought to Boston by his mother. He was educated in the Boston Latin School and Harvard College, graduating in 1886. He studied at Berlin and returned to take a Ph.D. from Harvard in 1889. From then until 1912, he taught there. In that year he resigned and left for Europe with a blast against American life. "The prevalence of insanity, of 'breaking down,' and of 'nervous depression' is one of the most significant things in America," he wrote. "It goes with overwork, not having a religion, or 'getting religion.'"

He lived and wrote in England, Paris, and Rome, where he died September 26, 1952.

His works include *The Sense of Beauty* (1896), *The Life of Reason* (5 volumes, 1905-6), *Character and Opinion in the United States* (1920), *Scepticism and Animal Faith* (1923), *Dialogues in Limbo* (1925), *Realms of Being* (4 volumes, 1927-40), *Persons and Places* (3 volumes, 1944, 45, and 53), and one novel, *The Last Puritan* (1935).

He never married, living instead with a few intimate friends and his books. At the end of his life he lived in a Roman convent, one of the strangest inhabitants of a religious retreat in history. He was a "devout atheist," deeply attached to Catholicism but entirely divorced from faith. He believed that there is no God and the Virgin Mary is His mother. He wrote:

My atheism, like that of Spinoza, is true piety towards the universe and denies only gods fashioned by men in their own image, to be servants of their human interests.

Whenever the name of Santayana is mentioned, the reader immediately thinks of the famous indictment of American philosophy he delivered under the title of "The Genteel Tradition," a womanish, backwater devotion to a misty spirit rather than the much more vital and enterprising technological tradition of American life:

> The chief fountains of this tradition were Calvinism and transcendentalism. Both were living fountains; but to keep them alive they required, one an agonised conscience, and the other a radical subjective criticism of knowledge. When these rare metaphysical preocupations disappeared — and the American atmosphere is not favorable to either of them — the two systems ceased to be inwardly understood; they subsisted as sacred mysteries only.

Royce was the philosopher Santayana was most directly criticizing. He considered Royce to be an "overworked, standardised, academic machine, creaking and thumping on at the call of duty or of habit, with no thought of sparing itself or any one else" as it attempted to show that "all lives were parts of a single divine life in which all problems were solved and all evils justified."

William James, on the other hand, Santayana felt, was the first great American philosopher to break with the genteel tradition. The break came, according to Santayana, for these reasons:

> On the one side came the revolt of the Bohemian temperament, with its poetry of crude naturalism; on the other side came an impassioned empiricism, welcoming popular religious witnesses to the unseen, reducing science to an instrument of success in action,

and declaring the universe to be wild, young, and not to be harnessed by the logic of any school.

Santayana was an evolutionary naturalist, a critical realist, maintaining that consciousness reveals Reality. The two historical sources for his thought are the ancient Greek philosophers and Spinoza. He rejected pantheism, believing that the word "God" is a useless repetition of the word "Nature."

In a letter to William James he wrote:

I am a Latin, and nothing seems serious to me except politics, except the sort of men that your ideas will involve and the sort of happiness they will be capable of. The rest is exquisite moonshine. Religion in particular was *found out* more than two hundred years ago, and it seems to me intolerable that we should still be condemned to ignore the fact and to give the parson and the 'idealists' a monopoly of indignation and of contemptuous dogmatism. It is they, not we, that are the pest.... What did Emerson know or care about the passionate insanities and political disasters which religion, for instance, has so often been another name for? He could give that name to his last personal intuition, and ignore what it stands for and what it expresses in the world. It is the latter that absorbs me; and I care too much about mortal happiness to be interested in the charming vegetation of cancer microbes in the system — except with the idea of suppressing it.

In *The Life of Reason*, Santayana wrote:

Fanaticism consists in redoubling your efforts when you have forgotten your aim.

•   •   •

SCHNEIDER, HERBERT W. (1892-   ): Author of *A History of American Philosophy* (1946), *Three Dimensions of Public Morality* (1956), *Morals for Mankind* (1960), and *Ways of Being* (1962), Herbert W. Schneider was born in Berea, Ohio, and educated at CCNY and Columbia (Ph.D. 1917). Granted an L.H.D. by Baldwin-Wallace College in 1960, he has taught at Columbia 1918-1957 and at Claremont Graduate School, in California.

• • •

SELLARS, ROY WOOD (1800-   ): One of the original seven critical realists, Roy Wood Sellars was the Canadian-born professor of philosophy at the University of Michigan, beginning in 1905. He wrote *Critical Realism* (1916), *The Next Step in Religion* (1918), *Evolutionary Naturalism* (1921), and *The Philosophy of Physical Realism* (1932).

• • •

SMALL, ALBION WOODBURY (1854-1926): One of the founders of American sociology, he was head of the department of sociology at the new University of Chicago, beginning in 1892. This was the first department of its kind. He believed passionately in the unity of the social sciences. The son of Thankful Small and a distant relative of Abraham Lincoln, Albion Woodbury Small was born in Maine and educated in New England and Berlin. Among his three hundred works are *General Sociology* (1905) and *Between Eras: From Capitalism to Democracy* (1913).

• • •

SMALL, WILLIAM (1734-1775): If Socrates deserves to be called a philosopher, even though he never published, so does Small, on a smaller scale.

His students turned out rather better than the old master's: instead of Alcibiades, Thomas Jefferson (*q.v.*).

Small never wrote, not even the most modest book. Yet his breadth of vision was impressive. He took an experimental, scientific, view of the world, taught the unity of knowledge, and considered every area of thought essentially connected to other areas. Philosophy, politics, and medicine were all interconnected. The man of affairs ought to know about them all. Small recommended a practical approach to theoretical problems.

A short time before Jefferson had enrolled at the College of William and Mary, most of the faculty had been fired. There were various kinds of misconduct, the most interesting of which was the case of Jacob Rowe. Not only had Rowe, the Professor of Moral Philosophy, been reprimanded for drunkenness, but he then became the leader of a gang fight between the students and town apprentices. The students were armed with pistols, knives, and other weapons. This was the familiar town-and-gown problem writ large. During the engagement, one of the members of the Board of Visitors ordered the sudents to stop fighting. The Rev. Professor Rowe pointed a pistol at the board member's chest.

When the excitement in town died down, the struggle in the board room began. Mr. Rowe was called to account, but cautioned not to bring his pistol. He was suitably meek, as befitted his not-quite-thirty years. He apologized for threatening the board member's life. However, he refused to apologize for the remarks he had made insulting the President of the College who, he insisted, richly deserved what had been said. The Professor was fired on September 29th, 1760.

At this point, as on other similar occasions, the College was practically without a faculty. They employed Dr. William Small from Scotland to fill this void. It was hard to operate a school without teachers. Small had an M.A. five years old from the University of Aberdeen. The turn of events being what they were, Small was practically Jefferson's only teacher.

Jefferson wrote in his autobiography:

241

It was my great good fortune, and what probably fixed the destinies of my life, that Dr. William Small of Scotland, was then professor of mathematics, a man profound in most of the useful branches of science with a happy talent of communication, correct and gentlemanly manners, and an enlarged and liberal mind. He, most happily for me, became soon attached to me, and made me his daily companion when not engaged in the school; and from his conversation I got my views of the expansion of science, and of the system of things in which we are placed. Fortunately, the philosophical chair became vacant soon after my arrival at college, and he was appointed to fill it *per interim:* and he was the first who ever gave, in that college, regular lectures in ethics, rhetoric, and belles lettres.

Small not only gave Jefferson an exceptionally liberal view of thought and science, but also secured for him some important friendships, He gave him an entree as a student of law to a place at the table of Virginia's able Governor Fauquier.

In 1763, after Jefferson had left, Dr. Small began to practice medicine in his spare time, both in the town and outlying areas of the county. At first the Board of Visitors overlooked this practice, but later they decided that no college teacher could have outside employment without written consent. They promptly presented this new assertion of authority to the faculty in the form of an oath of allegiance to be signed.

Small refused. In 1764 he left Williamsburg, never to return to America. It almost seemed as if he had been employed by destiny specifically to teach Jefferson.

A year later he took his M.D. degree and practiced medicine in the city of Birmingham (where Priestly was to move a few years later) until his death in 1775.

•　　•　　•

SMITH, SAMUEL STANHOPE (1750-1819): A common-sense Realist, like his father-in-law, John Witherspoon (*q.v.*), Samuel Stanhope Smith was born in Lancaster County, Pennsylvania, at Pequea, March the 16th, 1750. Educated at the academy which his father had founded, he entered the College of New Jersey (Princeton) when he was sixteen. Fascinated by natural science, he retained a spirit of free inquiry throughout his life.

He worked his way through "the fanciful doctrines of Bishop Berkeley," prodded by Witherspoon into common-sense realism.

Incredibly productive, he founded the Academy (now College) of Hampden-Sydney in 1776, returned to the College of New Jersey as professor of moral philosophy, and served after 1795 as its president. He had to raise money to repair the damage done by the revolutionary war. As soon as this had been completed, Nassau Hall was hit by fire, and the entire task had to be repeated.

It was suspected that the fire had been caused by careless or reckless students. Discipline was increased. This led (1807) to a student rebellion. More than half were suspended.

Smith did not neglect the improvement of the intellectual life of the college, despite the strain of all these events. He called in 1795 the first undergraduate teacher of chemistry and natural science in the country, and offered a unique course combining the sciences and the humanities. These educational innovations were, of course, subjected to intense and hostile criticism.

His main book is *The Lectures, Corrected and Improved, Which Have Been Delivered for a Series of Years in the College of New Jersey; on the Subjects of Moral and Political Philosophy* (1812).

• • •

SOCIAL PHILOSOPHY: American Philosophy has made some important contributions to the Theory of Society. By

its experience in the art of social engineering, by its deliberate constitution-making, it has provided a significant addition to the Greek theory of *politeia*.

John Adams (October 30, 1735-July 4, 1826) represented
the "constitutionalist" school of Federalism, flourishing in
New England. Thomas Jefferson (*q.v.*) and the Virginia
Republicans represented the "bill of rights" school.

John Adams, born at Braintree, Massachusetts, was a
Harvard graduate (1755). He taught school in Worcester
and considered becoming a minister. "Frigid John" Calvin,
however, was not to his liking, and instead he took to
reading law. Practicing law in Boston, he was gradually
drawn into political events. He cheered the Boston Tea
Party and urged unsuccessfully that the King should recog-
nize the "natural rights" of the colonists.

The term, "general welfare," was used to mean nothing
more than "common defense," and "commonwealth" meant
only the union of "justice and equality," law and order.
Adams called this "Novanglian" Federalism.

Adams said plainly:

It must be remembered, that the rich are *people* as
well as the poor; that they have rights as well as others;
that they have as clear and as sacred a right to their
large property as others have to theirs which is smaller;
that oppression to them is as possible and as wicked
as to others.

Adams favored a self-regulating order. Institutions should
be so constructed as to make private interest and public
interest identical. This could be done by depersonalizing
the law. Powers would be so distributed that no one particular interest could predominate. The natural equilibrium
would automatically do justice to all the factions. Checks
and balances were the key to his "scientific" theory of
government.

If you give more than a share in the sovereignty to

the democrats, that is, if you give them the command or preponderance in the sovereignty, that is, the legislature, they will vote all property out of the hands of you aristocrats, and if they let you escape with your lives, it will be more humanity, considerations, and generosity than any triumphant democracy ever displayed since the creation. And what will follow? The aristocracy among the democrats will take your places, and treat their fellows as severely and sternly as you have treated them.

Adams' *Discourses on Davila* (1790) are filled with observations on the inequalities found everywhere, made by God or Nature, which cannot be changed.

The second President of the United States, Adams was defeated in his bid for a second term by Thomas Jefferson, in 1800. He appointed John Marshall as Chief Justice of the Supreme Court, thus bringing more of the checks and balances which he believed to be the fundamental of good government.

SOCIETY [Lat. *societas*]: Ger. (5) *Gesellschaft;* Fr. (5) *société;* Ital. (5) *società.* (1) A biological COLONY, for which this latter term is preferable.

(2) Any social GROUP, for which this latter term is preferable.

(3) A commercial, scientific, or other organization for a special purpose.

(4) The public, others; as in the expressions 'the opinion of society,' 'to be in society.' Not technical.

(5) A social group characterized by some degree of reflective and voluntary CO-OPERATION. 'A number of like-minded individuals who know and enjoy their like-mindedness and are therefore able to work together for common ends' (Giddings, *Elements of Sociol.*).

(6) A naturally formed population occupying a defined territory (e.g. England, France, or the United States), of which, on the whole, definition (5) is true.

In the history of the concept of society, three questions of philosophical importance have arisen, namely: —

1) That of the essential nature of society; (2) that of the distinction between natural and political society; and (3) that of the inclusion of animal groups under the term societies. The distinction between natural and political societies was imperfectly made by Hobbes and Locke, and precisely made by Bentham (*Fragment on Government,* chap. i).

1. John Dewey:

(1). What nutrition and reprodution are to physiological life, education is to social life. — *Democracy and Education.*

(2). Society is one word, but infinitely many things. It covers all the ways in which by associating together men share their experiences, and build up common interests and aims. — *Reconstruction in Philosophy.*

(3). Society is the process of associating in such ways that experience, ideas, emotion, values are transmitted and made common. — *Ibid.*

(4). "Society" is either an abstract or a collective noun. In the concrete, there are societies, associations, groups of an immense number of kinds, having ties and instituting different interests. They may be gangs, criminal bands; clubs for sport, sociability, and eating; scientific and professional organizations; political parties and unions within them; families, religious denominations, business partnerships, and corporations; and so on in an endless list. The associations may be local, notion-wide, and trans-national. Since there is no one thing which may be called society, except their indefinite overlapping, there is no unqualified eulogistic cannotation adhering to the term "society." Some societies are in the main to be approved; some to be condemned, on account of their consequences upon the character and conduct of those engaged in them and because of their remoter consequences upon others. All of them, like all things human, are mixed in quality; "society" is something to be approved and judged critically and discriminatingly. "Socialization" of some sort — that is, the reflex modification of wants, beliefs, and work because of their share in a united action —is inevitable. But it is as marked in the formation of frivolous, dissipated, fanatical, narrow-minded, and criminal persons as in that of competent inquirers, learned scholars, creative artists, and good neighbors. — *The Public and Its Problems.*

(5). Society, in order to solve its own problems and remedy its own ills, needs to employ science and technology for social instead of merely private ends. This need for a society in which experimental inquiry and planning for social ends are organically contained is also the need for a new education. — *The Educational Frontier* (a Symposium, ed. by W. H. Kilpatrick).

• • •

SPAULDING, EDWARD GLEASON (1873-1940): One of the American Neo-Realists, Edward G. Spaulding rejected both the monism of absolute idealism and the relativism of Pragmatism. Born and educated in Vermont, Spaulding went on to Columbia and Bonn. He taught at CCNY and Princeton. He wrote *The New Rationalism* (1918) and served in the chemical warfare division of the Army. His other works are *What Am I?* and *A World of Chance, or Whence, Whither, and Why?* (1936).

• • •

STALLO, JOHANN BERNHARD (1823-1900): A Frisian philosopher, Johann Bernhard Stallo had come to America when sixteen to live with an uncle in Cincinnati. His father couldn't afford an advanced education, and the boy did not want to spend the rest of his life as a village school teacher. Once here, he completed his schooling and taught chemistry at St. John's in Fordham, New York.

In 1848 he published the *General Principles of the Philosophy of Nature,* written, as he said, "under the spell of Hegel's ontological reveries." The book introduced to American readers the philosophies of Kant, Hegel, Fichte, Schelling and Lorenz Oken.

Stallo went on to a varied career, studied law and became a judge. He defended the Cincinnati School Board against the clergymen who were trying to retain forced hymn-singing in schools.

The Concepts and Theories of Modern Physics was published in 1882, an essay in epistemology similar to Ernst Mach.

During the Civil War he was active in organizing the 9th Ohio Infantry. Afterwards he remained in public life, appointed minister to Italy by Cleveland in 1885.

• • •

STEPHENS, ALEXANDER HAMILTON (1812-1883): In 1856 Stephens challenged Benjamin Hill to a duel. Hill refused, remarking that he had a family to support and a soul to save, while Stephens had neither.

Known as "Little Elick," Alexander Hamilton Stephens was vice president of the Confederacy, congressman from Georgia, a brilliant parliamentarian, and an effective public speaker.

Author of *A Constitutional View of the Late War Between the States* (1868, 1870), he saw the book create a sensation. He responded with three other works, each less successful than the one before. Nevertheless, Stephens remains a learned and independent thinker on political and social philosophy.

After the war, Stephens was elected to Congress, serving well despite his cadaverous appearance, until 1882. Bored by retirement, he ran for governor of Georgia and won, but died after a few months in office.

• • •

STEVENSON, CHARLES LESLIE (1908-   ) Noted for his modern treatment of ethics, Charles L. Stevenson titled his major work *Ethics and Language* (1944). Born in Cincinnati, June 27, 1908, he was educated at Yale, Cambridge, and Harvard. He has taught at Harvard, Yale, and the University of Michigan, where he has been since 1946. *Facts and Values* is his second book (1963). He remarked that:

> ethical theory is given to the age-old quest for ultimate principles, definitely established. This not only hides the full complexity of moral issues, but puts static, otherworldly norms in the place of flexible, realistic ones. . . . The demand for a final proof springs less from hopes than from fears. . . . Living questions are too rich in their complexity to be answered by a formula.

T

TARSKI, ALFRED (1902-   ): A distinguished mathematician and philosopher, Alfred Tarski was born and educated in Warsaw, Poland. He taught at the University of Poland for fourten years. In 1939, as the Second World War began to destroy life in Eastern Europe, Tarski came to the United States. He was research associate at Harvard for two years, taught at CCNY for a year, joined the Institute for Advanced Study in Princeton in 1941-42, while Einstein was there. In 1942 he went to the University of California, where he has taught ever since.

He has written *Introduction to Logic* (English translation, 1941), *A Decision Method for Elementary Algebra and Geometry* (1948), *Undecidable Theories* (with others, 1953), *Logic, Semantics, Mathematics* (1956), and *The Completeness of Elementary Algebra and Geometry* (1967). With others, he has also produced books on the methodology of science and related questions.

● ● ●

THOREAU, HENRY DAVID (1817-1862): Although he preferred philosophy to the family business, pencil-making, Henry David Thoreau enjoyed more financial success with the latter than the former, at the time. His Concord contemporaries thought it more important to buy pencils than books, perhaps on the theory that it was better to have a pencil and an empty mind than an educated mind with no pencil.

In 1833 he entered Harvard, not very enthusiastically. He was taught Greek by Jones Very. Although his marks were poor, he read more widely than any other members of the graduating class.

He returned to Concord and, since college had prepared him for no occupation in particular, taught school. He lasted two weeks. A member of the school committee objected vigorously to Thoreau's lack of discipline, so the next day, to show how absurd whipping was, he whipped a half dozen surprised pupils and resigned that night.

The next year, Henry and his brother John started their own school, which ran with great success for two terms, and whipped nobody.

Thoreau next lived in the Emerson house, where he looked after practical matters. While there, his brother died, just sixteen days before Emerson's little Waldo.

In 1843 Thoreau actually lived outside Concord — for a year, in Staten Island. He met Henry James the Elder and Horace Greeley, but his efforts to sell articles to the New York magazines were generally unsuccessful.

He returned to Concord, where, on the 4th of July, 1845, he built himself a hut at Walden Pond, where he lived until September 6, 1847, and began, in Channing's words, "the grand process of devouring yourself alive," introspective writing.

Walden Pond is much larger than one might imagine. "Pond," in the dialect of New England, is the word for "lake." Thoreau used his solitude for meditation in the classic sense. America built no monasteries in the European sense. The faith that had grounded them was gone, even in Europe. But the fruits of solitude could be enjoyed, Thoreau maintained, by any who would open his eyes and actually see what was happening around him:

> I see young men, my townsmen, whose misfortune it is to have inherited farms, houses, barns, cattle, and farming tools; for these are more easily acquired than got rid of. Better if they had been born in the open pasture and suckled by a wolf, that they might have seen with clearer eyes what field they were called to labor in.

Thoreau's real meditation was society, its nature and improvement, if possible (and Thoreau was rather pessimistic on that point):

> Some of you, we all know, are poor, find it hard to live, are sometimes, as it were, gasping for breath. I have no doubt that some of you who read this book are unable to pay for all the dinners which you have actually eaten, or for the coats and shoes which are fast wearing or are already worn out, and have come to this page to spend borrowed or stolen time, robbing your creditors of an hour.

No man, says Thoreau, can:

> kill time without injuring eternity. The mass of men lead lives of quiet desperation.

The public officials of Concord thoughtfully provided Thoreau with a personal lesson in the workings of society by arresting him for non-payment of taxes. He opposed slavery, and it became an issue in the Mexican War. So he refused to pay his war taxes. He spent one night in jail, after which, to his disgust, one of his aunts paid the tax.

This act of the authorities became the occasion for Thoreau to write his famous essay, which has had a world-wide influence on such men as Tolstoy and Gandhi, *On the Duty of Civil Disobedience* (1849: originally entitled *Resistance to Civil Government* and later called *Civil Disobedience*):

> I heartily accept the motto, — "That government is best which governs least;" and I should like to see it acted up to more rapidly and systematically. Carried out, it finally amounts to this, which also I believe, — "That government is best which governs not at all;" and when men are prepared for it, that will be the kind of government which they will have. Government is at best

but an expedient; but most governments are usually, and all governments are sometimes, inexpedient. The objections which have been brought against a standing army, and they are many and weighty, and deserve to prevail, may also at last be brought against a standing government. The standing army is only an arm of the standing government.

This idea, that the government ought to wither away, which is recognized now as a staple of Marxist theory, has much in common with a similar theory by Henry James the Elder (*q.v.*). It grew up in this case entirely upon American soil, in the peculiarly American town of Concord, Massachusetts, completely removed from outside influences. It has been remarked, fairly, that Thoreau's political theory can be viewed as a logical extension of Jefferson's doctrines.

The problem which the essay does not face, is what to do when an extraordinary situation arises, such as the debate over slavery at that time. Lincoln observed that a lack of government led to the crisis.

Thoreau would no doubt reply that the case was one where certain men, as in the Mexican War, were making use of the government for their own purposes. Stephens (*q.v.*) had done so by his clever parliamentarianism.

Thoreau clearly stated his position:

Must the citizen ever for a moment, or in the least degree, resign his conscience to the legislator? Why, has every man a conscience, then? I think that we should be men first, and subjects afterward. It is not desirable to cultivate a respect for the law, so much as for the right. The only obligation which I have a right to assume is to do at any time what I think right.

The crux of the matter is the distinction between the law and the right.

Thoreau's description of life in prison is done with classic skill. His feelings on his release are profound. He felt that most residents of Concord were friends, in a phrase recalling Paine, "for summer weather only:"

> that they did not greatly purpose to do right; that they were a distinct race from me by their prejudices and superstitions, as the Chinamen and Malays are; that, in their sacrifices to humanity, they ran no risks, not even to their property.

In 1849, Thoreau published, at his own expense, *A Week on the Concord and Merrimack Rivers*. 200 copies sold. 750 copies were returned to Thoreau. He consoled himself wryly, remarking that his privacy was affected less.

Walden, or Life in the Woods (1854) did much better. Supposedly a book of natural history, it struck telling blows against the shams of society and government.

After *Walden*, Thoreau's short life was anticlimax. Tuberculosis began sapping his strength. He met Walt Whitman in 1856, and in 1859 became the first American to publicly defend John Brown following the raid at Harpers Ferry.

As the disease progressed, he took a fruitless journey in search of health to Minnesota, of all places. Doctors in Minnesota send their patients to Arizona. For all I know, doctors in Arizona may send their patients to Concord in search of health. Wherever you are, someplace else must be healthier.

Back in Concord, weaker than when he left, he at last was confined to the sickroom. Working feverishly to edit his manuscripts, at last the effort of even holding up the page was too much for him. At nine in the morning, May 6, 1862, he thought of the wilderness once again, said "moose" and "Indian," and died.

● ● ●

TILLICH, PAUL JOHANNES (1886-1965): One of the contemporaries of Einstein, Paul Tillich followed a similar route to the United States, coming in the same year Einstein resigned from the Prussian Academy.

Tillich's place in American philosophy is a matter for legitimate discussion. He is dismissed by naturalists as a hopeless religious figure. He is also dismissed by theologians on the grounds that he is hopelessly philosophical. The reason for this situation is that Tillich preferred to work, as he said, "on the borderline." Carnap had done so between physics and philosophy. Tillich did so between philosophy and theology.

The comment by John Herman Randall of Columbia was:

Paul Tillich stands in the classic tradition of Western philosophy, in that long line of thinkers stemming from the Greeks who have been concerned with the problem of being and wisdom. . . . In the recent German fashion Tillich is inclined to leave ultimate matters to a final "dialetic."

Tillich had a comprehensive mind ranging over the universal topics of Western thought, encompassing both traditional and existential themes. In his main work, with the rather unlikely title (from a philosophical point of view), *Systematic Theology* (3 volumes), the reader can receive summary information on every main argument in the history of Western thought. Tillich weighted philosophical criticisms of his concepts far more heavily than theological criticisms. His replies to Randall are far more extensive and careful than similar replies to Nels Ferre, for example.

Tillich views his own thought by remarking that:

There are many motives in my thought which point to a basic identity of theology and philosophy. Primary among these is the doctrine of the mutual immanence of religion and culture. I could say that in a perfect theonomy the philosophical analysis of the structure of being-in-itself would be united with a theological expression of the meaning of being for us.

Technically speaking, the philosophical position Tillich occupied when he came to America was as a representative of Schelling and Heidegger, whose thought he applied to the American stituation, largely through the use of theological symbols.

I. Life

Born at Starzeddel, in Brandenburg, August 20th, 1886, his father was district superintendent for the Prussian territorial Protestant Chuch. The life he led as a boy, he felt, was protected and privileged. His food and upbringing were better than his classmates at school.

He studied at Berlin, Tübingen, Halle, and Breslau (Ph.D. 1911). Ordained into the Lutheran Chuch, he joined the German Army as a chaplain in 1914, serving until 1918. Socially, this military experience demonstrated to him the split between classes, with the workers viewing religion as in league with the ruling class. He became a religious socialist. Intellectually, he, and the other soldiers, discovered Nietzsche, reading *Thus Spake Zarathustra*, which struck them with the force of a new revelation. Further, "the belief in special Providence died in the trenches," as the paths of machine gun bullets were not deflected by family prayers.

Following the war, Tillich taught at Berlin (1919-1924), Marburg (1924-1925) where Heidegger was also teaching, Dresden (1925-1929), and Frankfurt (1929-1933). Then, "I was immediately dismissed after Hitler had become German chancellor. At the end of 1933 I left Germany with my family and came to this country." He was 47, and did not know English.

Union Theological Seminary, in New York City, took him in as visiting, associate, then full professor of philosophical theology. He taught there until his retirement in 1955.

During this period, his works included *The Protestant*

Era, which he had intended to entitle *The End of the Protestant Era?* until the publisher informed him that no question mark could be permitted in the title to a book, or it would not sell (1948), *The Shaking of the Foundations* (1948), the first volume of the *Systematic Theology* (1951), *The Courage to Be* (1952), *Love, Power and Justice* (1954), *The New Being* (1955), and *Biblical Religion and the Search for Ultimate Reality* (1955).

In 1955, to help save the Harvard Divinity School from extinction, Tillich was invited to come up and bring his reputation with him. Here he taught as university professor from 1955 to 1962. *Dynamics of Faith* and the second volume of the *Systematic Theology* were both published in 1957. The latter book is notable in the history of thought for revising the central concept of the first volume. He had affirmed that the one non-symbolic statement necessary to get his system going was that God is being itself. In the second volume he states that the one non-symbolic statement is "that everything we say about God is symbolic." Although Tillich insists that the difference is slight, there still is a considerable difference. Another work of extraordinary worth was the *Theology of Culture* (1959). Clearly, Tillich's years at Harvard were most productive.

The author became a student of Tillich's in 1957, at a class taught in the Semitic Museum, in a room past an enormous picture of some ancient city burning — perhaps it was Tyre. Having just come from California, the campus seemed like some ancient set, especially the year Tillich taught in the old Harvard Hall, in the Yard.

In 1962 he became Nuveen professor of theology at the Divinity School of the University of Chicago. He hesitated to complete the *Systematic Theology,* to put the last period after the last sentence of the last paragraph. Six years passed before he could be persuaded to complete his task. Finally, in 1963, volume three was published. *Morality and Beyond* (1963) and *The Eternal Now* (1963) also appeared during this period, as did *The Future of Religion,* only a small part of which was written by Tillich.

On the 22nd of October, 1965, he died in Chicago.
Posthumously several books have been published which are primarily old lecture notes unrevised and unimproved, works which Tillich would have preferred not to have been published. He had intended the *Systematic Theology* to be his great work, to go beyond the split between naturalism and supernaturalism, and his judgment on the central place of this set-of books remains valid.

• • •

TRANSCENDENTALISM: (John Dewey's definition) — Ger. *Transscendentalismus;* Fr. *transcendantalisme;* Ital. *trascendentalismo.* (1) The philosophy of the TRANSCENDENTAL (*q.v.,* 2) in the Kantian sense. An explanation of the possibility of an *a priori* knowledge of objects, together with a systematic inventory of the concepts which may thus be applied, and of the principles which result from their application under proper conditions.

2) Kant's successors attempted (through the elimination or transformation of the Kantian thing-in-itself) to unify the ultimate subject und object of knowledge, and thereby to give complete and not merely phenomenal value to the concepts of absolute or pure thought. This did away with the Kantian distinction of transcendent and transcendental; and transcendentalism comes to mean any theory asserting the dependence of the world upon the activity of reason, provided a systematic attempt is made (as in Fichte's *Wissenchaftslehre* and Hegel's *Logik*) to give a methodic development of reason into the particular categories that constitute the world of experience.

(3) In a loose sense, any philosophy which emphasizes the intuitive, spiritual, and supersensuous; any mode of thought which is aggressively non-empirical or anti-empirical. Thus we hear of the transcendentalism of Emerson, &c.

• • •

TWAIN, MARK (SAMUEL CLEMENS, (1835-1910): Not an American philosopher, Mark Twain in his last book, *Letters From the Earth* (1962), nevertheless produced a vivid critique of the teleological argument for the existence of God in every way as effective as **Voltaire's**:

Man is the Religious Animal. He is the only animal that has the True Religion — several of them. . . . He is not content to be pious all by himself, he requires his neighbor to be pious also — otherwise he will kill him and *make* him so. Yes, if that neighbor declines to lead a holy life, he will take an ax and convert him.

V

VEBLEN, THORSTEIN (1857-1929): The most considerable and creative social thought in America was produced by Thorstein Veblen. His first and principal book was *The Theory of the Leisure Class* (1899), with the theory of conspicuous consumption.

Born in a Wisconsin Norwegian community, he was sent by his father, a passionate believer in education, to be educated at Carelton College, Northfield, Minnesota. He went on to study philosophy at Yale with Noah Porter (*q.v.*). After he received his Ph.D. degree, he found that the only job he could get was working on a Minnesota farm. After four years he married Ellen May Rolfe, a wealthy young woman whose father's prosperous business promptly failed. They spent three years on a farm in Stacyville, Iowa, waiting for something to turn up. Nothing did.

At the age of thirty-four he decided to go back to some graduate school, and use that as a fresh point of departure. He went to Cornell. The man he impressed there, Laughlin, took Veblen along to Chicago, when he joined Harper's (*q.v.*) new faculty there. At $520 a year, Veblen finally had made it into academic life.

His life was disturbed by marital difficulties. In 1904 his wife reported one of his amorous relationships to the authorities at the university, and he was obliged to leave. He went to Stanford in 1906. Temporarily reunited with Ellen, another unconventional relationship with a woman forced him to leave in December of 1909.

After this, he taught at Missouri, edited the *Dial*, and served on the faculty of the New School for Social Research. He wrote *The Instinct of Workmanship* (1914), which he

261

considered his best book. *An Inquiry into the Nature of Peace* (1917) charges that both patriotism and business are useless to the community at large, and the principal obstructions to a lasting peace. *Higher Learning in America* (1918) attacks the "conduct of universities by business men." In *The Vested Interests and the State of the Industrial Arts* (1919) he defines a vested interest as "a marketable right to get something for nothing," and states that the aim of business (as opposed to industry) is to increase profits by sabotaging (restricting) production.

In 1920 his second wife died (Anne Fessenden Bradley, a divorcee with two daughters), and he felt tired, ill, rootless. In 1925 he turned down the presidency of the American Economic Association because "they didn't offer it to me when I needed it."

In 1926 Ellen May Rolfe died, and Veblen returned to his cabin in Palo Alto, living there with his step-daughter until his death three years later, August 3, 1929.

●   ●   ●

VLASTOS, GREGORY (1907-   ): Stuart Professor of Philosophy at Princeton since 1956. Gregory Vlastos is a native of Constantinople, born there July 27, 1907. Educated at Roberts College, Constantinople (1925), he took a religious degree from Chicago Theological Seminary (1929) and the Ph.D. from Harvard (1931). He taught at Queen's University, Kingston, Ontario (1931-1948), Cornell (1948-1955), and Princeton. An industrious contributor to journals, he is closely associated with *The Monist Dialogue*, and *The Canadian Philosophical Review*. A member of the Institute for Advanced Study in 1954-55, Gregory Vlastos is an expert on Greek political theory and philology.

W

WATTS, ALAN WILSON (1915-   ): A popularizer of Eastern philosophy, Alan Watts has written four books on the subject of Zen Buddhism alone. Born in Chislehurst, England, he went to King's School, Canterbury (1928-32). He came to America in 1938. He has seven children, and has been married three times. His major academic position was at the University of the Pacific, where he taught comparative philosophy (1951-57). Since then he has been an independent writer and lecturer, writing nineteen books, including *The Wisdom of Insecurity* (1951), *Beyond Theology* (1964), and *The Book On the Taboo Against Knowing Who You Are* (1966).

•   •   •

WAYLAND, FRANCIS (1796-1865): Described by Schneider as something of an oddity — "an educated Baptist" — Francis Wayland was president of Brown University and author of *Elements of Moral Science* (1835), a book which sold 200,000 copies.

Its distinction lay in abandoning Paley's attempt to prove that man by nature is intended for eternal happiness. Adopting a radically anti-utilitarian stance, he retained Butler's theory of conscience, emphasizing the intent rather than the consequence of the deed. Not prudence and policy, but conscience and duty were the basis of ethics, both individual and social.

Besides, most of the book was practical rather than theoretical. It was intended to be a book in moral "science."

Wayland's theories of education led to the banishment of any textbook from the classroom. The "analytic method" was employed to keep the student alert, develop habits of close reasoning and precise statement.

He proposed that a national university would be the best use of the Smithsonian money. Several years later he suggested a radical reexamination of the collegiate system in the country, with a view to making its services more widely available and more directly contributory to the needs of society.

• • •

WEISS, PAUL (1901-   ): The travelling Sears scholar (1929), Paul Weiss has been called the foremost speculative philosopher in America. Born in New York City, the son of an immigrant tinsmith, he was educated — after having dropped out of high school — evenings at CCNY. Soon he quit his job and went full time, studying with Morris Cohen (*q.v.*). He went to Harvard for graduate work, studying under Alfred North Whitehead (*q.v.*). and graduating in 1929. He taught at Harvard, Bryn Mawr, and Yale. His major works are *Reality* (1938), *Nature and Man* (1947), *Man's Fredom* (1950), *Modes of Being* (1958), *Our Public Life* (1959), *World of Art* (1961), *The God We Seek* (1964), and *Right and Wrong* (1967). In 1969 he joined the faculty of the Catholic University of America in Washington, D.C.

• • •

WHITE, ANDREW DICKSON (1832-1918): Born at Homer, Andrew Dickson White always wanted to go to Yale. His mother said Geneva College (Hobart) would be better, but he could only stand one year. When his parents forced him to go back the next, he went into hiding instead. Finally his father agreed to let him go to Yale.

He became a professor of history, married Mary Outwater and went out west, to the University of Michigan.

In time he founded his own college, dedicated to freedom

of learning, and free from church control, Cornell. Church opposition to such startling innovations was fierce. 1868 was not as liberal a year as White had hoped.

As opposition increased, he found himself studying the history of religious reaction to science through the centuries. The fruits of this study, which lasted for a long time, were published as *A History of the Warfare of Science with Theology in Christendom* (1896). An amazingly complete work, it contains information on religious opposition to the sciences of biology, geology, astronomy, archeology, anthropology, ethnology, meteorology, chemistry, physics, medicine, psychology, philology, mythology, political science, and literary criticism.

Another of his works was the *Seven Great Statesmen in the Warfare of Humanity with Unreason* (1910).

He is classed as one of the disciples of Darwin and Spencer.

Besides an academic career, he also was active in politics and international diplomacy. He died in 1918.

• • •

WHITEHEAD, ALFRED NORTH (1861-1947): The outstanding process philosopher in America, Alfred North Whitehead spent the first part of his life teaching mathematics at Cambridge University. Born at Ramsgate, England, on the 15th of February, 1861, he said that his life was lived in three successive epochs. The first was from birth to 1914, the second during the war of 1914 to 1918, and the third after the First World War.

After a classical education, he became a fellow of Trinity College, Cambridge, at the age of twenty-four. The loss of certainty, which the philosophers had experienced earlier with Hume and Kant, was repeated for the scientists when they tried to explain radiation phenomena. Newton's grand scheme of thought failed. Whitehead learned what he called "the fallacy of dogmatic finality." When he was later asked, "At what period of your life did you begin to feel that you had a grasp of your subject," Whitehead replied, "Never."

In 1890 he married Evelyn Wade, daughter of an Irish military family. They had three children.

During these years he wrote *A Treatise on Universal Algebra* (1898), *Axioms of Projective Geometry* (1906), *Axioms of Descriptive Geometry* (1907), *An Introduction to Mathematics* (1910), and with Bertrand Russell, the epoch-making *Principia Mathematica* (3 volumes, 1910-1913). *The Organization of Thought* (1916) was the last book from this period.

In mid-career he pulled up stakes, moved to London, and took "a bottle-washing job" at London University, beginning in 1910. His two sons fought in the war. One, Eric was killed. Any attempt at consolation, said Whitehead, even by the English master poets, "only trivialized the actual emotions."

He wrote *An Enquiry Concerning the Principles of Natural Knowledge* (1919), *The Concept of Nature* (1920), and *The Principle of Relativity with Applications to Physical Science* (1922).

By now he was sixty-three years old. The letter from Harvard, inviting him to teach, came as a complete surprise. "What do you think of it?" asked his wife. He replied, to her surprise, "I would rather do that than anything in the world."

During the next twelve years he taught philosophy and wrote his most famous books: *Science and the Modern World* (1925), *Religion in the Making* (1926), *Symbolism: Its Meaning and Effect* (1927), *The Aims of Education* (1929), *Process and Reality: An Essay in Cosmology* (1929), *The Function of Reason* (1929), *Adventures of Ideas* (1933), *Nature and Life* (1934), *Modes of Thought* (1938), and *Essays in Science and Philosophy* (1946).

The day after Christmas, 1947, he began to be paralyzed. Four days later, December 30, 1947, he died, in his 87th year.

Whitehead wrote:

A clash of doctrines is not a disaster — it is an opportunity.... The clash is a sign that there are wider
truths and finer perspectives within which a reconcilia-
tion will be found.

Philosophy is the search for pattern in the universe,
an attempt to express the infinity of the universe in
terms of the limitations of language.

The universe itself is in process. It can never be confined
by a formula or a dogmatic generalization:

There are no whole truths; all truths are half-truths.
It is trying to treat them as whole truths that plays
the devil.

● ● ●

WHITMAN, WALT (1819-1892): A philosophical poet,
Walt Whitman celebrated the principle of equality, the
"divine average," the value of the common man. Certainly
the cities where he worked and died testify to his faith in
the common: beautiful Brooklyn and scenic Camden, New
Jersey.

A prophet for "world democracy," Whitman saw the
Civil War, during which he served the wounded soldiers in
the huge hospitals, as a crusade for democracy and the
common man.

His great book, *Leaves of Grass* (1855, 1856, 1860, 1867,
1871, 1876, 1881-2, 1882, 1888-9, 1891-2) was an instant
failure. Only after many years and anonymous laudatory
reviews written by himself, was the book appreciated as
the masterpiece it is. When it was banned in Boston (as
a dirty book) it became a best seller in Philadelphia, selling
3000 copies in one day.

A great admirer of Spinoza, Whitman tried to infuse
pantheism into the philosophy of democracy, feeling much

like the American deists, that a new form of politics required a new religious base.

Nevertheless, Whitman never wished to form a new dogmatism, declaring: "I leave all free. I charge you to leave all free."

●　●　●

WILD, JOHN D. (1902-　　): Born in Chicago, John Wild was educated at Harvard (Master's degree) and The University of Chicago (Ph.D. 1926). He has taught at Harvard, Northwestern, and Yale. He edited *Spinoza* (1929), and wrote *George Berkeley* (1936), *Plato's Theory of Man* (1946), *Introduction to Realistic Philosophy* (1948), *Plato's Modern Enemies and the Theory of Natural Law* (1953), and *The Challenge of Existentialism* (1955). He also maintains an active interest in phenomenology and eastern philosophy.

●　●　●

WITHERSPOON, JOHN (1723-1794): Witherspoon lived two lives. The first was in Scotland, as an articulate conservative clergyman, a kind of clerical William Buckley, crusading against the efforts of fellow churchmen to learn the humanism of arts and letters. When one clergyman actually dared to write a play, Witherspoon exploded in anger, publishing *A Serious Inquiry into the Nature and Effects of the Stage: and a Letter Respecting Play Actors* (1757; a second edition, much encouraged by the burning of a theater in Richmond, appeared in Virginia in 1812). Attending plays, he said, was a "crime." It was a shame to witness the "wanton gesticulations of actors." Actors are not thrifty, said the Scotsman. They are paid too much, and they spend it too freely.

His second life began in 1768, when he became the President of the College of New Jersey (Princeton). Like Alfred North Whitehead later, Witherspoon came to America and here changed his vocation significantly. No longer was he the conservative. He did not so much modify his views, as they seemed altered by the new climate. Some pious followers of Jonathan Edwards looked upon his mild version of the typical Edinburgh course in moral philosophy as "infidelity reduced to a system."

Significantly, Witherspoon joined the American Enlightenment by his active interest in freedom. His famous "rebellion" sermon of May 17, 1776, delivered to the Princeton students (*The Dominion of Providence over the Passions of Men*) argued that it was the sovereign will of God which was arousing the "disorderly passions" of the American colonists against their English oppressors: "The wrath of man in its most tempestuous rage, fulfills his will, and finally promotes the good of his chosen." The loss of civil liberty, he asserted, always meant the loss of religious liberty as well: "If we yield up our temporal property, we at the same time deliver the conscience into bondage."

Witherspoon is also to be credited with importing and popularizing Scottish "common sense" philosophy in America He had no sympathy with subtle or abstract intellectual formulations. He denounced Berkeleyanism, popular in many American circles, and exterminated its influence at Princeton. He insisted on the worth of solid empirical doctrines. Some of the successors in in this line of thought include Witherspoon's son-in-law, Samuel Stanhope Smith (*q.v.*), professor of moral philosophy at Princeton (1779), and James McCosh (*q.v.*), a later president of Princeton.

Witherspoon was active in politics as county delegate (1774), chairman of the county delegation (1775-6), leader in the movement to imprison the royalist governor of New Jersey, and delegate to the Continental Congress (1776). On July 2, he delivered a dramatic speech in Philadelphia urging action when others were counseling delay: "it was not only ripe for the measure (the Declaration of Independence) but in danger of rotting for the want of it."

As a member of Congress until November of 1782, he was appointed to more than one hundred committees, including the board of war and the committee on secret correspondence (foreign affairs).

He spent his last years (1782-1794) attempting to rebuild the college, which had been closed, damaged by the war. In 1774 he had appealed for all "to declare the firm resolve never to submit to the claims of Great Britain, but deliberately to prefer war with all its horrors, and even extermination, to slavery." Now, due largely to troubles made by the war, his own last years were sad and difficult. The college treasury was nearly empty. His own purse was depleted. Soon his wife died.

In the spring of 1791 he married Ann Dill, the widow of Dr. Armstrong Dill. As he was then sixty-eight and his bride twenty-four, the marriage caused considerable coment. They had two children, one of whom lived. A year later he went blind. Within three years he was dead on Tusculum, his farm.

Witherspoon's influence, Scottish common sense realism, lasting from 1800 to 1875, was on that period in American Philosophy called by Santayana "The Genteel Tradition," in both its Calvinistic and transcendental aspects. The reader is referred to the article on Santayana for further information on this classification.

• • •

WOODBRIDGE, FREDERICK JAMES EUGENE (1867-1940): Leader of the American "realist" movement (he called it "naïve realism"), F. J. E. Woodbridge was dean of the graduate faculties at Columbia. With Butler and Burgess he is one of the three who organized Columbia into a true university. Born in Ontario, Woodbridge attended the Michigan Asylum and Amherst College. He studied at Berlin (1892-4) and taught at Minnesota before going to Columbia.

The sources of his thought were Aristotle, Spinoza, Locke, and Santayana. He used Aristotle to criticize idealism and the Cartesian epistemological tradition.

His main works were *The Purpose of History* (1916), *The Realm of Mind* (1926), and *Nature and Mind* (1937).

He was an enthusiastic pragmatist by temperament. The moral lesson of natural teleology is that the world can be improved. Ours is the best possible world only because it has the capacity to engender and support the effort to make it better.

•   •   •

WOOLMAN, JOHN (1720-1772): One philosopher who really lived up to his name was John Woolman. He refused to wear clothes that had been dyed because of his strong convictions against the slave industry, which produced the dye.

Alfred North Whitehead (*q.v.*) pays tribute to Woolman in the *Adventures of Ideas*, saying that he was "that Apostle of Human Freedom" the first in modern times to deliberately set out to abolish slavery.

His method was economic boycott, refusing to patronize any industry that was based on slavery. He objected in later years to the use of sugar for this reason.

He was convinced that he was right by the doctrine of the Inner Light, a characteristically Quaker doctrine (cf. William Penn). According to this view, the human mind may directly intuit truth, in a mystical apprehension. What keeps this from becoming purely subjective solipsism (assuming that it is in fact so kept) is the society of like-minded persons (in this case the Quakers, the Society of Friends) who, given a chance to meditate upon the issue, become of like mind.

In 1776, at John Woolman's urging, the Philadelphia Yearly Meeting disowned those members who refused to free their slaves.

Born on the 19th of October, 1720, at Ancocas, West Jersey (now Rancocas, New Jersey), he descended from people of substance. His grandfather was a Proprieter and his father a candidate for the provincial assembly.

His formal education was limited to that provided by the neighborhood Quaker school. Afterwards, he continued to read widely.

Becoming a tailor by trade, he prospered fabulously in Mount Holly. He also handled such things as surveying, drawing wills, and executing bills of sale. In his spare time he taught school, publishing a primer that ran through several editions.

At this point in his life Woolman wrote: "I saw that a humble man, with the Blessing of the Lord, might live on a little, and that where the heart was set on greatness, success in business did not satisfy the craving; but that commonly with an increase of wealth, the desire for wealth increased."

He entered the Quaker ministry, travelling widely throughout the colonies from New Hampshire to North Carolina. He was active, as were other Friends, in various social causes. He opposed military draft and taxes, sought the conversion of Indians, and opposed slavery, "reaping the unrighteous profits of that iniquitous practice of dealling in Negroes." During a trip to Virginia in 1746, he wrote: "I saw in these Southern Provinces so many Vices and Corruptions increased by this trade and this way of life, that it appeared to me as a dark gloominess hanging over the Land, and though now many willingly run into it, yet in the future the Consequence will be grievous to posterity. I express it as it hath appeared to me, not at once, nor twice, but as a matter fixed on my mind."

He wrote *Some Considerations on the Keeping of Negroes* (1754), and *A Plea for the Poor* (1763), which was later reprinted as a Fabian Society Tract. His most famous work was *The Journal of John Woolman's Life*

272

and Travels in the Service of the Gospel, not published until 1774, two years after his death.

He died in York, England, October 7, 1772, having contracted smallpox while on a walking tour on behalf of the poor—he had given up horseback riding as too vain. He was 51.

Woolman's doctrine of the inner light was not a rival, but a supplement to natural reason. He declared that direct communication is possible between God and man. The knowledge gained in this way can be used to correct other processes of thought. The inner light was particularly useful as a guide to conduct, reminiscent of Socrates' *daimonium,* furnishing a basis for choice and serene confidence in the future. It was available, he taught, only to pure spirits, souls purged of selfishness and willing to follow its lead.

• • •

WRIGHT, CHAUNCEY (1830-1875): Human calculator for the *Nautical Almanac,* Chauncey Wright later lived the quiet life of a bachelor at The Village Blacksmith's house at Harvard. A thorough-going naturalist, he was a forerunner of William James. His most valuable article, "Evolution of Self-Consciousness," illustrates the quality of this thought. He held an instrumentalist conception of mental activities. As might be guessed, Wright opposed Transcendentalism, on the grounds that no single, inclusive metaphysical system could serve as a foundation for matters of fact and evaluation. Also, like Henry James, he contended that religion and morality are not necessarily linked.